MR MOO
CONFESSION

MR MOON HAS LEFT THE STADIUM

But Paul is a determined man and asked me to come in for a chat anyway. Maybe I could give them advice on how they could improve the announcements on a match day? So I agreed. Just to poke about behind the scenes if I'm honest. It's not every day a lifelong fan gets invited to the club offices.

I've worked around football clubs throughout my broadcasting career, but I still felt a buzz as I walked into the stadium. It would be awesome to be involved here. Instead of paying for a season ticket, imagine getting paid for working for West Ham United? Getting paid to watch the team I loved was quite a thought. The idea made me giggle a bit, I thought it was in my head, but it may have been out loud, as the receptionist gave me an odd look.

I started visualising myself walking out onto the pitch, microphone in hand. I had to remind myself I wasn't going to be the announcer, I was just going to help them out. Yes, that was it, I had some expertise in a certain field and my club needed to consult me. I was, of course, greatly honoured to be able to help, but I would leave the stadium still a fan who paid for his ticket and reserved the right to shout at them, as well as for them.

Paul Aldridge was a tall, broad, charming man. He asked me what I'd thought of the stadium announcements during the previous season. I had to admit that I hadn't heard many of them. The speakers in the West Stand had seen better days. The sound quality was awful, either too quiet to hear or too distorted to understand. There didn't seem to be any middle ground, I told him.

Harry Redknapp's West Ham team used to take to the field with the announcement, 'Please welcome 'Arry's 'Appy 'Ammers.' I told Paul I didn't much care for the contrived triple 'A' alliteration. He may have thought I was being a bit Professor Higgins about it, but he nodded his head in agreement.

I can't remember commenting on much else, other than the sarcastic use of music. If your team has just been spanked, I don't find it amusing to leave the stadium to the sound of 'Things Can Only Get Better' or 'The Only Way Is Up'.

The club was replacing the entire public address system ready for the new season. The previous announcer, who organised travel tours in real life, had been sent packing.

My name had been suggested for the job as I often spoke about West Ham on BBC Greater London Radio. I was presenting the breakfast show at the time and some-one at the club had heard me.

We chatted for a while and had a cup of tea. It was all very pleasant, especially when he showed me the trophy room. I didn't even know we had a trophy room and surpris-ingly there were quite a few trophies in it. Closer inspection showed a lot of them to be plates and bowls that we'd been presented with on overseas tours. We hadn't won anything since 1980; the year I used my head in my A levels and Trevor Brooking used his to nod in the winning goal in the cup final against Arsenal. The badge that I loved, with the crossed hammers and the castle, was everywhere, even the toilets had blue walls with claret cubicles. It was so inviting, Paul was so friendly, they clearly wanted me to do the job and those colours were so damned enticing. There's something about claret and blue that is so reas-suring. As a kid when I left the Glade Primary School in Clayhall to go to big school, I was scared stiff. Instead of being able to walk to school, I would now have to go on a bus. But then I found out that Ilford County High School wore claret blazers with claret and blue ties and I couldn't wait to start.

I could feel the claret and blue working its magic again; if I wasn't careful I was going to be tempted into taking this job. Where would my broadcasting career be then? I quickly left, heading back to my Docklands flat, having once again turned down the chance to be the new announcer.

The ever-determined Paul told me to think about it and he'd give me a call in a few days to see if I'd changed my mind. My Dad thought I should take the job. My girlfriend Charlotte wasn't keen as it would mess up our weekends together. It was important that I didn't let my heart rule my head. Being the voice of West Ham was a powerful draw but it would certainly interfere with my career.

I say career, but I've never really had a career. I've stumbled from one job to the next and usually but not always ended up on my feet. All my jobs have involved talking in one form or another, usually on the radio, but most recently on television. At the time I'd just finished a spell as a TV presenter on Channel Five, fronting their sports shows *Turnstyle*, *Sick as a Parrot* and *Live and Dangerous* as well as anchoring their live football coverage. I was now back on the radio presenting a breakfast show, but that didn't mean I'd turned my back on sports presenting. All through my career I've flip-flopped between news, sport and light entertainment on both TV and radio. Committing myself to West Ham would mean ruling out Saturday afternoons. No commissioning editor was going to give me a sports show if I asked for the day off every time West Ham played at home. On the other hand, the TV channels weren't exactly queuing up for my services. As a season ticket holder I'd not missed a home game in two years.

So I decided to sleep on it. It was a nice problem to have, as football managers say about team selection when everyone's fit.

That night I had a dream. I say night, it was the afternoon. Early-morning presenters exist in a strange time zone. Breakfast is another country, they do things differently there.

In the dream West Ham's Rio Ferdinand was playing for England in the World Cup Final in Paris. It was unclear who England were playing. It started off as Germany but at some point it seemed to have changed into France. Continuity issues have always plagued my dreams and they could never be made into films. But there was no doubt who won the match. Rio Ferdinand rose above everyone in the box to head home a corner. England had won the World Cup for the first time since Bobby Moore and the 1966 team.

Back in real life at the start of the 1966/67 season Bobby had been welcomed onto the pitch at Upton Park along with his West Ham team mates Geoff Hurst and Martin Peters. The World Cup-winning captain and the men who'd scored all four goals between them ran out to enormous cheers from the crowd. West Ham hadn't won the cup entirely on their own, but England couldn't have done it without us.

In my dream the 1998/99 season started with Rio Ferdinand running onto the pitch ahead of the rest of the players. Thunderous applause greeted him, but as the camera panned round there was no sign of me clapping. I wasn't in my usual seat in the West Stand, I was down on the pitch. I was holding the microphone. I was the new stadium announcer!

I woke up with a start. I'd dribbled out of the corner of my mouth onto the sofa. Alan Devonshire had nothing on me when it came to dribbling in the afternoons.

I made myself a cup of tea and had a good think about things. I'd really enjoyed being the announcer in my dream. It felt good. I was part of history, even if it hadn't actually happened yet. A West Ham player was going to win the

World Cup and I was going to coordinate his triumphant homecoming.

After having the Rio dream for three days running, and some of the nights too, I rang Paul Aldridge and agreed to be the new West Ham United stadium announcer.

That summer Rio Ferdinand travelled with the England squad to the World Cup Finals in France. He was an unused substitute in the tournament. He didn't make it onto the pitch for any of England's matches. They lost on penalties to Argentina in the last sixteen. Rio had to watch from the bench.

My dream turned into a nightmare when David Beckham was sent off for petulantly kicking out at Diego Simeone and quickly became public enemy number one. England arrived home before their postcards.

The trouble with dreams is they have a habit of fading and dying. As a West Ham fan I should know that. It's in our song.

When the fixtures came out for the new season, West Ham's first home game was against Manchester United. My debut as announcer would see me read out the name 'David Beckham'. Instead of welcoming a hero onto the pitch, I was destined to welcome a villain.

SHEFFIELD SATURDAY

West Ham's biggest name in 1998 was Ian Wright-Wright-Wright. Wright signed from Arsenal in the summer. For brevity I would usually announce him as just Ian Wright. I'd never been a big fan, because he played for the Arse. Now I suddenly found I was a huge admirer of his work. It's funny how that happens.

Wrighty scored in my first game since becoming the announcer, although I didn't announce anything. It would have been frowned upon as it was an away match at Hillsborough. The Sheffield Wednesday announcer might not have appreciated a soft southerner grabbing the microphone. In the announcers' world that would be considered as taking the mike. Instead I contented myself with singing, 'Ian Wright-Wright-Wright, Ian Wright-Wright-Wright,' at the top of my voice. It wasn't a song I'd sung before, but I found that amazingly I seemed to know all the words.

I'd been dreading going to Hillsborough. The last time I'd been there was in 1989 to commentate on an FA Cup semi-final between Nottingham Forest and Liverpool. I was working for BBC Radio Nottingham. It became the worst day of my life. Ninety-six Liverpool fans lost their lives in a huge crush. I went down onto the terracing with a delegation of journalists. We walked in total silence amongst the twisted crash barriers and down into the tunnel where most of the victims died. We won a New York Academy Award for best coverage of a breaking news story, but I take no pride in that. It was just a horrible day.

As I drove into Sheffield to watch my team, images of that day nine years before kept creeping into my head. I had a tear in my eye as I walked into the ground, remembering those that had also entered with such high hopes a few years before. I'd watched as many of them were carried away dead or dying on advertising boards used as emergency stretchers.

Once the game began, I started to feel OK again. I was surrounded by my people. Unless you are a football fan, you won't know what that feels like. Every weekend, you can go to watch your team and you feel at home, even if you are away. I didn't know all these people personally, but they were my family. They wore claret and blue, the colours I'd grown up with. They sang the songs I'd sung all my life.

A few of them recognised me from the TV. Not many, because the Channel Five signal was poor in the early days. In Scotland I had a huge fan base, as their signal was strong from day one. On one trip to Glasgow, to present the World Cup qualifier between Scotland and Latvia, I discovered I had a large female following. Fortunately I managed to shake her off on the way to the ground. When the signal improved nationally I was replaced by someone better-looking.

On that sunny day in Sheffield, I surveyed our crowd. West Ham fans are a bit special. They were singing their hearts out. They chastised the northerners for the aggression of their tackles and their dubious parentage. There were positive songs too about why East London is wonderful and the delights that it's full of.

I sat with curly-haired pop star David Essex; the club had probably sorted out tickets for both of us. Between us sat his twin boys and they had an enormous bag of pick and mix. Life couldn't get much sweeter. It was like sitting in a West End musical version of my favourite things. I was watching my childhood heroes, who'd just asked me to work for them, there were pear drops and cola bottles on tap and I was sitting with Che Guevara. It was going to be a good day after all.

We won the game 1–0 and left the ground as Happy Hammers. The only worry for Hammers fans was how we were going to afford Wright-Wright-Wright on the back of our replica shirts.

As I drove out of Sheffield, I thought again about the Hillsborough victims. I thought about how badly we treat football supporters in this country, how they are herded around like animals.

I made a decision then that I would always treat away supporters with respect in my time as the announcer at West Ham. I would love my team, but not hate anybody else's. I was going to be like Dave Allen, the stand-up comic who mainly sat down. His motto was 'Whatever your religion, may your god go with you'. I was going to be like Dave, except I wasn't going to drink whisky or smoke or lose a finger in an accident. It was mainly the respect bit that I was going to copy, and possibly the sitting down.

I headed back down the motorway to London thinking about my debut: West Ham at home to Manchester United the next weekend. All the talking was over, now it was time to start ... talking.

BOOING BECKHAM

In the summer of 1998 Tony Blair was still a popular Prime Minister and Harry Redknapp was the manager of West Ham. Work had just started on the Millennium Dome, Princess Diana had been dead less than a year and Pluto was still a planet.

Things were going to go downhill for Tony, Harry and Pluto. We should have guessed Pluto wasn't a planet because of its name. Mars, Venus and the rest were named after Roman gods, Pluto was a Disney dog. It all went goofy in 2006 when it was downgraded to a dwarf planet. Even then the name didn't sit right; a dwarf planet should be named Dopey or Bashful, maybe Sneezy if it's prone to eruptions.

Nowadays Harry Redknapp is a pantomime villain when he returns to West Ham as manager of the sleeping giant from down the lane, but back in 1998 he was still Our Harry. He'd been manager since 1994; assistant manager to Billy Bonds before that. Billy is one of my all-time favourite players. He played with his socks rolled down and I would pretend to be him in school football matches, especially when it was muddy. It always seemed to be muddy when Billy played. Maybe that's why he rolled his socks down.

The club had been promoted or relegated four out of five seasons under Billy. It was like being stuck in a lift with a small child who kept pressing the buttons; you were never sure which level you'd be on next. Harry brought stability. In 1994/95 we finished thirteenth, in 1995/96 it was tenth. The 1996/97 season was nearly a disaster when Harry saw the Bosman ruling as an invitation to go Euro shopping. He bought some disastrous players like Paulo Futre and Florin Radiciou. Harry says he was called Florin because he was worth about 'two bob'. We were heading fast for the relegation trapdoor that season and only the arrival of strike duo John Hartson and Paul Kitson kept us up with a stream of goals.

The 1997/98 season was much better. Hartson and Kitson were up front with an exciting midfield that included Eyal Berkovic and Trevor Sinclair, and we finished eighth.

Then came the biggest signing of all, in my world anyway, I joined the club in the summer of 1998 ready for what promised to be a great season.

I arrived at the ground in plenty of time for my debut as the announcer. I'm a confident person, maybe even a little arrogant, but I still get nervous before doing new things. There are two things I am never without when starting a new job. One is my little statue of Bobby Moore and the other is a packet of Boots Diareze tablets. One is for good luck and the other is to bung me up – I hope you can guess which is which.

Everyone shows their nerves in different ways. I spend most of my time before big events on the toilet. They say an army marches on its stomach; mine lets me down every time there's a sign of trouble ahead. Not even trouble, just new territory.

It was the same for my first ever show on university radio, my first show at each new radio station since, my first live TV show, the first night presenting live on Channel Five, first dates with girls, first after-dinner speech, first awards show, first keynote conference speech, the list goes on. That statue has been around the world with me and I've contributed to the healthy share price of Boots for many years running.

The thing that worries me is a lack of preparation. I worry that I haven't done enough research and I will come a cropper. For this reason most of my reference library is in my toilet. I have shelves and shelves of football books, about half of them West Ham-related, all in my downstairs loo.

Once it is too late to do any more research I stop worrying. I'm not actually nervous when speaking, just beforehand. I know that I'm good at thinking on my feet, so if anything goes wrong I'll be fine. The only thing that can go wrong is if I've not researched my subject.

On Saturday 22 August 1998, I went into a gig more prepared than I have ever been in my life. I'd been a broadcaster for twelve years and I'd supported West Ham since I was a boy. I was totally confident in my head that I could do this. Sadly my head hadn't told my bottom. I'd been up most of the night with worry, but now the Diareze seemed to have control of the situation. Either that or I was totally empty.

The club were very worried about the abuse that David Beckham was getting. A banner had been pinned to the gates at West Ham reading, 'Beckham, 22 August = hell'. It had been pictured in the papers alongside a photograph of an effigy of David hanging by a noose outside a pub. It later emerged the pub was the Pleasant Pheasant in South Norwood in the middle of Millwall territory, but that didn't stop the papers having a field day. According to one report, hooligan group The Inner City Firm had threatened Beckham's parents over the phone. It must have been a dodgy connection because the ICF stands for Inter City Firm. I suspect it was some kids having a laugh, but there was no doubt there was a lot of anger against Beckham from the whole country.

Today he's widely respected, but back then it was a different story. Becks was going out with Victoria Adams, the poshest member of the Spice Girls. A London butcher put two pigs' heads in his window and labelled them David and Victoria. You know you've lost the public when the butchers start turning against you.

At the Charity Shield match against Arsenal, Becks was booed every time he touched the ball. While we were playing at Sheffield Wednesday, Manchester United were at home to Leicester. Becks had an easy ride in front of his home fans, scoring at the end.

As the game at West Ham approached, the pressure was building. Some supporters were planning to hold up red cards at public enemy number one. Politicians were making their usual 'it's only a game, can't we all just get along' speeches.

The police were so worried they contacted supporters' groups and fanzines and pleaded for them to help defuse the situation. I had to have a couple of meetings with the police and officials at West Ham. I promised not to say anything that would inflame the situation.

I was caught between a rock and a hard place. As an England supporter I was furious with David Beckham. What an absolute plonker, I thought, there's only a World Cup every four years and he blew it not only for himself, but the whole country. This was a really good chance for us to win it. We'd gone so close at Italia 1990 and we'd not qualified for USA 1994. France 1998 was going well until a moment of petulance from Beckham ended our dreams.

However, as the West Ham announcer I was the voice of the club. The world would be watching. Anything I said would be taken as being the club's view. I wanted to yell, 'You robbed us of our dream! You are an idiot! Your girlfriend isn't posh and she's the worst singer of a bad bunch!' I wanted to hold up my own red card and shove it right into his annoyingly handsome face, but that wouldn't have been a good idea.

The players ran out for a kick-about. I welcomed them onto the pitch from the safety of the announcer's box, a cabin I called the Shed down in the corner of the West Stand and the Bobby Moore Stand. I ran through the team sheets on the desk microphone. It was forty-five minutes until kick-off and the ground was only a quarter full, so it was good to get a few announcements under my belt. Beckham was loudly booed as he ran out. I booed quietly in the shed with the microphone turned off, grinning to myself at how childish I was being.

As soon as I finished the first announcements I felt better. I took a drink of water, as my throat was totally dry with nerves. Nowadays I run training courses on how to cope with speaking in public, but my career up to this point had been as a TV and radio presenter. I wasn't used to seeing my audience. On radio I would talk to my guests, my producer and maybe the newsreader. On TV you just spoke into a camera. If someone didn't like what you said, you couldn't hear them shouting at you from their home.

The next announcements would be harder. Just before kick-off I would take to the pitch with the radio microphone. That was scarier, because there's always the chance your knees will buckle and you'll go down like one of those guardsmen who faint on parade. That has never happened to me, but I've never been in the guards.

There was half an hour until kick-off, so I relaxed a bit. Everything had gone fine so far. The ground seemed fairly quiet. Maybe it wasn't going to be so bad after all.

Then the phone rang. It was the Bobby Moore receptionist. That's the receptionist from the Bobby Moore Stand. My Bobby statue doesn't have his own receptionist. He was just standing quietly next to the CDs.

She put through a caller from Cyprus. He was requesting a minute's silence for an East Londoner who'd emigrated. He had been killed in a road accident. The caller said the victim was from the West Ham area originally and he was a huge Manchester United fan. As we were playing Man Utd that day, he thought it would be very fitting if we observed a minute's silence for his friend. I felt very mean, but I said no.

The caller was insistent. He would be very grateful if we did observe a silence. He was clearly very upset, but I was firm. On a day already filled with all the anti-Beckham emotion, a silence would not be a good idea. The caller went on and on. I let him speak because he clearly needed to talk about his friend, but there was no way I could allow an impromptu minute's silence on a day as potentially volatile as this one.

I like to think I was acting thoughtfully and calmly, but inside every impassive announcer there is a fan just waiting to get out. On reflection I know I made the right call. But it's also true that West Ham fans do not like Cockney Reds or Manchester United fans that live anywhere in the world apart from Manchester. There's no doubt they are a fantastic club and I will always cheer for them when they play in Europe representing our country, but we believe you should support your local team. We get fed up hearing Cockney Reds saying how well 'we' are doing in their London accents, never having been to Old Trafford in their lives. It breaks our hearts when little children from generations of good West Ham stock ask for a Manchester United shirt for Christmas.

So no, I didn't think the silence would be a good idea for the East London-born, Manchester United-supporting ex-pat in Cyprus. The team he supported against his local team was not in fact a perfect scenario. It could turn ugly and I was not going to do it.

Calls like that will usually be cut off at the switchboard but I think the Cypriot had been unusually persuasive and so he'd been put through. I felt bad about having to turn down his request and annoyed that he wouldn't take no for an answer. In the end I had to interrupt him and just say goodbye. We'd been on the phone for ages. I put down the receiver and looked up. There were fifteen minutes to kick-off and the ground had filled up since I last looked out of the window.

The adrenaline was pumping in my body. I hate confrontation of any sort. I hoped the Cypriot didn't feel too bad about his friend.

I was joined in the shed by Carl Bailey, a former Australian rugby league player now in charge of the West Ham dance troupe, the Hammerettes. He was still Australian but no longer played for the London Broncos. Carl played the CDs while I ventured pitchside with a stick microphone in hand.

There were 26,039 people there that day. I know because I announced it later on. But for the time being I just had to get through that team sheet. It's the scariest thing I've ever done. Suppose I opened my mouth and nothing came out? What if my voice made that funny high-pitched sound it sometimes makes under pressure? At thirty-five years of age I wasn't confident that my voice had fully broken. Occasionally on the radio, when I was least expecting it, my voice would jump up to a much higher pitch. Usually it would come in the first word spoken for a while. I'd say 'Hello, I'm Jeremy Nicholas and you're listening to GLR breakfast' and the first syllable of hello would sound like a soprano, with the rest sounding like a tenor. Would my high-pitch 'hell' affect me now?

I opted to say 'good afternoon' rather than 'hello'. In my experience the word 'good' was far less likely to cause high-end problems.

As soon as I stepped out onto the pitch I felt happy. It was good to stand on the grass. I felt I was on home turf. My people were all around me – most of them didn't know me from Adam but we all shared one passion. Every time I'd felt sad over the years, they had felt the same. They'd been on the same emotional rollercoaster that I'd been on. They'd tasted the highs and lows at the same time as me. They'd cheered when Trevor used his head and cried when Bobby died.

These were my people and they were about to boo me.

The club and the police had laid down strict guidelines on what I could and couldn't say. Everything was written down, so there were no worries about remembering it. As long as I could read out loud, I would be fine.

I flicked the switch on the bottom of the microphone to the 'on' position. The switch on my bottom was firmly in the 'off' position. Thanks, Diareze! My knees showed no signs of buckling. My big fat tenor was sitting firmly on the boy soprano at the back of my vocal cords. Nothing could go wrong.

It's a tradition to read the away team out first. When I reached number seven, David Beckham, a wave of booing cascaded down from the stands. It washed over me like a tsunami of hate. It came from all four corners of the ground. No one heard me say number eight, Nicky Butt, or number nine, Andy Cole; the booing was relentless and hostile. It was incredibly intimidating. I couldn't hear myself above the noise. The only thing that got me through it was knowing my Dad would be booing, my friends would be booing, and if I was still a season ticket holder in the West Stand, I would be booing too.

Forget what I said about not being scared once I start talking, I was petrified. There's nowhere to hide when you are standing on the pitch, surrounded by baying fans on all sides. I looked across at David Beckham and he didn't seem bothered by all the hostility; he'd gone into the zone, preparing himself for the match. I needed to get myself into a zone as well and control my breathing. The boy soprano at the back of my vocal cords was beginning to wriggle free. I took some big breaths, to give the big fat tenor the extra oxygen he needed to hold him in check. Then I read the West Ham team. It was amazing. Every name was cheered. I don't know why I was surprised, of course they were cheering. It was nothing to do with me, it could have been a trained parrot reading out the names and they'd still cheer. But I felt so very, very happy. I'd got through the hard bit and this was the reward. The crowd had booed the villain and now they were cheering the heroes. I stood there just soaking it all in. What a brilliant, brilliant moment in time. I was floating on air. It could have been the euphoria or it could have been because my tank was running on empty.

Just then I noticed the referee was glaring at me and seemed keen to start the game. I'd almost forgotten there was going to be a football match. I'd been so worried about the Beckham business. I floated off the pitch and into the shed.

'Good on you, mate,' said Aussie Carl. 'You've got a good voice there.'

And with that I sat down to watch the game. A flask of tea and some triangular sandwiches had arrived. I needed to refuel, so this was great news. Life couldn't get much better. I had my own private suite with full hospitality and colonial staff. I could see most of the pitch and Carl seemed to know how the sound system worked.

The thousands of red cards in the crowd didn't materialise. The fanzines had acted with restraint, but the chanting against Beckham was horrendous. Questions were asked about his wife's favourite position – and I'm not talking about the checkout till at Armani. Further questions were asked as to whether his team-mates had also had a go. Again I'm not talking about shopping. Becks declined to answer any of the questions, quite wisely in my view. If they couldn't hear me with a radio mike, how would they hear him without one?

The icing on the cake for me would have been a goal on my debut. It didn't come. I would have to wait to announce one of those. Still we managed a 0–0 draw with Manchester United in the season where they went on to win the treble.

Since that day Beckham has rehabilitated himself. I was annoyed with him for a long time, until his incredible free kick right at the end against Greece in 2001, which secured qualification for the World Cup Finals in Korea and Japan. He's a remarkable player and as an East London boy it's a tragedy that he never played for West Ham. He's done OK at other clubs and has become a great global ambassador for the beautiful game, but I think it would be fitting if he ended his playing days back home. He'll always be assured of a warm welcome at West Ham. He certainly got a very hot reception on my debut in 1998.

Season in a Nutshell 1998/99

Some of the football was fantastic with lots of flair bu
were better at attacking than defending. When we did lose,
we often let in quite a few. Amazingly, despite finishing fifth
we ended the season with a negative goal difference. The
last five games sum up the season. After beating Derby 5–1
at home, followed by a 2–1 win at Spurs, we then lost 5–1 at
home to Leeds with three of our players sent off. After losing
6–0 at Everton, the topsy-turvy run ended with a 4–0 win at
home to Middlesbrough.

Highlight – Announcing my first goals in the second home
match. We scored three against Wimbledon.

Lowlight – Later in the same game, announcing four goals
for Wimbledon to lose the match 4–3 as the Wombles
cleaned up.

International highlight – being called up by England to
announce at under-21 level.

Worst moment – West Ham striker John Hartson hit the
target during training. Unfortunately the target was his
team-mate Eyal Berkovic's head. Sky cameras filmed it
and it was shown over and over again on news channels.

Heroes – Marc Vivien Foe added strength to the midfield.
Paolo Di Canio arrived and became an instant star. Joe
Cole broke into the side looking like a player we should
build a team around.

Villains – John Hartson was sold to Wimbledon after the
twin shame of the Eyal incident and appearing in adverts
for hair transplants.

Team news – Frank Lampard Junior announced he wanted
to be known as plain old Frank Lampard despite his dad
with the same name also working at the club. Nobody ever
confused the two; one of them puffed a lot after a run and
the other was our assistant manager.

It shouldn't happen to an announcer – Against Southampton I announced the releasing of two thousand balloons. A few got away, but most took to the air still trapped in the giant net. The crowd cheered. The net was later found on the beach at West Mersea still containing many balloons. Amazingly it was found by Ron Read, a West Ham season ticket holder in the East Stand.

New this season – The 50/50 draw ticket was introduced. Dancing girls, the Hammerettes, would sell tickets before games and I'd pick out the winner at half-time on the pitch.

Missed games – Just one, I already had a holiday booked to Madeira with Charlotte. My friend Tim deputised for me. He's a broadcaster and West Ham fan. He says it went OK, but his girlfriend told him the crowd were booing him.

Did we win at Anfield? – No, we drew 2–2.

My bald patch – The size of the bottom of a tea cup.

Three-Legged Stool Review

Job leg – Delighted to be nominated for a Sony Award for GLR Breakfast. There was talk of some network radio presenting and I'd landed a dream job with West Ham. So job leg was rock solid.

Relationship leg – Charlotte moved out of our Docklands flat to be closer to her job in Cambridge. This leg is wobbling, but hasn't yet fallen off.

West Ham leg – We finished fifth and qualified for Europe and the boys won the FA Youth Cup. The West Ham leg of the stool was holding up well. Only the Boys of '86, with third place, had finished higher.

AND THE AWARD GOES TO...

There's no secret to being a good announcer, you just need to have something to say. If you don't have anything to say the best thing is to keep quiet.

In my view the worst announcers are the ones who like the sound of their own voice and they go on and on, just rambling and rambling, with no real purpose, relentlessly talking, talking, talking, rambling and meandering their way through the various thoughts that pop into their heads, and churning them out, never pausing for breath, not bothering to make them into easy bite-size little chunks that we can take in, rather going for long paragraphs of speech, with no complete sentences, no full stops, no pauses, just rambling rubbish with little commas in between, while they breathe, often through their mouths, because this sort of approach attracts mouth-breathers.

I prefer to be brief. Short little sentences are best. Pause for thought. Stand and deliver. I'm adamant about this. Ridicule is nothing to be scared of.

As far as I know there are no awards for announcers, at least not in this country. Maybe the mouth-breathers are holding their own dinner once a year and not telling the rest of us about it, but that seems unlikely.

At the end of each season we do hand out an award for Hammer of the Year. It's for the best player of the season, as voted for by the supporters. There's a runner-up and a junior Hammer award too, as well as one for the best Academy player. As the nomination forms appeared towards the end of my first season, I wondered who would win. First, though, I was up for an award myself.

The Sony Radio Academy Awards of 1999 were memorable for me; it was the one time where I went into a gig completely unprepared. I was totally speechless. You've probably guessed by now that I'm a bit of a control freak, who likes to prepare thoroughly for all my various speaking engagements. However, this wasn't a speaking job, we were just there for a celebration. There'd only be a speech if we won, and we were confident we wouldn't.

The GLR breakfast show was nominated for a Sony Award. We were never likely to win, because there were two categories: best speech breakfast show and best music breakfast show. We were a mixture of speech and music. We'd entered the speech category with no expectation of making the shortlist.

The other nominations were BBC Radio 5Live breakfast and the TalkSport breakfast show. They didn't play any music and they were both national networks. GLR always had ideas above its station, but that station only broadcast to London. We were the black sheep of the BBC local radio family, but we were still local. There was no way we were going to win, so we didn't even think about writing an acceptance speech. You can guess where this is going, can't you? Actually you're wrong.

We put on our best black ties and headed for a good night out at the Grosvenor House Hotel on Park Lane. Fortunately this was where the awards were being held. The great and the good from the radio industry were all there, plus about five hundred others.

At the arrivals drinks a rumour began to spread. People told us they'd heard we'd won. We didn't take much notice, distracted by the splendour of the occasion. There were sixty round tables, each set for ten people, with lots of bottles of wine. Each table had a giant Chinese-style paper lantern in the middle. The breakfast team were usually tucked up in bed early, so we were determined to have a good time. Our bosses had officially sanctioned us sounding a bit rubbish the next day, as reward for the nomination.

I read the programme over and over again. It definitely did say GLR Breakfast in the Best Speech Breakfast category. Well, it was lovely to be nominated, never mind about winning. While my co-presenter Clare McDonnell and the rest of the team soaked in the occasion and quite a lot of the wine, I had a chat with Fiona Fullerton, one of the most beautiful actresses this country has ever produced and definitely the Best Bond Girl Ever. Fiona and I had co-hosted an awards show for the Tommy's premature baby charity a few weeks earlier. She was also presenting an award at the Sonys and she'd heard we'd won the award in our category.

It was midway through the evening. We'd had the first lot of awards and dinner. The wine flowed freely and our award category was the first one after the break. As the rumour that we'd won the Gold Award grew and grew, we started believing it. Someone from Radio Two and then someone else from Radio Four came over to our table and gave us those nods and winks that suggested they knew something. When one of the judges, albeit not in our category, came and slapped us on the back, we were putting on the running shoes ready for a lap of honour. When I returned to the table with news that the Best Bond Girl Ever reckoned we'd won as well, we started panicking. Nobody had thought of actually going up to accept an award. An awful lot of alcohol had been consumed, and that's not like me. I never drink when I'm speaking, but that was the trouble, I didn't think I'd be speaking onstage.

I hastily wrote an impromptu acceptance speech on the back of my invitation. I was marginally more sober than

Clare and besides I was used to stadium gigs. Compared with twenty-six thousand a crowd of six hundred would be a breeze, even if they were all broadcasters or producers.

The show restarted. Our award was announced.

'And the Sony Bronze Award goes to ... GLR Breakfast.'

We hadn't won. We'd come third. Out of three. Having got used to the idea of winning, our table let out a collect-ive sigh of disbelief. It might have been the sheer force of that group exhalation or maybe someone knocked the table, but somehow the flame of the candle set light to paper around it. The Chinese Lantern caught fire at the base and rose into the air like a hot-air balloon. It floated gently upwards towards the high ceiling, taking with it our forlorn hopes of glory. There were gasps of disbelief from the tables around us; it looked like a protest at the decision. This was not the BBC way to behave. Inform, Educate and Entertain was the corporation's philosophy, now it looked as if GLR, the black sheep of Auntie's family, had let the side down again. If anyone was in any doubt as to where these bad losers were sitting, a blazing beacon hovered above us, illuminat-ing our burning cheeks of embarrassment. We protested our innocence to anyone who would listen, but with the station's reputation for being a bit different, nobody seemed to believe us. This was the station, after all, with maverick ideas like combining rock music with intelligent speech. We were clearly not to be trusted. The Gold Award went to BBC Radio 5Live and rightly so. I congratulated their presenters Victoria and Julian afterwards.

I left GLR shortly afterwards. Not because of the lantern protest. I wanted to be able to live a normal life again. Presenting a breakfast show is deemed the most prestig-ious in a radio station's schedule, but it ruins your life. Every time I've presented breakfast in the past it's made me tired and fat. And I already have a tendency to be tired and fat.

The Sony award, even if it was bronze, had brought me to the attention of a few national broadcasters. The future looked bright, so I packed in the show without too many worries. I told my friends and family that if I ever said I was going to present another breakfast show, they should shoot me. Steve Redgrave, the Olympic rower, said a similar thing about rowing, but he returned to the water and competed in an amazing five Olympics in a row. A few years down the line I 'did a Redgrave'. I accepted an offer to present another breakfast show, on the most unlikely radio station.

Man of the Match

Meanwhile, back at West Ham it was my job to announce the winner of an award at each match. Just before the end of the game I would wait until the ball had gone out of play for a goal kick and then read out the name of the man of the match. During my first season this would more often than not be awarded to Ian Wright. He had an OK season with us, he was popular with the fans and he scored a few goals, but there was no way he was man of the match every week.

The man of the match at West Ham is chosen by a group of people in a corporate box who've paid for the privilege. For the money they'd get to pick the winner of the award and then meet him afterwards in their box. It was the notion of meeting him afterwards that would sway the voting.

At the time Ian Wright was one of the most famous people in the game. After a glittering career at Arsenal he was still scoring goals for us and embarking on a media career. The prawn sandwich brigade loved having their picture taken with him. It meant that less famous, less photogenic players in the West Ham team were regularly overlooked for the award.

Rio Ferdinand was immense in defence and Eyal Berkovic showed some great skill in midfield, but they rarely won the award. Wrighty was a real character; there was no doubt he was good value; he was a dream player for the hospitality department. Everyone wanted their picture taken with Wrighty.

So week in and week out I'd announce the man of the match... Ian Wright. At first there'd be gasps of surprise, then groans and towards the end of the season some boos. It was embarrassing. People would stop me outside the ground and ask me how I could announce him as the man of the match.

It wasn't an ideal system. If you cast your vote knowing that whoever you vote for may end up being the prize, it's bound to affect your decision. No democratic system would allow voting like that. Even if it was fair, have you ever been in a corporate box? Just because you've paid a bit more to watch the game doesn't mean you know any more about it. In fact just the opposite is true in some cases. No disrespect to corporate fans – I love speaking at their company dinners – but I wouldn't trust some of them to sit the right way round on a toilet. Like I say, no disrespect and I am available for weddings, funerals and bar mitzvahs.

Ian Wright only lasted one season at West Ham. He was one of three West Ham players sent off in the 5–1 home defeat to Leeds. While Steve Lomas and Shaka Hislop left the field without problem, Wright decided he'd pop into the referee's room in the tunnel. In a moment of madness he trashed it, while the ref was still out on the pitch. He didn't win the man of the match award that day. It wasn't his finest moment, but he did get a fine. We loaned him out after that.

Wrighty didn't win the Hammer of the Year trophy either, despite all those man of the match awards. He wasn't even runner-up; supporters are much better judges of players than anyone across the course of a season. Defender Ian Pearce came second in the awards, with our goalkeeper Shaka Hislop winning Hammer of the Year. In a season where we'd let in so many goals, it might seem strange that a goalkeeper and a defender should be rewarded, but hey, that's the West Ham way.

YOUTH CUP FINAL

The highlight of my first season was winning the FA Youth Cup, although I was too old to be in the actual team. West Ham have a proud tradition of developing young talent, our academy is second to none. We'd lost in the Youth Cup Final to Liverpool three years earlier, with a team that featured Frank Lampard and Rio Ferdinand. Now we'd another great youth team with Joe Cole and Michael Carrick leading the way.

It's amazing how many of our youth team went on to be regulars in the England side. The tragedy is that they'd usually moved on to other clubs by then. Our youth team must have earned the club a fortune in transfer fees over the years. I've always said that the most important figure at West Ham during my time with the club has been Tony Carr, the man behind our academy.

Manchester United also had a reputation for home-grown talent in the 1990s. While Beckham, Giggs, Scholes and Butt stayed at Old Traffford, we lost the cream of our crop. How great might West Ham have been if we'd kept hold of Rio Ferdinand, Frank Lampard Junior, Michael Carrick, Jermain Defoe, Joe Cole, John Terry and Glen Johnson?

Actually we nicked Jermain Defoe from Charlton's academy, we let John Terry go at fourteen because we didn't think he was good enough and Frank Lampard Junior didn't take much spotting as his dad was our assistant manager. But let's not spoil a good story.

On a Friday night in May, two days before the end of

the season, we played Coventry City in the 1999 FA Youth Cup Final with a team that contained Lampard, Carrick and goalkeeper Stephen Bywater. Having beaten them 3–0 at Highfield Road, the second leg at the Boleyn seemed a formality. It was live on Sky, so the club officials weren't expecting a large crowd. However, you should never underestimate West Ham fans' hunger for success. We'd suffered nineteen years of hurt, since the FA Cup triumph over the Arsenal. The silver polish in the cupboard was well past its 'use by' date.

You didn't need a ticket for youth cup matches. It was pay on the door, and lots of people did. Twenty-three thousand turned up, mostly at the last minute. The scent of glory is enticing, but supporters like to keep their priorities right, and you do have to pass a lot of pubs on the way to the ground.

It was a great night, but it caused problems for the stewards. This was in the days when the ground capacity was twenty-six thousand. At first just the West Stand was open, but it soon filled up. Then the two ends were opened. Still the people kept coming. Kick-off was delayed and the East Stand was finally opened as the game started.

On the pitch West Ham were well in control. Off the pitch it was a different story and led to me upsetting someone I held in high regard.

As the cup final was being played, people were walking around the pitch in front of the stands. Most seats were now full but there was space in the newly opened East Stand. Kids were racing to get the best seats. Families were getting separated.

With a high percentage of youngsters in a crowd, anything can happen. Kids are more likely to run onto the pitch and songs will be sung in a higher key. The pitch invasion is the more serious of the two, unless you are a dog with sensitive hearing.

West Ham's kids were scoring at will. As the goal tally went higher, so did the pitch of the singing and the anxiety levels of the stadium manager, John Ball.

He asked me to read out an announcement urging the fans not to come onto the pitch at the end. The wording was along the lines of, 'In the interests of safety, do not come onto the playing surface at the end of the game. After the whistle a presentation will be made to the winning team. This presentation will not take place if anyone comes onto the pitch.'

He made me read this out six times during the second half. I felt like a teacher in front of a class of known troublemakers.

And then I was a little bit naughty myself.

The last time I read out the message was just before the whistle. West Ham were leading 6–0 on the night, 9–0 on aggregate. It seemed unlikely that Coventry were going to make a comeback at this stage.

So after saying, 'presentation to the winners', I added the words, 'whoever they are!'

There was a loud cheer.

It didn't go down well with the Coventry officials.

The whistle blew.

Nobody ran onto the pitch. Amazingly, after winning the cup 9–0 on aggregate, in front of a largely juvenile crowd, nobody came on the pitch. It was a great result on both counts.

I did that. I made that happen. I was a little bit of a hero too, in my own head. My first season at the club had ended in silverware that wasn't cutlery.

The club were pleased with me. We'd had a few pitch invasions in previous years and were still on a suspended sentence. A subsequent invasion could have cost us dearly. We could have been fined or forced to play a game behind closed doors.

My 'Goodbye Mr Chips' routine had saved the day.

I was invited to the Chairman's Lounge for a drink to celebrate a job well done. It might have been to celebrate winning the youth cup, but in my mind it was also to acknowledge the crowd control skills I'd displayed to the full.

Not everyone was happy with my performance, and an hour later I was pinned up against a wall by Gordon Strachan, the Coventry manager. I don't know if you ever saw him play, but he was not the sort of man you'd want to mess with.

He was a short, ginger-haired, tough-tackling, no-nonsense Scottish midfield general. I don't like to stereotype short, Scottish redheads, but he just happened to be quite short-tempered. It was probably just a coincidence. In short, he was not the sort of person you'd want to argue with.

He seemed unhappy about something. I decided to listen and let him make his point.

'I've got sixteen-year-old lads crying their eyes out downstairs, because of what you said.'

He moved his face even closer to mine.

'It was bang out of order. You shouldn't say things like that.'

I knew Gordon. He'd been a guest on my BBC Radio 5Live show *Sick as a Parrot* a few months earlier, a light-hearted sports quiz show that I wrote and chaired. We were recording on a Saturday evening at the Pebble Mill studios in Birmingham. Gordon was an ambitious booking as Coventry were playing Arsenal that afternoon at Highbury. But he was confident he could make the programme in time. We were recording three shows back to back and Gordon was in the last one.

However by the start time of show three there was no sign of Gordon. The crowd were getting restless. I started telling some of my after-dinner stories. Then resident captain Stuart Hall regaled the audience with tales from his *It's a Knockout* days. It looked like we might have to resort to rival captain Phill Jupitus standing in the door-way with a baseball bat, when Gordon suddenly arrived.

There had been a meningitis scare at his kid's school. Strachan Junior had the symptoms. Gordon had arrived back from Highbury, taken the kid to hospital, got the all-clear and then driven across to Birmingham. Most football managers would have pulled out of the programme, but Gordon is a determined man. He was good on the quiz too, getting most of the answers right and being witty in the process.

I liked him a lot. However, just a few months later, he didn't seem to like me much. In the Chairman's Lounge after the cup final, the ginger was going nuts. I didn't seem to be getting any answers right as far as he was concerned.

I was aware of people at the periphery of my vision, star-ing at us. I didn't like to turn my head in case it angered Gordon further. I hoped I looked in need of saving.

'When you are announcing at a stadium, you should show respect for both teams. You disrespected my players.'

I should have pointed out that the reason those lads were upset was they'd just lost a cup final 9–0. The biggest day of their lives so far had gone badly wrong, and it had been live on Sky, in front of all their friends. But I kept quiet. Please don't laugh, Jeremy, I thought, because he is really angry.

At this point I was saved by a West Ham director. He commiserated with Gordon and said all the polite things that directors say to people from other clubs they have just thrashed. After Gordon had left, the director apologised to me for 'having to be put through that'. Apparently I'd done a great job and we weren't at Wembley so we didn't have to be totally unbiased. My announcements had been fine.

I was relieved that I hadn't let my club down, but I think deep down I know the last announcement was wrong. I did disrespect those Coventry kids and Gordon was well within his rights to stand up for them. But that's football. I was just excited at winning a cup. And at the end of my first season too. There's no manual on how to be a good stadium announcer. There's no British Association of Football Announcers. But I made a note that I wouldn't do that again. It wasn't the West Ham way. Mind you, nor was winning trophies!

It had been a funny old night. I would have to think carefully about announcements next season. With a crop of youngsters like this, surely the good times were just around the corner. Now that is a very West Ham thing to say!

WE'RE ALL GOING ON A EUROPEAN TOUR

'**W**here are we in relation to Europe? Not far from Dover!'
– Harry Redknapp.

You'd think fifth would guarantee you a place in the UEFA Cup, but it didn't. It was just our luck, UEFA were messing about with the rules of qualification, something to do with coefficients. We had to make do with entry into the Intertoto Cup. It was held in such low esteem throughout Europe that some teams that qualified didn't bother taking part. But at least we qualified for something. There was a time when Harry's only chance of competing in Europe looked to be writing a song for Bucks Fizz. Our strong finish to the season meant we could now use the football route to the continent.

At the start of my second season, after the shortest of summer breaks, the Happy Hammers climbed aboard the Trans Europe Express. Named after the dog in *The Wizard of Oz*, rumoured to be Sepp Blatter's favourite film, the Intertoto Cup was a competition for losers. Well, not exactly losers, but those who hadn't quite won. Only the munchkins of European football were allowed in. You qualified by finishing behind those who qualified for the Champions League and the UEFA Cup. The ridiculously early start to the season put off many of the qualifiers.

When I saw our first game was 17 July I thought they were pulling my leg, especially as the opponents were FC Jokerit. We made a good start against the Finnish side and progressed to beat SC Heerenveen of the Netherlands and then played FC Metz of France.

Having lost the first leg 1–0 at home, hopes weren't high about the away leg. I'd already booked to go on holiday with my girlfriend Charlotte to Tuscany, not expecting the football season to be under way so early.

I'd met Charlotte in Tuscany in the early 1990s. My mate Roger from university had organised a combined stag and hen week with his future wife Louise. He'd condensed stag and hen to give it the appealing name of a Shag Week. Single men and women from the future bride and groom's circle of friends were duly invited. Roger was a splendid host and organised a boules tournament under the blistering Tuscan sun. First prize was to kiss all the girls and with that incentive there was no stopping me. My boules were on fire and I claimed my winnings. I carried on kissing Charlotte long after we arrived back in the UK.

After seven years of dating and then living together in Docklands, her work had taken her to Cambridge. She'd bought a house of her own and we'd drifted apart. We still saw each other at weekends, but something had to change. The return to Tuscany was to see if we could make a go of it or if we should part as friends.

I don't think she was too impressed when I wandered away from the villa one night with my radio in hand. I needed higher ground to get a better signal. I sat down on top of an Italian hill, listening to my team amazingly beating Metz 3–1 on French soil. Charlotte thought football was far too important in my life, which was a shame because we'd been together for seven seasons. She didn't mind me watching football, but did I have to watch it 'every' weekend?

The sun was setting on my time with Charlotte. As I watched it disappearing behind a field of sunflowers I wondered what the future held. I was back on the market,

I hadn't dated in years and West Ham had qualified for a proper European tournament.

By beating Metz we'd won the Intertoto Cup. There were actually three winners, for reasons nobody understood. Along with Juventus and Montpellier we now qualified for the UEFA Cup.

When the draw is made, fans always hope for a trip to a tourist destination like France, Spain or Italy, hoping to avoid anywhere cold like Russia. We were drawn against NK Osijek of Croatia. It's a beautiful country, but the conflict between the former Yugoslav states hadn't long finished and the authorities were worried about fighting of a different nature. Whenever English teams travel abroad there's always an overreaction from our continental cousins who remember our hooligan past. Thankfully there's been little trouble from English teams in recent years, but it meant I was invited to travel with the team to Croatia. Worried about crowd trouble, the Croatians wanted someone to do the safety announcement in English to our supporters. I wasn't complaining; I was going abroad with West Ham to represent my club on a European stage. There probably wouldn't be a stage, but I'd stand next to the pitch with a microphone so it still counted as being officially brilliant.

We flew from Stansted in a specially chartered plane, parking our cars right next to the terminal building. The plane was just the other side. You could have chipped a ball from my car and hit the plane. You'd have been thrown out, because airport security is very tight, but that's how close it was. There was none of this 'park in a field and get a bus' nonsense, and no long walk to find your boarding gate. I think I found that short distance from my car to the plane one of the most exciting things about the whole trip. This was the executive lifestyle and I was living it.

There were no instructions about seating but a natural order emerged. The players automatically sat at the front, the journalists went to the back. The club officials sat in the middle, forming a buffer between the players and the press. The players took two seats each so they could spread out. The rest of us only had one seat. I didn't mind, I was just happy to be asked to go.

We spent a night in the capital city Zagreb, before flying to Osijek on a smaller plane. The in-flight meal was a cheese roll in a paper bag. The roll was white but the bag was brown.

The fourth largest city in Croatia, Osijek suffered terribly in the fighting as it's very near the Serbian border. It's full of history. In 1526 Sulemain the Magnificent, the longest reigning sultan of the Ottoman Empire built a five-mile-long bridge at Osijek. It was constructed from wooden boats and was considered by some as the eighth wonder of the world. Suleiman definitely liked it, but I'm not sure how much we can value his opinion if he called himself 'the Magnificent'. It's a bit like Paul Ince calling himself 'The Guvnor'. A grand nickname only has value if someone else picks it.

West Ham fans were more interested in other local attractions. The first brewery in Croatia was founded in Osijek in 1697. Osjecko Pivo is regarded as one of the best beers in the land. Its taste is described as bready and yeasty, with a light lemon background. It's considered very light on the palate. On a hot day East London beer aficionados were tasting large quantities of Osjecko Pivo with vigour. Some forgot to spit it out.

While the fans enjoyed the local hostelries, I went for a look around a beautiful church in the centre of town with some other journalists. I'm not much of a drinker and I like a bit of sightseeing, which is in line with my no drinking when working policy. It's hard enough to pronounce names properly, without being half-cut.

The church was riddled with bullet holes from the

conflict. It was hard to find buildings that didn't have holes. It was as though we'd wandered into Cheese Town and were now in the Swiss Quarter.

I've only ever known war from the movies. I count myself lucky to have been born in a time when I didn't have to go and fight. One hundred and thirty thousand people lost their lives in the conflicts surrounding the break-up of Yugoslavia. The Croatians were at war from 1991 to 1995. Sitting in the cool of that church it was hard to believe that just four years before there had been running street battles outside. It didn't bear thinking about.

We emerged into the heat of the afternoon to walk to the stadium. There was a lot of shouting and chanting coming from the main square. I feared the worst. English football hooliganism had surely reared its ugly head and my team was going to be dragged through the dirt. The politicians and the tabloids would have a field day. Osijek was a war zone again.

I would have to stand by the side of the pitch giving messages in English and people would probably boo me. It was going to be like David Beckham debut day all over again. Except this time people might throw things, stuff they'd kept handy in case the Serbs popped back.

Our European dream had hardly started and we were going to be banned from the competition. It just wasn't fair. In 1986 we'd finished third in the league, but had missed out on Europe because all English teams were banned for five years, after Liverpool fans rioted at Heysel.

On one side of the main square the Croatians were drinking, chanting and waving their flags. On the other side were our lot, drinking and singing 'We are West Ham's Claret and Blue Army'. In the middle of the square the two forces had come together. I hardly dared look.

I needn't have worried. At the top of their voices they were singing, slapping each other on the backs and swapping scarves. Croatians it seemed spoke little English, but they did seem to like us. They appreciated our backing in their conflict with the Serbs and the West Ham fans were greeted like liberators.

The two groups of fans walked to the stadium together. There seemed to be little or no segregation. Maybe after all the years of conflict the Croatians had no will to fight. Our fans behaved themselves impeccably. After nineteen years away from Europe they were enjoying the adventure.

At the match, I went onto the pitch and read out the announcements in English. I wasn't booed by the Croats and the West Ham fans gave me a big cheer. We won the game 3–1, 6–1 on aggregate. It took ages to get back on the coach. West Ham's Igor Stimac was a local hero and we had to wait for him to sign autographs. He took forever. As we'd all come on the same plane, we had to wait for him. The other journalists moaned and moaned, but I just sat back in my seat smiling. My team were back in Europe where they belonged and I was going to savour the moment. Good times were ahead.

We lost to Steaua Bucharest in the next round.

HE WHO MUST NOT BE NAMED

There's one footballer whose name is never ever mentioned at West Ham. Not just because it's hard to pronounce, but because he did something so selfish and ridiculous, that the club banned all reference to him in the matchday programme.

I am speaking of Manny Omoyinmi. How stupid do you have to be to not know if you played in a game or not? Manny cost us a Worthington Cup tie in 1999 because he was cup-tied.

We'd loaned him out to Gillingham earlier in the season. During that time he'd played for them in a cup match. The rules of cup competitions are different from the league. If you play for one team in the cup, you can't play for a different team later in the season in the same tournament. It's to stop teams reaching the final and then buying up all the best players for Wembley.

Manny played for the Gills against Bolton in the second round of the cup. He actually played in both legs, but somehow forgot to mention it on his return. Nobody at West Ham noticed, so he was in the squad to play against Aston Villa in the quarter-final. Midway through the second half of extra time, I announced Manny's arrival into the tie. He only played the last few minutes and had no effect on the result.

The game ended in a draw and went to penalties. It was such a close match, I remember calling for a round of applause for both sides just before the penalties started.

One of these teams was about to go out. I stood on the concourse at the back of my shed, because I only needed to see one half of the pitch and the penalties were at my end. The atmosphere under the floodlights was fantastic, especially with it being a cup tie that had to be decided on the night.

We beat them in an exciting penalty shootout in which Manny played no part, apart from maybe congratulating his team-mates who scored. It was a great night, capped off by victory on penalties.

We were through to the semi-final, or we would have been until someone pointed out that Manny was ineligible. Somebody had grassed us up. Despite having no effect on the match Villa were well within their rights to report us, once it was brought to their attention.

There were calls for West Ham to be thrown out of the tournament. It would have been fair enough to be honest. One of our players had broken the rules. He either forgot he'd played for Gillingham or he knew he'd played, but thought no one would notice. He was either downright thick or incredibly naive.

We were lucky that the authorities were lenient and allowed the game to be replayed. But we lost it and the cup dream was over, thanks to the selfish actions of a half-wit. Manny Omoyinmi never played for West Ham again and Club Secretary Graham Mackrell resigned.

I wrote a programme column about Manny. It was largely based around how to pronounce his name, because I'd heard so many mispronunciations in the previous few days. Many papers had also been spelling his name 'imni' instead of 'inmi'. The article never made it into print. Harry Redknapp was so furious he outlawed any mention of Omoyinmi in the programme. My column was banned by my own club!

Our chances of silverware ended too. We'd gone into

the original Worthington Cup game in December having already been knocked out of the FA Cup. For some reason the third round of the FA Cup was held the second weekend in December that season, and we'd lost at Tranmere. To beat Villa a few days later in the quarter-finals of the League Cup had been a big boost. The replayed game wasn't until January, and by then we didn't have the same sparkle and we lost.

Manny Omoyinmi suffered the ultimate punishment of being sent on loan to Scunthorpe United; Harry really was angry! There was no way back for him and he was loaned out again, this time to Barnet. I don't know if he played for them, and I shouldn't think he does either. He was finally offloaded to Oxford United.

The Strange Case of Mr Hyde

The Manny story doesn't reflect well on footballers, but they're not all like that. In the same season, about an hour and a half before a game, I was sitting in the shed sorting out my CDs, trying to find the perfect combination to build the atmosphere to fever pitch. It was a Premiership game against Watford, so it was important to check no Elton John songs had crept into the running order. There was a knock at the door of the shed, which was already open. In came an athletic chap in a Watford tracksuit. He asked if I was the man announcing the teams, and then said, 'the number eight for Watford is pronounced Miker Hyde'. I thanked him very much for the information. On the team sheet it was spelt Micah Hyde, because that's how you spell it, but I would have pronounced it Meeka Hyde. That's how all the commentators had been pronouncing it this season, so I'd assumed that was the correct way. I smiled at the man in the Watford tracksuit and thanked him. It's not every club that is forward thinking enough to send a representative to check the announcer knows how to pronounce their players' names.

He grinned back and I asked him his name.

'I'm Micah Hyde,' he said, and with that he ran off to join his colleagues who were just emerging from the tunnel for a first look at the pitch. It was a bit of a surprise. Poor old Micah had obviously been so frustrated at his name being mispronounced around the country that his first job on arrival at a new stadium was to seek out the announcer and put him right. I have nothing but admiration for the man.

THE GAME THAT HAD EVERYTHING

By the time we'd buried a millennium time capsule in Dad's back garden, West Ham were out of both cups. But there was one game to come, which had all the thrills and spills of a whole cup run, condensed into just one game. It was in February that West Ham played Bradford City in a nine-goal thriller. It started badly when goalkeeper Shaka Hislop broke his leg in the first few minutes. Young Stephen Bywater, who'd been in the youth team that had won the cup the previous season, went in between the sticks. In a game he would surely remember, the young lad had an absolute nightmare. He let in four goals and we found ourselves 4–2 down at home. Paolo Di Canio was furious we were playing badly and he wasn't getting any joy with the referee. He felt he should have had a penalty. As the decisions continued to go against him, the volatile Italian sat on the ground and motioned to the bench that he wanted to be substituted. He wasn't injured, he'd just had enough. He couldn't cope with the way his teammates were playing and made that rolling motion with his hands that is the international sign of a substitution. Harry Redknapp doesn't speak Italian, but he understood that gesture. Some managers when they see a player give up like that would take him off, thinking his mind wasn't on the game, but Harry was having none of it and insisted he continue on the pitch.

The match came to a head when West Ham won a penalty after Paul Kitson was fouled in the box. Frank

Lampard stepped up to take it but Paolo had other ideas. For a while Frank and Paolo both had hold of the ball and neither showed any sign of letting go. Steve Lomas stepped up as a King Solomon type figure. Maybe the ball would have to be cut in half?

Frank was the designated penalty taker that day and it looked as if he would get his way, except Paolo wouldn't let him. In the end seniority won the day and Frank walked away not looking happy. Paolo of course scored the penalty, even though the keeper guessed which way he'd put it. It was a superb penalty: low to the left and just inside the post. It summed up Di Canio: a mercurial talent who didn't play by the rules, but was capable of moments of brilliance.

West Ham went on to win the game 5–4. It was the busiest I've ever been. The winning goal was scored by Frank Lampard, which I was delighted about. Much as I admired Paolo's efforts, it was fitting that Frank should score the winner, having lost the wrestling contest. I've never announced nine goals before or since.

BROADCAST NEWS

Radio Gaga

The time had come to leave GLR, the early starts were getting to me and I kept thinking about football. One day I presented the Breakfast Show from Elstree Studios, home of *Star Wars*. The props and photos seemed to be crying out to me. R2D2 – scoring draw. C3PO – home win. When Darth Maul came on with his red and black face he looked like an AC Milan fan. I'd thought Darth was a first name but it turns out it's a title like Lord. So you have Darth Maul, Darth Vader, Darth Crooks, that sort of thing.

I'd started presenting a few shows on BBC Radio 5Live. There was no conflict with GLR as it was all BBC. I'd worked there before, reading a few sports bulletins and hosting a World Cup spoof in 1994 called *Route One USA*. After that I'd developed a niche in funny thirty-minute sports programmes, co-hosting *You Cannot Be Serious* with Kevin Day and then devising and hosting *Sick as a Parrot*. But now I was being offered some serious work, hosting full-length sequence programmes. First of all I covered for Adrian Chiles on the Saturday morning show, which was just up my street, as it was light-hearted banter about sport and life. That went well and I started being his regular fill-in host.

After that I was asked to be the stand-in host of the 5Live afternoon show, which was presented by Ian Payne. I spent a day with the programme, to find out how it all fitted together. I'd lots of questions to ask, but as I sat in the control room with pen poised to write down everything that I needed to know, something happened that made me keep quiet. Everyone was very helpful and friendly and I had a good feeling about the programme, but something seemed to be going on beneath the surface. People started talking in hushed tones in little groups. Producers moved in and out of the studio rather more quickly than normal. I started to get a feeling that something was wrong, like when you see a policeman running. Reports were coming in of a breaking story in West London. If it was true it was horrific, and it was a story that touched us all, because it concerned one of our BBC colleagues.

We were getting reports that TV presenter Jill Dando had been shot dead on the doorstep of her home. After that there was disbelief in the control room as the production team tried to first of all confirm the story, and then report the details as they emerged across the afternoon. I didn't know Jill personally but a lot of the people I was working with did, and it was an ordeal for everyone at the BBC that day. It left me with a great deal of admiration for how a team reacts to a breaking story in such dreadful circumstances.

Four days later I was presenting the 5Live afternoon show, not fully understanding how everything worked, but totally confident that I had a fantastic team behind the glass.

On Digital

After the Croatia trip with West Ham, I found myself flying to Europe regularly. After packing in the GLR breakfast gig I'd landed a job fronting the European football for On Digital, ITV's new digital channel. The big European game was on ITV on Wednesday night, presented by Des Lynam. But there were also two live games on the Tuesday night, one hosted by Jim Rosenthal and the other hosted by me.

Jim preferred to stay at home, so I was given all the foreign games. I went to Eindhoven, Stockholm, Marseille and all sorts of exotic places including Glasgow. One time I was spotted buying an Arsenal magazine in a supermarket while wearing a West Ham leisure shirt. An old boy in the queue behind queried the purchase, wondering what I was playing at. I told him I was buying it for research for a trip to Florence to cover the Arse in the Champions League for television. He asked if he'd ever seen me on TV. I told him he would know that better than me, as we can't see out of the television into homes when we're presenting.

As my matches were all presented on location there was no studio. I presented from the stadium. To promote the new channel, they wanted more on-air branding, so jackets were ordered for me and the rest of the team. When they arrived they were cracking jackets, top of the range with On Digital neatly stitched in big letters on them. It didn't help with on-air branding though, because some bright spark had decided the logo should be on the back of the jackets, so nobody ever saw it!

The stitching also completely invalidated the jacket's fantastic waterproofing. The rain came seeping through the holes and we all ended up with wet backs. Not surprisingly On Digital went bust after a short time, so my football trips were just to West Ham after that.

Talksport

After filling in again on the 5Live weekday afternoon show I was offered more work, but it wasn't for another four months. Honestly, Ian Payne and Adrian Chiles were very selfish, if they'd taken more time off, I'm sure I could have made it big on that network. Instead I joined TalkSport hosting a lunchtime weekday show and a phone-in programme with Tommy Docherty at the weekend.

Season in a Nutshell 1999/2000

The ridiculously early start to the season because of the Intertoto Cup meant we hit the ground running and were third in the league after five games. It caught up with us later in the season, as injuries and tiredness began to tell, but we still finished in the top ten for the third season in a row.

Team news – Ian Wright, Wright, Wright turned out to be Ian Wrong, Wrong, Wrong and was loaned to Nottingham Forest, before joining Eyal at Celtic. Stuart Pearce signed to fill the hard-tackling, psycho left-back role that Julian Dicks had filled with distinction for many years.

Highlight – Paulo Di Canio won the goal of the season with a stunning volley against Wimbledon that showed the most incredible timing. Moments like that were worth the admission fee alone, especially as I didn't pay to get in.

Lowlight – We lost 7–1 to Manchester United.

International highlight – Travelling with West Ham as part of the official party on our European adventure.

Worst moment – Manny Omoyinmi's memory lapse ending a promising League Cup run.

Villain – Paolo Di Canio for sitting on his backside and demanding to be substituted when we were 4–2 down against Bradford.

Hero – Paolo Di Canio for getting off his backside and inspiring the team to turn the game around and beat Bradford 5–4.

It shouldn't happen to an announcer – I was invited to Sol Campbell's birthday party, despite never having met the chap and him being a Tottenham player. I took my Spurs mate Tara, who was very excited, but we couldn't get in because he'd invited the whole of the London media and they'd all turned up, leaving massive queues. We stood outside with Olympic athletes and soap stars and then gave up. Tara was gutted and for the first time I felt bad about a Spurs fan being unhappy.

New this season – I experimented with playing cockney knees-up music, like we used to sing around the old Joanna. It wasn't well received as old Joanna had long since moved to Billericay to live with her sister.

The new Fila kit was gorgeous, with more claret than usual and a thick blue stripe down the arm. The blue wasn't quite the colour I'm used to – it was more of a baby blue – but it was a stylish kit from the Italian makers.

Missed games – None.

Did we win at Anfield? – No, we lost 1–0 to a Titi Camara goal.

My bald patch – The size of the bottom of a mug.

Three-Legged Stool Review

Job leg – I left GLR, which had been so much a part of my life. It was one of the most innovative radio stations ever. But I'd left before and this time I had work lined up as a fill-in presenter at BBC Radio 5Live, before landing a regular show on TalkSport and covering Champions League football for ITV.

Relationship leg – After the sadness of ending with Charlotte after seven years, I was looking forward optimistically to a new start with Catherine. She was far too tall for me but I was optimistic about growing a bit, now I'd given up the early-morning breakfast shifts,

West Ham leg – After a fun run in Europe we finished ninth in the Premiership.

THE OTHER HALF

The great loves of my life are football, music, comedy and women. Obviously I like lots of other things too, like walking by the Thames, thrashing round a golf course, pub quizzes, playing tennis, a chilled cider, falling asleep in a deckchair listening to *Test Match Special*, psychological thrillers, drinking pina colada and getting caught in the rain, but the four things that have always been top of my list are football, music, comedy and women. I say always, I imagine in my pre-school days that Lego and colouring were probably contenders too.

I'm beginning to sound like Nick Hornby, whose character in *High Fidelity* was always compiling top ten lists. However, if you've read this far, expecting a West Ham version of *Fever Pitch*, you'll have realised I'm no Nick Hornby.

Over the years the order has changed. Football was the most important from the age of six to about fourteen, when music started to rival its supremacy. By seventeen women were firmly on top, with music close behind and football coming in a poor third.

By the time I left for university, football had slipped to fourth spot. It was just too hard to keep up with the latest news. I went to college in the north. I should imagine it's a university now, because it was then, and they don't often take away university status. It was a long way from home up the M1, in a grim setting, surrounded by dark satanic mills. Many people arrived a little bewildered, having hoped to reach a different destination. A lot had come via somewhere called Clearing. Ironically it was during my time away that West Ham had some of their best form, finishing third in the table in 1986.

From 1990 I was safely back in London trying to integrate two of my great loves, by taking women to watch games. As any football fan knows, it is tough fitting fixtures into your social life, if your partner is not a fellow enthusiast. I've always tried to include my girlfriends in my love of West Ham, but it's never really worked out.

Typically whenever I met someone new they'd be excited about going to a game. There was a mystique about going to a match. It was a bit like the theatre, but without knowing whether it was going to be a tragedy or a comedy. They enjoyed the spectacle of it all, especially the singing and the banter. After a while they'd start losing interest. As the team started to slide down the table or, more significantly, when the temperatures began to drop, the excuses for not going to games would begin. 'Why don't you see if one of your friends would like my ticket?' was always a good one. It showed a caring side, a compassion for others rather than a lack of enthusiasm. In the end, pretty much without fail, they all decided they'd rather go shopping.

As West Ham is such a big part of my life, I'd try everything to get them interested, but with no great success. I'd talk about the skills of Paolo Di Canio, the cheekiness of Joe Cole and the eating records held by Razor Ruddock. I'd try and win them over using topics that would appeal to them like the hairstyles of David James and the fashion shoots of Freddie Ljungberg. But all to no avail.

My girlfriend for much of the 1990s, Charlotte, used to come to games with me in the days when I had two season tickets. She'd alternate with my sister and my Dad – except during the winter when Dad seemed to get the nod most weeks.

Once, Charlotte and I were queuing for a brew at the highly rated Frank Lampard Tea Bar. In a film of this book Charlotte would be played by Catherine Zeta Jones, probably a young CZJ from *Darling Buds of May* days. I don't know how that would work without the use of a time tunnel, but it's unlikely there will be a film, so let's not worry about it. The real point is that I had a girlfriend who looked like CZJ. Her previous boyfriend thought she looked like Winona Ryder, but she didn't. She was much prettier and he was a half-wit.

So I was punching above my weight in the girlfriend stakes, but the counter staff at the FLTB weren't pulling their weight, it was taking ages to get served. I kept checking my watch. We were in danger of missing the kick-off. Like a Frank Lampard Senior tackle in the later stages of his career, we were going to be a bit late.

Charlotte had a plan. I would have rather she kept it to herself, but she decided to say it out loud. She has quite a posh accent for someone who grew up near Bromsgrove. Her brother's a Villa fan with a proper Brummie accent, but Charlotte sounds like a duchess. She's a lot posher than Zeta Jones, who goes a bit Welsh when she's had a few.

'Jeremy, why don't we take our seats and get the drinks at the interval?' Charlotte enquired in a pure cut-glass accent. A few people turned round and grinned at me. I went red. It was like going to a match with Margo from *The Good Life*. It wasn't an ideal time to be called Jeremy either. Still, at least it wasn't Jerry.

I explained that the interval was actually known as half-time. We couldn't pre-order the drinks and emerge at the interval to find them neatly laid out next to a raffle ticket with our number on it. That might work for gin and tonic at the Royal Shakespeare Theatre but it didn't work for Bovril and a Wagon Wheel at the Boleyn. Not that we were ordering Bovril or Wagon Wheels. I'm just trying to regain a bit of street credibility having been called Jeremy in a posh voice.

If you're a football fan, you don't get called Jeremy. It's perceived as an upper-class name more at home on the golf course or rugby club. My West Ham mates have always called me 'Jel' and my family usually call me 'Jem'. 'Jeremy' just doesn't sound right, especially not at West Ham.

We opted to leave the queue. I used the excuse that I didn't want to miss the kick-off, but in reality I was too embarrassed to stay. Charlotte stopped coming to games shortly after that, maybe because of the tea incident, possibly because she came from a family of Aston Villa fans, or most likely because we split up and she started seeing someone else. It was a shame because I enjoyed being able to wear my claret and blue scarf on visits to her parents, without getting any funny looks. Apart from the times when I wore it indoors.

Now I had a new girlfriend. My friend Tara had always said she had the ideal life partner for me. Who says Spurs fans aren't useful? Catherine was a doctor of sexual health who'd also acted in comedy shows at the Edinburgh Festival. A sex doctor with a sense of humour, what's not to like? She also had a brain the size of a planet. In fact the only downside was her height. She was five foot eight, the same as me, but in heels she towered over me. She looked great, but I fear I may have looked a little comical alongside her. In the film, which they aren't going to make obviously, she would be played by Helen Hunt, from around about the *Twister* era. In fact once in Covent Garden an American asked for Catherine's autograph thinking she was Helen Hunt.

When there are important decisions to be made, I often like to have a walk to ponder matters. On the important matter of deciding on a new partner, I combined my walk with a game of golf. There were three choices, go back to Charlotte, ring an old friend who I'd always liked, or call Dr Destiny. This was the name assigned to Catherine by Tara, because she was apparently my destiny, as we had the same sense of humour.

There was no one else out on the course as it was a foul day. I put down three balls on the edge of the green about forty to fifty feet from the hole. It was a slightly sloping green from right to left. I assigned a ball to Charlotte and hit it five feet beyond the hole to the left. The second ball bearing the hopes of the old friend, who didn't even know she was in the contest, landed a couple of feet short and to the right. The third ball was for the good doctor. As she was my destiny, I decided to close my eyes. I struck the ball cleanly and started walking. As I opened my eyes, I could only see two balls. The third ball was nowhere to be seen, until I reached the hole. There it was nestling at the bottom of the cup, staring up at me, daring me to make that phone call. I rang later that night and made an appointment to see the doctor.

Our first date was the GLR night of comedy for Children in Need at the Shepherd's Bush Empire. I met her there because she had come straight from a surgery. The first time I met her was when she edged along the row of seats towards me. It was of course a ridiculous idea to have a first date at a theatre. She was late and the show had already started. That meant we couldn't talk until the interval. So it was a fifteen-minute speed date, followed by the second half.

Afterwards we went to try and find her car. In the rush not to be too late, she'd parked it in a side street off Shepherd's Bush Green. We couldn't find her car though. Worse still she couldn't remember what sort of car it was, as she'd only just bought it. I couldn't get my head around someone not knowing what sort of car they drove. It turned out to be a Peugeot 406 when we stumbled across it, so fair enough.

The second date at a curry house was much better. We talked and talked and got on fabulously. She came from a family of six-footers, so whenever I visited her folks it was like a trip to *Land of the Giants*. I was slightly worried when I was invited to dinner that they might eat me. But despite the Spurs connections I converted her to a West Ham fan and she was soon coming to games, sitting with me in the announcer's box, helping out by collating the birthday requests. Like most of my girlfriends I suspect she tolerated West Ham rather than fully embraced them.

BEHIND THE SCENES

Betty the Tea Lady

I've worked with some lovely people over the years at West Ham. One of my favourites was Betty the tea lady. Every match day Betty would bring me a flask of tea, first to the shed and later up to the announcer's box. She must have been well into her seventies when I first joined the club, and worked into her eighties.

She was a real character, reminding me of my Nanna. She'd always stop for a few words, probably to get her breath back. The move from the shed at pitch level to level three of the West Stand was not a popular one with Betty. Lift or no lift, it was still a long way from the kitchens.

She'd come to me after she'd taken the players their drinks, giving me an idea of their form by saying things like, 'Paolo's in a good mood, laughing and joking. I reckon he'll score today.' Or she'd say, 'Some of them look a bit tired, I reckon we're going to get done.'

She was a popular figure behind the scenes, everyone got on well with Betty. But there was one man she couldn't stand. Referee Graham Poll was Betty's arch-enemy. In her opinion Poll didn't like West Ham. Whenever he refereed one of our games, Betty would be in a bad mood. She'd bring me my tea, piping hot in a flask, and then she'd spend a good few minutes letting off steam. I could have earned a few bob as her therapist.

'He never gives us nothing. I said to him, when are you going to give us a penalty? He never said a word. I don't

know what we've ever done to him. I tell you what, Jeremy,
I ain't sure he's ever given us a throw-in.'

With that Betty would get off laughing and everyone
in the announcer's box would laugh with her. She was
West Ham through and through, having organised travel
to away games with her husband in the 1950s and 60s.
When he died she still loved being part of the club, making
teas on a match day.

One day Betty was in a very jolly mood, a bit of a surprise
when you looked at the officials named on the team sheet.
'We've got that Graham Poll again today,' she said, having
just taken tea and biscuits into the referee's room for the
four officials.

'I've give him plain digestives and he says to me ain't
you got no chocolate ones. I says no, we've run out, but I
tell you what, Jeremy, we have got some. Look, I've brought
you some, I told him they've run out, 'cause I know they're
his favourites. He don't ever give us nothing.'

Poll had made the mistake of once telling Betty he loved
his chocolate digestives. From that day, whenever he was
officiating at West Ham, the chocolate digestives mysteri-
ously disappeared. He was lucky to get plain digestives as
Betty thought about giving him Rich Teas but she wasn't
a vindictive woman.

I don't remember Graham Poll being biased against
West Ham. I think in general he was a good ref. He fancied
himself a bit and liked to be the centre of attention a bit
too much, but he was certainly competent. Poll must have
thought that West Ham's catering suppliers were very slack
in topping up the chocolate digestive supplies. Little did he
know it was just our Betty's way of settling a score. She
thought he didn't give us anything, so he missed out on
his favourite biscuits. When it came to referees, Graham
Poll wasn't Betty's cup of tea.

She even started telling the other refs about it. I feared

someone would grass her up and she'd get into trouble, but they never did. Say what you like about refs, they're not whistleblowers.

When Betty retired she came for a chat on the microphone with me before a game. She went to live with her sister in the northeast and died soon after. I like to think she's now watching games from the great grandstand in the sky. Knowing Betty she'll have it organised, with her husband on one side and Bobby Moore on the other. She'll be in the middle with a huge flask of tea and some biscuits, and I bet they're all chocolate digestives.

MC Hammer

Often we'd play the last game of the season wearing the new kit for the following season to boost sales during the summer months. I was told I'd be given a new shirt and I could have my name or whatever I wanted printed on the back. I asked for 'MC Hammer' with a number six. All of my West Ham shirts have had the number six on the back, after my first West Ham hero, Bobby Moore.

MC Hammer was the 1980s rap artist with the unfeasibly large dancing trousers. In a way I'd always regarded myself as MC Hammer, not because of my fashion sense but because I'm master of ceremonies for the Hammers.

On the last day of the season I arrived early at the ground, eager for the first sight of the new kit. I couldn't wait to try on my new shirt and hear the gasps of amazement as fans appreciated the wit and thought that had gone into my name selection.

You know that song 'Big in Japan' by Alphaville from the mid-80s? I always remember dancing to that with a pint of lager snakebite in one hand, singing 'Big in the Pants tonight'. They were happy carefree days and we deliberately sang the wrong words for comic effect.

Trousers were enormous, with massive pockets. It was a waste because we had nothing to put in them; mobile telephones hadn't been invented and we didn't have any money.

Back to the future and on this last day of the season, I was going to be big in the pants, MC Hammer pants. I had on the baggiest trousers that Next for Men sold and just needed my personalised shirt to complete the look.

Walking down the tunnel singing 'U Can't Touch This', I caught sight of Eddie the kit man. He's a top man, now retired, but he obviously wasn't a fan of the artist formerly known as Stanley Kirk Burrell. Eddie held up my new shirt and it was lovely. He turned it round, oh dear, not so lovely. On the back was the anticipated number six, but above it were just two letters. Instead of MC Hammer it said 'DJ'. This might have been an economy drive, or a protest against the increasing influence of rap music in popular culture, but it was just a mistake. Eddie couldn't remember what I'd asked for. He knew it was something to do with music, so he guessed 'DJ'.

I still have that shirt and wear it to the gym sometimes. But I've only ever once worn it with big trousers, the day I nearly pulled off the funniest visual gag seen at the Boleyn in years.

Legend has it that once in the days of black-and-white football, a ball went into the crowd and a player went to retrieve the ball for a throw-in. The 'ball' was thrown back and he caught it. It was very cold, much colder than you'd expect a ball to be. Close examination revealed it to be a frozen turkey, although some variations of the story say it was a chicken.

There have been hilarious songs and chants but that is probably the funniest sight joke ever seen at West Ham. My MC Hammer shirt was going to be the only serious contender to knock the 'frozen turkey/chicken' off its perch. I was robbed of that moment by Eddie. Of course I forgive him, but I've never sent him a Christmas card since that incident. Or indeed before it.

The Men in Black

On a match day I often have to talk to the Men In Black, which is a bit scary. I've grown up hearing that they have dubious parentage, enjoy their own company and have poor eyesight. The second thing may have led to the third. By the way, I'm talking about referees, not Will Smith and Tommy Lee Jones. It would be great to see Tommy ref a game at the Boleyn though. You'd get no truck with players misbehaving if Will got his shooter out.

Will and Tommy are dedicated to rooting out illegal aliens. They are trained to spot those who are not of this world, who act in a strange manner, which brings us right back to referees.

Actually most refs are a dream to work with, especially now Graham Poll has retired. Once in the days when I announced from the box high up in the corner of the stand, I couldn't see how many minutes were being added on at the end of the first half. Poll was the fourth official and he was meant to show the electronic numbers board to all corners of the ground, but he didn't. He just held it straight above his head. I told the crowd I couldn't see how many added minutes were being indicated, but they could hopefully see for themselves. There was laughter. He still didn't spin it round. Instead he put the board down and later mentioned my 'misconduct' in his match report. He didn't do his job properly and I got ticked off! Thanks, Graham. Still, at least I had chocolate biscuits that day and he didn't.

I'll often ask the referee what time they are planning to walk the players onto the pitch, so I can coordinate the playing of 'I'm Forever Blowing Bubbles'. If I've done my job properly the song will reach its peak just as the players emerge from the tunnel. Occasionally I'll give the signal to start the anthem, and then find the ref has changed his mind, because one of the teams is not ready. By then it's too late and we sometimes have to have a second chorus of Bubbles.

If it's a live TV game, then there's no point in talking to the ref. My point of contact will be the TV floor manager, who will decide when the players walk. The ref might appear to be in charge, but TV really runs the show. If the teams emerge while the adverts are still playing, then someone is going to be in trouble.

When I'm driving home from West Ham, I always listen to the radio phone-ins where referees are slaughtered. Every football fan is convinced they are biased against their team. It's ludicrous to think that, they just have good days and bad days like anyone else.

People are always convinced they've been robbed. I can only smile, yet a few years before I became the announcer, I was absolutely sure in my mind that the ref had it in for us. Keith Hackett's performance in our FA Cup semi-final defeat to Nottingham Forest in 1991 set a benchmark in low refereeing standards. He sent off Tony Gale and ruined our day out. And his guide dog made a mess of the pitch.

My memory of the day is that Tony was very hard done by. Watching it now, video evidence suggests a yellow card would have been more appropriate, but Keith will tell you he had no choice but to send Galey off, because of a tightening up of the law on fouls.

If you want to know why West Ham fans are so special; watch the video of that game. It was 0–0 when Tony Gale was sent off. We lost 4–0, but you wouldn't have known it, we never stopped singing. It was the same chant, over and over and over again, 'Billy Bonds' Claret and Blue Army' repeated hundreds of times until the final whistle. It was tuneless but hypnotic, futile yet glorious.

It is one of my proudest memories of supporting the club, yet you won't see the footage on any West Ham Greatest Moments videos. Marketing people don't under-stand why defeat can be glorious. A focus group wouldn't come up with a 4–0 defeat as a highlight, but it was. It showed when it comes to support through thick and thin we are right up at the top of the league. Stoke and Portsmouth are noisy. Liverpool singing 'You'll Never Walk Alone' at the end of a match is inspiring. Spurs on a European night is a bit special and Millwall can create an intimidating atmosphere. But when it comes down to pure, raw, unbridled passion, you'll be hard pushed to find more committed supporters than West Ham fans. They're made from special stock and they're different gravy.

Free Parking

One of the perks of being the announcer is being allocated a parking space, close to the ground. Over the years my space has got closer and closer. To start with I was given a space in car park C, which is the playground of a school in Central Park Road. After a few years, I was promoted and given a spot in car park B, which is the car park of the claret and blue school right next to the ground on the way to the tube. You have to be really important to get a place in car park A, where the top officials park, but so far that's only happened on youth and reserve games. And then there's the player's car park, but I'm never going to get in there … not at my age. I'm happy with car park B where we've got snakes and ladders painted on the tarmac!

Lucky owners of a parking space are given a coat hanger-shaped pass to hang on the rear view mirror. One year my car park pass was number 100. That felt lucky.

Another year my pass number was my age at the start of the season but after November it wasn't my age any more. I still have all my coat hanger-shaped laminated passes in a nostalgia box. How sad is that?

For an evening match I have to arrive for a meeting at 3:45. At that time car park B is still being used as a school playground. The kids don't like it when you try and reverse into a space they are using for hopscotch, so the B team are given permission to use the hallowed car park A, but only on a temporary basis. After 4 p.m., a message goes out to all members of staff in car park A that they have to move them over to car park B.

I drive a fairly old car, but at least it gets me from A to B.

HARRY REDKNAPP

I liked Harry Redknapp a lot. He was the first manager I worked with as announcer and I was sorry to see him go. Harry played for West Ham when I was a kid, alongside assistant manager Frank Lampard. Harry and Frank were big mates and married two sisters from Barking. They'd both fathered footballers; Jamie Redknapp was at Liverpool and Frank Lampard Junior was at West Ham.

I'd met Harry quite a few times before I started as announcer. He likes the media and is very good at interviews. He'd been a guest on TV and radio shows that I'd presented. I remember playing darts with him on *Turnstyle*, a Saturday morning show I fronted alongside Chris Hollins on Channel Five. The great thing about Harry is he's himself. He's totally natural when onscreen, funny in real life and he's a dream for journalists as he gives good quotes.

Once when we were in make-up together at Meridian Studios in Southampton, I asked him how he copes with pressure. 'Football's not pressure,' he said. 'Pressure is when you are lying by the side of the road after a crash and a policeman puts a blanket over your face saying, this one's dead.'

Harry went to watch the World Cup in Italy in 1990 with his close friend Brian Tiler, the managing director of Bournemouth. We all remember Italia 1990 for the penalty shootout defeat to Germany in the Turin semi-final. Gazza cried and the nation wept with him.

For Harry it was more serious than that. He was involved in a horrific car crash in Italy. His friend Brian was killed and Harry suffered facial injuries. As he lay by the side of the road his knowledge of Italian words was good enough to know they thought he was also dead.

To this day he's not let the pressures of football get to him. His injuries left his facial muscles damaged and he has a twitch. Heartless fans refer to him as 'old saggy chops' and sing 'he's going to twitch in a minute'. It's very mean, but football fans have a habit of being mean.

However, whenever he comes back to West Ham he always gets a good reception from the true fans, those that remember him bombing up and down the wing as a player. One time two teenage girls ran onto the pitch to kiss him during a game. He wasn't a bad manager either, certainly our most successful in recent history. He's a local boy too, born in Poplar. His grandmother was an illegal bookies runner in the East End. Harry would often come home from school to find his nan being taken away by the police. Harry likes a gamble, but he thought he was on safe ground as the season came to an end.

He'd only gone into chairman Terry Brown's office for a chat about the future. Harry had been outspoken in the *Over Land and Sea* fanzine about not having the funds he needed. The chairman wasn't impressed and before you knew it, he was off. The club say it was by mutual consent but Harry is adamant he was sacked. Frank Lampard Senior went with him and not surprisingly, having seen his uncle and his dad depart, Frank Lampard Junior was soon following them out of the door.

Harry left for Portsmouth, where he was a hero saving them from relegation. He then became a villain because he went to rivals Southampton. But he took Southampton down, regaining his hero status again with the Pompey faithful. He returned to Portsmouth to cement his place in

Fratton Park folklore, before spoiling it all by leaving in a hurry for north London.

His career hit a new low when he became the manager of our arch rivals Tottenham Hotspur, the only team named after a Shakespeare character. Harry took the Spuds from bottom of the table to the Champions League. I wonder if he could have done that at West Ham. What would have happened if he'd stayed with his home club, if he hadn't gone into the chairman's office that day and had an argument?

There have been lots of stories about Harry's business dealings. He's been investigated a few times. I was in court reporting on his case with Milan Mandaric over allegedly misleading the Inland Revenue over payments, during their time together at Portsmouth. As he walked into court, Harry nodded at me, probably wondering what on earth I was doing there. I was asking myself the very same thing, It was another one of those strange quirks of the reporter rota. I hadn't been in court for years and could just about remember the restrictive rules of reporting.

The other downside to Harry is the way he became West Ham manager. He was originally Billy Bonds' assistant. One day Billy was sacked and Harry became the gaffer. Billy is one of my all-time favourite West Ham players, second only to Bobby Moore. Harry was Billy's best man at his wedding but they don't talk any more, which is a real shame. A lot of West Ham fans blame Harry for Bill's departure, although Harry insists he didn't stab his mate in the back.

Harry is always being touted as an England manager. I would love that, because he's a real man manager and would get the best out of the players. However, one of his greatest skills is in the transfer market and that's no use as an international boss. They won't let the England manager buy a top foreigner and play him in the national team. The only Brazilian you can buy is at the beauty parlour. And you have to be very lucky not to get the sack.

I'll always remember my first manager with fondness. He's trod on a few toes in his time, and he's the manager of our arch rivals, but I still look forward to his visits to Upton Park.

I wondered at the time if we'd get a new manager who could take us to the next level, someone with bags of experience who could turn our team of entertainers into a team of winners. We didn't.

TWO FRANK LAMPARDS

'Two Frank Lampards, there's only two Frank Lampards!' West Ham have had two players called Frank Lampard. One played for us when I was a kid, the other played during my early seasons as announcer. Now they were both gone, collateral damage in the Harry Redknapp/ Terry Brown argument.

My first meeting with a Frank Lampard had been a very scary one. I used to go to football training at Redbridge Sports Centre when I was eleven or twelve. Les Allen was our teacher, a member of the famous Allen family. He's Clive and Bradley's dad, as well as being Martin and Paul's uncle. Les was also a member of the Spurs team that did the double in 1961, but let's not talk about that. One week Les couldn't make it, so we were told there would be a last-minute replacement. We sulked like a bunch of kids, because that's what we were, until we found who the substitute was. There were gasps of amazement when West Ham first-team player Frank Lampard turned up. In those days he wasn't senior. He had a shaggy beard and he threw himself around like a wild man. To be frank, he was a little rough for my liking, but I had grown up with three sisters so I'd always had to play nicely. Much as I idolised Billy Bonds, I played like Trevor Brooking, with none of this tackling nonsense, just lots of flair. To my young eyes Frank seemed to be getting stuck in a bit more than Les used to. He didn't wear any sports shoes so he didn't hurt us. But it also meant he could come sliding into tackles using his socks on the indoor surface.

It's all a bit of a blur and the next thing I can remember is having a drink afterwards. Redbridge Sports Centre had a vending machine that served ice-cold orange drink. For two pence you could have the sweetest, coldest drink in the world, in a white plastic cup. I'm sure it should have been diluted, but they'd just forgotten. You'd get an instant 'ice cream headache' as soon as you had a sip. When Dad came to pick me up, he found me by the drinks machine suffering from frostbite and sugar shock. I must have looked shocked, because he asked how I was.

All I could say was, 'We had Frank Lampard and he was sliding into tackles and everything.' Dad rolled his eyeballs upwards. He always reckoned I needed toughening up. Most times when we were drying up after dinner, he'd flick me with the tea towel and provoke me into an impromptu boxing lesson. Dad had learnt boxing in the army; anyone would think he was a regular soldier the way he went on about it. He'd only been in for two years doing national service before becoming a pharmacist. As a small child, I thought this meant he helped on a farm, but it didn't. He was a white-collar worker, but he wanted me to be able to cope with the rigours that life could throw at me.

For the next week, Dad practised slide-tackling me in the garden, which he enjoyed immensely. I didn't find it quite as much fun, so I invested in a set of shin pads from Ted Fenton's sports shop. The next week I was ready for Frank Lampard and his sliding socks, but rather disappointingly it was Les Allen once more. In fact Frank Lampard never came back. Dad says he'd probably been scared off by news of my intensive training regime, but I think it was just that Les was available again.

When I started as matchday announcer, Frank Lampard had been renamed by deed poll as Frank Lampard Senior.

He was now the assistant manager to his old mate Harry Redknapp. Frank was always very friendly, always nodding when he saw me. Maybe he remembered me from all those years ago, although I'd put on a lot of weight in the meantime.

Harry Redknapp may seem like a confident chap, but he used to worry about the crowd putting pressure on the players. Most managers like the crowd roaring on the team, but not Harry. He'd send Frank along to see me pre-match with a few words of warning. Frank would tell me not to build up the game too much by being too vocal on the microphone. If the crowd were too pumped up before the game, it might get to the players. I thought it might have a positive effect. I know if I was a West Ham player I'd love nothing better than walking out to a full stadium and the crowd singing, but Frank was not to be swayed. He'd always preface any instructions with 'Harry says'.

So in the Redknapp era, I would deliberately try to not create an atmosphere. Each manager has their own ideas. Alan Pardew was at the opposite end of the spectrum, he wanted the stadium rocking. I'm there to serve whoever is in charge of my team. I try and steer them towards the West Ham way, but in the end if they want bells and whistles, that's what they get. Fans who've listened to my announcements over the years must think I have multiple personalities. I can go from the loudest announcer in the world to the most laid-back in the change of a manager.

One time Frank Lampard Senior came to see me before the game. 'Harry says can you not make a big thing about welcoming back Tony Cottee. The last time you did, he scored against us.'

I pointed out that we always welcome back old players, it's the West Ham way. But Frank Lampard Senior was having none of it.

'Well Harry says don't do it, so don't. From now on he doesn't want you to welcome back any old players.'

So when I read out Tony Cottee's name on the team sheet, I didn't welcome him. I did pause after his name and the crowd cheered and I waited until the cheering stopped before continuing. I'd complied with instructions, but I'd also respected a hero. Players like TC should always be welcomed back. The science that suggests the welcoming back of a player leads to a goal is nonsense. The feel-good factor induced by the cheering is also likely to make the player feel bad about scoring against us. Even if it doesn't, I think it's important to do things right.

When Harry Redknapp first returned to West Ham as a manager in the opposition dugout, I was tempted not to welcome him back. It was what he would have wanted, I thought. However, I was determined to pursue my policy of doing it the West Ham way, especially as there was very little chance of him scoring. He received a terrific reception from the fans. The media seemed surprised by this. He was asked in a post-match TV interview if he was taken aback by the warmth of the home crowd. He said he wasn't; he'd been a West Ham man and boy, and he knew West Ham always welcomed back their own. I smiled when I heard this – he was right, but it was no thanks to him. I like Harry a lot, he says it like it is, and he's great company.

Over the years the warmth of his reception has cooled, but that's his own fault. He did become Spurs manager and that's never going to endear you to the Upton Park faithful. Still, I like to think there's lots of us that still remember him with affection.

I don't know who Harry uses these days to convey important messages to the announcer. Frank Lampard Senior parted company with his gaffer after their spell at West Ham. Frank's other big part in my life was in the beverage department.

Most of the tea bars in the old West Stand were named after old players. All except the Anne Boleyn Tea Bar. Anne did have a trial with West Ham but we had to let her go. She kept losing her head in the box.

I liked the Anne Boleyn Tea Bar, but in my view the best cup of tea in the ground was served at the Frank Lampard Tea Bar. It was also the closest to my seat when I was a season ticket holder, so that may have been a factor. The walk from the ABTB was just a bit too far. I like to let my tea brew naturally for three minutes, just the right time to walk to my seat from the FLTB.

The tea bar was named after Frank Lampard, the bearded West Ham defender of my childhood, and not his son. Frank Lampard Junior may well have eaten a lot of chocolate and crisps from the tea bar, but it was named after his dad.

In those days Junior was a promising young midfielder who I felt never really earned the respect he deserved from the home supporters. There was a feeling he only made the team because his uncle was the boss and his dad was assistant boss. It was also felt by some of the slim-line members of our crowd that he was a little chubby, hence my childish comment about the snacks. When Young Frank left West Ham for Chelsea he matured as a player and went on to become a top-class international midfielder. He's still called 'Fat Frank' by the West Ham faithful though. This was particularly ironic in the days when we were sponsored by Icelandic airline 'XL'. Whether your shirt was small, medium or large, you still had XL in large letters on the front. When we played Chelsea, our fans would sing to the tune of 'skip to the loo my darling', 'Big Fat, Big Fat Frank, Big Fat, Big Fat Frank, Big Fat, Big Fat Frank, Big Fat Frankie Lampard' .

This would be sung by overweight gents with replica shirts encasing their stocky frames. Above their bulging bellies were the letters 'XL'. The object of their attention didn't have an ounce of fat on him and proved it by running for ninety minutes. Amazingly for such a 'fat' gentleman he never seemed to miss a game either.

I was sorry to see him go. I always felt he was a great talent. At the time Joe Cole grabbed all the headlines with his ball-juggling skills. Michael Carrick was a solid holding midfielder who was also highly rated. Frank never won over the Upton Park faithful.

Since then he's received a lot of barracking from West Ham fans whenever he's returned. I don't think he deserved that, well not at first anyway.

I always made a point of shaking his hand when he returned. Until one day when I went to watch West Ham at Chelsea. Frank was getting his usual abuse, but he started giving it back. He made gestures at the West Ham fans. I wasn't impressed. When Chelsea won the game, he made more gestures as he left the field.

But I'm still a fair-minded man. It can't be much fun getting stick like that. So on his next visit to the Boleyn Ground, I walked out to shake his hand as he walked off.

'Hello, Doc,' he said.

He thought I was one of the doctors! After all the times I'd defended the plonker in front of my mates, he thought I was one of the club doctors. Big Fat Frank thought I was a medic. Did he think I was coming over to check his BMI or fit him with a gastric band? Or had he been stuffing his fat face so much with chocolates, it had affected his eyesight?

Childish as it maybe, I resolved not to seek him out to shake his hand again. I wouldn't shun him, though, because that would be wrong. If he came over to shake my hand or ask medical advice, I would shake his hand. I also decided that I would no longer wear a stethoscope at matches.

Season in a Nutshell 2000/01

Paolo Di Canio, Joe Cole and Trevor Sinclair made watching West Ham an absolute joy. The skill and flair that they brought to the team was phenomenal. Leeds United paid a British record fee of £18 million for our highly rated defender Rio Ferdinand.

Highlights – Coming from behind to beat Manchester City 4–1, and beating Charlton 5–0.

Lowlight – Selling Rio Ferdinand, I'd watched him grow from a boy to a man. He's a proper West Ham player in the Bobby Moore mould, with the ability to move the ball intelligently out of defence.

Golden moment – Paolo Di Canio's goal against Fabien Bartez to beat Manchester United in the FA Cup at Old Trafford. Bartez tried to con Paolo into thinking he was offside, putting his hand up like a gendarme stopping the Paris traffic. The Italian motored on to make it 1–0 to the cockney boys.

Worst moment – Losing to Spurs in the FA Cup quarter-final.

Hero – Joe Cole was called up by England.

Villain – Croatian signing Davor Suker was rubbish, a big name who didn't live up to his golden boot reputation.

Team news – Freddie Kanoute joined along with Suker. Rio left and Julian Dicks had his testimonial.

It shouldn't happen to an announcer – Harry kept signing foreign players that were difficult to pronounce. I could cope with Titi Camara and Christian Bassila, but Ragnvald Soma didn't seem to have enough vowels. Fortunately he was happy to be called Raggie.

Missed games – None.

Did we win at Anfield? – No, we drew 1–1, with a Paolo penalty cancelling out Steven Gerrard's opener.

My bald patch – The size of the bottom of a ramekin, the sort you'd make a soufflé in.

Three-Legged Stool Review

Job leg – I was enjoying broadcasting on TalkSport. It was great to work with a legend like Tommy Docherty and we built up a great rapport.
Relationship leg – Things were going well with Dr Destiny. Catherine moved in to my Docklands flat.
West Ham leg – With the other two legs locked firmly onto the stool, this was the wobbly leg. We finished fifteenth and Harry Redknapp was sacked just before the end of the season, after an argument with the chairman about how much money he could spend on new players.

ROEDER NOWHERE

I returned to my first love, radio, in 2002. I was contacted by entrepreneur Vince Power, the man behind the Mean Fiddler organisation which puts on lots of music events. He'd been an avid listener to my GLR afternoon show in the 1990s and vowed that if he ever owned a radio station, he wanted me to present the breakfast show. Hooray! He'd bought a radio station. Hooray! It was a country music station. Oh!

I started broadcasting a weekend show on Mean Country 1035AM from their studios, which were within sight of Wembley Stadium. I had to look in my A–Z to find it as I hadn't been for a while. I was given the weekday breakfast show, completely forgetting how much I hate getting up in the mornings. I enjoyed being back on air, without having TV producers in your ear telling you what to do. I even started liking the songs. Listening to country music is a lot like following West Ham; it can be very depressing at times but the followers are devoted and talk about nothing else.

West Ham replaced Harry Redknapp with an experienced manager. The trouble was his experience was all at a lower level and at the wrong end of the table. The way West Ham played under Glenn Roeder, coupled with my daily fix of country music, it was a wonder I wasn't put on suicide watch.

Glenn Roeder was only West Ham's ninth manager in our hundred-year history. That's quite an amazing fact, isn't it? They gave the manager's job to Glenn Roeder!

Maybe he just happened to be hanging around in the corridor when Harry was sacked and so they asked him to take over. That can be the only explanation, surely? I wonder if he even applied for the job. He'd been out of work for a while and Harry had done him a favour by offering some coaching work. It worked out well for Glenn and ended in tears for us.

Roeder's one big talent was working with young players. It was maybe his only talent. He'd earned some brownie points at Watford having spotted Kevin Phillips playing non-league football. When they flogged him to Sunderland for five million they built two new stands at Vicarage Road. We didn't really need any help in spotting youngsters as we had a brilliant academy. What we needed was someone to help build the club so the youngsters didn't have to leave to pursue their careers. Rio and Frank Junior had left. Joe Cole and Michael Carrick would surely follow them, unless we moved up to the next level.

During his time at the club he had my full backing, as any West Ham manager always will. However, in the light of what happened, and bearing in mind I've been a fan a lot longer than I've been the announcer, I think now a decent passage of time has passed, I'm allowed to let off steam a bit about this awful period in our history.

Roeder was way out of his depth in my view and has the distinction of achieving relegation with one of the most talented West Ham squads ever assembled. His managerial background was to have narrowly avoided relegation with Gillingham and he left Watford when they were in trouble. He'd played for both Gillingham and Watford. He was later to go on to manage another of his former clubs, Newcastle United. He didn't do very well there either. The Newcastle link led to him having a season as Chris Waddle's assistant at Burnley and he nearly took them down.

He never played for West Ham, but had supported the

club as a boy. It was a cunning plan. Never mind his disastrous record as a coach, let's give him the top job because he knows the area. It will save money on a Sat Nav.

You might detect that I was less than enthusiastic about the appointment. Glenn might have grown up a Hammer, but he was no Harry. He looked like a bank manager when he stood on the touchline. He couldn't inspire the players and his tactics just didn't work.

I asked Glenn Roeder when he arrived if there was anything special he'd like me to do on a match day. He told me to carry on doing what I was doing. I think he probably did that with everyone to start with. That's why the first season wasn't too bad. With players like Paolo Di Canio and Trevor Sinclair the side didn't need much coaching. In fact it was only when Glenn started having ideas of his own that everything started to go wrong.

For a bank manager he didn't mind splashing the cash. Fat Frank had been sold to Chelsea for eleven million pounds and Glenn didn't leave the money in the vaults very long. England goalie David James from Villa was a great signing for the experience he brought, not to mention his wide range of haircuts. Glenn twice broke the club's transfer record. Scottish bad-boy midfielder Don Hutchison joined for five million pounds, a lot of cash for someone with a reputation as a hell-raiser off the field. Then, like all good bank managers, he authorised the signing of a Czech. Tomas Repka may have been a hero to some fans, but he was not my sort of player. I've never been a fan of martial arts.

To be fair, at the end of his first season, our new manager wasn't the disaster we'd all feared. After a bad start we'd had a good run thanks to our home form. The season ended on a disappointing note though, which for me summed up the problem with Glenn. He may have looked like a bank manager in his dress and demeanour, but managing wasn't his strong point. Glenn was great at the science of football, he brought in lots of new technology at the training ground, but he lacked the human touch that would have brought out the best in his players. His inability to manage a temperamental talent like Paolo Di Canio was to prove his downfall later.

Steve Potts, though, was a dream for a manager; he'd been at West Ham for as long as anyone could remember. A former club captain, Steve had been Hammer of the Year twice and this was to be his last season. He'd been on a total of 399 league appearances for the club and needed just one more to make a nice round 400.

Steve had been named as a substitute a few times that season, but he'd never come on. There was a clamour from the fans to give him one last game to reach that four hundred league appearances landmark. We beat Bolton 2–1, but sadly Steve Potts stayed on the bench. Despite the fans singing his name, Glenn didn't send him on. He almost seemed to be making a point: he was the manager, he had a game plan and he wasn't about to change it for sentimental reasons. Towards the end there was activity on the bench, the electronic board was being readied. I looked down at my clipboard, here we go, I was ready to give Pottsy his rightful send-off.

He didn't take his tracksuit off, instead amazingly on came John Moncur and Richard Garcia for just a few minutes of a game that we already had in the bag. There was no good reason why Steve Potts couldn't have had a run-out, giving the fans a chance to thank him for everything he'd done for the club he'd joined as an apprentice, nineteen years before.

I sat in the press conference after the game, where Glenn was asked why he didn't give Potts his moment in the sun. I can't remember what he said, but I remember the look on his face. Sentiment didn't come into his thinking. He was a tactics board manager who liked his performance statistics and the look of disdain he showed the questioner suggested any sentimentality would be seen as a weakness in his book. I found that disappointing, sad and it definitely wasn't the West Ham way.

Victory for us meant we'd finished seventh in the table, because rivals Spurs lost at Leicester. All in all it hadn't been a bad season. Maybe I was being a bit overly sentimental about the Steve Potts incident. Perhaps we did need someone at the helm who was a bit ruthless and cold, but it still didn't sit right with me. I know I bang on a lot about the West Ham way, but I think it's important we do things in the proper manner. I was lucky, I had the chance to shake Steve Potts' hand and wish him all the best, but those supporters in the stadium that day were denied the chance of cheering a loyal servant of the club. What was the point of that? However scientific your approach to the game is, you can't beat the human touch.

I did my best to make amends for the lack of class shown by our manager by giving Steve Potts a special mention at the end. He walked around the pitch in the traditional end of season lap of honour, applauding the crowd, as they in turn applauded him. It was a special moment, but it wasn't as special as it should have been.

I was disappointed in Glenn Roeder that day, but I forgave him, because we were a winning team. However if you're going down the cold, clinical approach to management, you'd better keep winning. If you don't get the results it can be very lonely being aloof and clinical.

PARKLIFE

While my Saturdays were spent in the Premier League, on Sundays I'd drop down a few leagues in the football pyramid structure.

I played for Heart of North London FC in the Camden Musicians League. We were a team of media types, but with very few musicians. Fortunately there were no auditions to enter the league. We did have Mark Chase, the lead singer of rock band World of Leather in our attack. He was a luvvie too as he'd presented *Sex Talk* on Channel 4. We'd picked the musicians league because we thought they might not kick us as much as the players in our previous league. I can't remember the name of the old league, but I think it was something to do with rehabilitating psychopaths. I often kept my shin pads on in the bar afterwards.

Our captain was Tim, the one who'd been booed when he filled in for me as announcer in my first season. He'd been my producer during the days when I presented *Sports Talk* on Talk TV, a short-lived channel on the Granada Sky platform. He was always a dreamer, with grand ideas for the team. We had our own fanzine, prestige fixtures, overseas games and everyone had at least one nickname. Once he arranged a pre-season friendly in Paris just after the Channel Tunnel opened. While the rest of the team settled down on the Eurostar at Waterloo, Tim wandered off to find a cappuccino on the platform. When he came back the train had gone with his colleagues and his bags, leaving him stranded, while everyone else sipped the cappuccinos, which of course they served on the train. We wore the Brazil kit, but that was where the similarity between us and them ended. At thirty-five I was the youngest member of the back four and the yellow gave the misleading effect that we were a bit tubby, so we bought a new set of the blue away kit. When mine arrived it was number twenty-five with Jeraldo on the back. We all had Brazilian names; one of our veteran players was very proud of his shirt with the name Senior Baiano.

I loved playing for Hearts and carried on until I was forty. We played in Regent's Park against teams with brilliant names like Red Star Belsize and a team of graphic designers called A3 Milan. Once we played the Royal Household staff at Kensington Palace. During the game the ref blew his whistle and everyone had to leave the pitch. A helicopter landed in the centre circle, a tiny figure emerged and the chopper flew off. It was King Hussein of Jordan, who is the smallest king I have ever seen. Everyone carried on with the match as if nothing had happened. When the ball went into the bushes at the back of the Palace, one of our midfielders went to retrieve it. A security officer emerged from a bush, handed him a ball and returned to the foliage, never to be seen again.

I only scored one goal in the whole of my Sunday League career. I was the left back, even though I'm right-footed. I wasn't as good as the right back, so he picked the position he wanted. If you're a big strong lad you can play up front or in the centre of defence. If you have a great engine you can play in midfield. If you're quick you can be a winger. But if you are short and slow, then you are destined to be a full back, and you'd better hope the team doesn't have any fancy ideas about playing a wing-back system.

When we played Damon Albarn's team, I found myself marking Phil Daniels. It was lashing with rain and it took a while for me to recognise the *Quadrophenia* star. It was such a shock that the rest of the game is a bit of a blur. For me the broadcasting world seems perfectly normal, I've worked in it all my career, but I still couldn't get my head around playing in a game against someone from a movie. It was a similar incident in reverse that led to me not getting my nose broken. We were playing against a team called Good Mixers who were based at the Camden pub of the same name. They certainly liked mixing it; they were very physical. My role was to mark an aggressive-looking skinhead who spent the first half kicking everyone in our team. Early in the second half he elbowed me in the face and I went flying. The ref didn't even give a free kick, so I picked myself up and went charging after him. I didn't really challenge him; I just kicked his legs from underneath him. He went down like a sack of spuds and came up very red-faced. He strode over to me shouting all sorts of abuse and pulled his fist back. There was no doubt he was going to punch me in the face. But he stopped mid-punch, looked at me in a puzzled way, put his fist away and ran off, looking back over his shoulder and frowning.

The ref booked me for retaliation and then the game continued. That meant I had to resume my position marking the skinny head. I jogged alongside him, just waiting for trouble. He leaned in a bit too close for comfort and said, 'You're on the telly.' Then he ran off. I'm not sure if he didn't hit me because he was so surprised to see someone from the TV playing against him in a football match or if he was a good person who didn't want to damage a TV presenter's career by breaking his nose. Whatever the reason, I survived and retired soon afterwards to concentrate on tennis and golf, where nobody could hurt me.

SITTING IN THE SHED

For the first few seasons, my workplace was a shed in the corner of the ground. Nestling in the corner between the West Stand and the Bobby Moore Stand, it was a tiny room at ground level, with two windows, one looking sideways along the West Stand towards the Centenary Stand and the other directly across the pitch towards the East Stand. So you had to decide which half of the game you fancied watching; if you wanted to see the whole pitch all in one go, you had to go outside.

The West Stand in those days was called the Dr Martens Stand. It was quite a nice stand, as stands go, but it didn't go that far. It was like a good convent girl, it didn't go all the way for religious reasons. It stopped at the edge of the penalty box because there was a Catholic school in the corner at the back of the stand.

The Catholic church on Green Street is still there to this day, but the school has gone. The players' car park on a match day used to be the school playground. When the West Stand was redeveloped into the towering monster we have today, the club came up with an ingenious solution; they bulldozed the school to the ground. Now the stand goes the whole way to the corner of the Bobby Moore Stand. That might sound a bit harsh, but before they demolished the school, the club paid for a new one to be built a few yards down the road towards the tube station. It's a striking building as it's painted claret and blue. On a match day its playground is where I park my car.

The shed was always the coldest room in the ground. My first thoughts were not good. Why on earth had I swapped my cracking seats in row G of the top tier of the West Stand for a ground-level restricted view in an ice hollow?

The shed had a door at the back, which if left open would lead to all sorts of people wandering in. Spectators from the Bobby Moore Lower would walk by and shout things. People would stick their heads in and ask for messages to be read out. They'd never fully come in, so I'd have to turn my head away from the action and risk missing a goal. This was a problem as there was no action-replay monitor in the box, just an old-style small square portable TV which had Ceefax, the old BBC text service which clicked round very, very slowly. Nowadays you can watch Sky Sports News and as soon as you see Chris Kamara flapping and twisting his head around, you know there's been a goal behind him. In those days you had to wait for a reporter to ring in a goal. Someone at Ceefax HQ would then input the data and finally the goal would pop up on page 303. Even then you had to wait for the page to click round. For alphabetical reasons, we'd be on page 4 of 4.

Every Premier League fan's favourite Ceefax page was 324, the league table. It would be split into two pages. The first gave you the top ten, and the second page, which was usually our page, gave you the bottom ten. One of the saddest things about relegation was knowing you would not visit page 324 for at least a year. Instead it was page 325, which was rubbish. Page 325 just didn't have the glamour of 324. It was very much the ugly sister of its numerical neighbour.

The worst thing was page 325 not only gave you the second-tier standings, it also gave you the third tier. It was spread over four pages, top and bottom of what's now the Championship, followed by top and bottom of what's now

League One. That meant there were four pages to click round, to reach the page with West Ham on, usually page one of four. If you weren't nifty with the hold button, it would carry on clicking and you would have to go round again. You were exposed to all sorts of small teams in that time. It was very dispiriting, a bit like being kept down a year at school. You wanted to shout out, 'We don't belong here, we should be in the top flight. This is only a temporary situation for us. Don't bother making friends with us, because we won't be here long.'

The old square portable TV in the shed wasn't up to much. The Ceefax pages had been left on for so long, they'd started to burn in. Even when you were watching Grandstand or Football Focus, you could still see the Ceefax text from days gone by showing through, a ghostly reminder of the perils of relegation. One day the old square TV wasn't there. It had been replaced by a newer one, which had a much better picture, but tragically didn't have Ceefax. I reckon a portable television cost about £100 in those days, while a set with teletext cost £110 and could receive Ceefax and Oracle. Ceefax was the BBC service and Oracle was on ITV. I always used Ceefax as a dyed in the wool BBC man. Oracle had adverts, so it was slower. I had a friend who had two cats called Ceefax and Oracle. Funnily enough, Oracle was the slower of the two. But that was because she was much older, not because she carried adverts.

For the sake of ten pounds, I now had a TV which didn't do the one thing I needed it to do, give me the scores at other games. Fortunately the old square Ceefax TV had been put in storage below the stand. I have no idea why. Were they waiting for old square box TVs to come back into fashion?

So ghostly Ceefax TV came back and I kept the new one as well. Result! I now had a state of the art announcing booth with two cassette players and two CD players plus a receiver for the two radio microphones. The mikes had a limited range which meant I had to work close to the West Stand touchline, between the shed and the halfway line.

I worked in the shed during the Harry Redknapp era, but when the old West Stand was demolished I moved to a new all-purpose announcer's box high up in the third tier of the stand, in the corner with the Bobby Moore Stand. It was warmer and the view was stunning, but the sound was awful. You could hardly hear the crowd due to double glazing. It made it very hard to know if you were talking loudly enough. I worked in the new box during the Glenn Roeder era, so perhaps it was best I couldn't hear what the crowd were singing. Later, when Alan Pardew took over, I moved down to my favourite position in the dugout, which is far and away the best place to be for the announcer.

Season in a Nutshell 2001/02

We started badly but rallied in the second half and finished a very respectable seventh in the league, although we were a massive eleven points off sixth place. We were effectively the leaders of a chasing pack still coming round the final bend while the leaders were sipping their isotonic drinks and talking to Sally Gunnell. We won twelve of our home games in the league, so the atmosphere was good, but on the road it was a different story as we lost 7–1 at Blackburn, 5–0 at Everton and 5–1 at Chelsea.

Highlight – Signing England goalkeeper and man of many hairstyles David James. Many of the highlights that season were in his hair.

Lowlight – James was injured and by Christmas he'd made more trips to the hairdressers than appearances in the team.

Worst moment – Steve Potts was left sitting on the bench in his final game for the club, on 399 league appearances for West Ham. It was a pointless, stubborn, dreadful example of man management from Roeder. It was not the West Ham way.

Hero – Steve Potts never moaned about the snub, held his head up high and was warmly applauded all the way round his post-match lap of the pitch by the fans that had all stayed in their seats to thank their former captain. That was very much the West Ham way.

Villain – Record signing Tomas Repka was sent off twice for West Ham and once for the Czech Republic in the space of a few weeks. He'd had three red cards before he'd written any Christmas cards.

Team news – Frank Lampard left for Chelsea and the eleven million was invested in the petulant Repka and the injury-prone Don Hutchison. Hutch injured his knee in

February, was out for nearly a year and was later sold to Millwall.

It shouldn't happen to an announcer – I thought it would be a good idea to introduce some wrestling-style nicknames. 'Deadly' Don Hutchison seemed to go down well with the crowd, but Tomas 'The Hit Man' Repka never really took off, mainly because it was rubbish. After a while I stopped, fearing Tomas was taking his nickname too literally.

New this season – Barclaycard sponsored the Premiership. It was like Barclays couldn't be bothered and they plonked one of their cards on the table and said, 'Put it on that'.

Missed games – None.

Did we win at Anfield? – Don't be silly. We lost 2–1.

My bald patch – The size of the top of a ramekin, the sort you'd make a soufflé in. (Haven't we had this one before? No, that was the bottom, this is the top. The sides are slightly angled, so it's a bit bigger.)

Three-Legged Stool Review

Job leg – TalkSport gave me the boot for being 'too BBC' as I kept giving both sides of the argument. I started freelance TV reporting work for BBC *East Midlands Today*. It was a bit of a shock moving to regional TV, especially as it wasn't my region, but I loved acquiring the new skill of using pictures in my reports.

Relationship leg – Catherine and I had a great year, but then she moved out and never came back. It's fair to say this leg fell off and the stool was wobbling around a lot.

West Ham leg – I needed this leg to keep firm to stop the stool collapsing. It wobbled a bit with the disappointing news that youth-team coach Glenn Roeder was to be our new manager. But to be fair to him, he wasn't a disaster ... until the following season.

WHO IS MR MOON?

We've had some characters over the years at West Ham. Lovers of silky skills will applaud the likes of Sir Trevor Brooking, Alan Devonshire and Paolo Di Canio. If you like your football a bit grittier, look no further than Julian Dicks, Tomas Repka and Billy Bonds.

Everyone has their own favourites, but there's one man who's warmly welcomed without fail every time he turns up at the ground. And his career has lasted longer than any player in Hammers history. I speak, of course, of the famous Mr Moon. A man revered in Hammers history, yet nobody has ever met him.

Mr Moon is a legend at the Boleyn Ground. His arrival is cheered enthusiastically. He never stays very long and his departure is cheered with equal vigour. Few people know who he is. I count myself lucky that I am one of those entrusted with the legend that is Mr Moon.

I can't tell you the whole story or I will be sacked. But I can tell you how the name came about. The select few who know the whole truth are sworn to secrecy. Like the people entrusted with the exact formula for Coca-Cola, they're not allowed to travel on the same aeroplane, in case it goes down taking the legend with it.

So before I reveal the truth, the half-truth and something like the truth, let me just tease you a little bit.

For as long as I can remember at West Ham there's been this mysterious announcement during some games.

'Will the stadium manager please note Mr Moon is in the stadium.'

There's always a huge cheer. He's obviously a popular chap; everyone is glad to know he's arrived.

After a while, usually about ten minutes, there is a second announcement.

'Will the stadium manager please note Mr Moon has left the stadium.'

A football crowd can be a fickle bunch. Just ten minutes after welcoming this mystery man, they now cheer just as loudly at the news of his departure. Yet very few of the people cheering have any idea who Mr Moon is, and why his arrival and departure are so important.

Here's the secret, or as much as I can tell you without getting the sack. Mr Moon is a coded message to the stewards. It tells them something has happened and they need to do something. Until Mr Moon leaves they are on a higher state of alert. It's nothing to worry about, by the way. If you look at a steward the next time the announcement is made, you'll see some of them are smiling. He's like an old friend to them.

Lots of organisations have coded messages. Certain names are used for certain messages. On the underground they use the name Inspector Sands, in theatres it's Mr Sands. But neither Inspector Sands nor his plain-clothes brother is accorded the ovation Mr Moon commands.

The Mr Moon message is odd because it is announced while the match is being played, without waiting for a break in play. Not even lost children or the man of the match are accorded that honour. The only other announcement when the ball is in play is the number of added minutes indicated by the fourth official.

When I became the West Ham announcer I was told the secret of Mr Moon. It didn't affect my job as it's an automated message, in those days a tape recording. After a few seasons the Mr Moon system received an upgrade. Now the recording was to be digital. To celebrate, the club decided to pay a small fortune to re-record the announcement. Then they decided against that and asked if I would do it for free.

Would I do it for free? Of course I would! This was the highest honour that could be bestowed on a lifelong West Ham fan. After years of wondering who this shady figure was I was to become the voice of Mr Moon. There was a lot of dancing in the streets that night.

Now when you hear 'Mr Moon has left the stadium', it's my voice. Scarily, if I'm talking in real life and the recording plays, it overrides me. It appears that I am interrupting myself.

One day Mr Moon arrived well into the second half of a game, just as I was announcing a substitution. The announcement kicked in over the top of me, so many people will have thought that Mr Moon actually came on and played the last twenty minutes. He's not the sort of person you'd want to throw on to protect a one-goal lead. In all the years I've been coming to West Ham, I've never known him stay for a whole game. This time he sloped off just after the full-time whistle, having arrived late. It interrupted the triumphant playing of Bubbles. He's a bit selfish like that. As long as he gets away in time to get a seat on the tube, he doesn't care. I don't think he's someone I'd want to meet. I don't have much time for fair-weather fans.

One day, out of the blue, I received a phone call that chilled me to the bone.

'Hello, Jeremy, you don't know me, but I am, well, I'm Mr Moon.'

Could it be true? The elusive figure who slipped in and out of the ground at will had tracked me down? No, of course it wasn't. He's only a coded message. This was a real-life human being, but he had some very interesting information. He'd heard I was writing a book with Mr Moon in the title, and he could add some very valuable information to the legend.

His name was indeed Mr Moon and he used to be a steward at West Ham, many moons ago. He explained that it was during his time there that the club introduced a new system of messages over the PA. They needed a name that stewards could listen out for. It had to be an uncommon name. It would have been no good picking Mr Smith or Mr Jones. The club didn't want hundreds of people wondering why their name had just been read out.

At a steward's meeting they'd been asked to come up with a rare name. One of his friends had put his name forward, as it was unlikely there'd be many Moons at a game.

I arranged to have a coffee with Mr Moon, to put a face to the name. I made a note of his phone number and asked his first name. There was a pause and then he said, 'It's a bit unusual, it's Dickon. It's a Cornish name.'

Born in Redruth, he'd moved up to London. His stewarding days are long since over. Nowadays he prefers his balls a different shape. Dickon Moon is the Director of Rugby at London Cornish Rugby Club based at Roehampton.

When I recorded the stadium announcements for the FIFA 10 video game, I decided to add Mr Moon. So now there's a global audience who hear the 'Mr Moon has left the stadium' announcement and wonder what it means. Only the West Ham fans recognise it, and of those only a few who've ever been stewards know the full meaning.

EVERYONE'S AN EXPERT

The trouble with talking to football fans in pubs is that everyone is an expert. It's the one topic where everyone knows they are right. In fact the less they know the more they are convinced about it.

I was doing an after-dinner speaking gig on HMS *Belfast* the other day and a slightly tipsy businessman was saying how much he used to enjoy listening to London radio station LBC football coverage years ago. If only he could remember the name of the presenter? I suggested it might be Tony Lockwood, but then he remembered it was Jonathan Pearce. Now I know JP, so I suggested to the tipsy businessman that he must be thinking of Capital Gold where JP worked before 5Live and *Match of the Day*. No, no, it was definitely LBC because he remembered him doing a double act on the commentary with Billy Bonds. He remembered when Billy lifted the cup at Wembley. He'd been touched that Billy had wiped his muddy hands first, so he didn't get the Queen's gloves dirty.

That didn't sound quite right, especially when he said he remembered listening to the first programme after Billy died. Billy is very much alive and although he had twice lifted the FA Cup at Wembley, I realised he was talking about was Bobby Moore, the incident was the World Cup Final and it was definitely Capital Gold, where Jonathan and Bobby worked together.

When I pointed this out in my slightly anoraky way, he looked at me as though I was completely mad. He was used to football conversations where you spout rubbish and everyone waits until you finish and then starts spouting rubbish of their own. No one was meant to interrupt with factual corrections; that's not the English way.

I've spent hours at weddings and networking events listening to armchair pundits holding court on all sorts of nonsense. The more they drink, the more they seem to know. Now, if I was sitting next to a nuclear physicist it wouldn't cross my mind to correct them on matters relating to fusion and fission. As far as I know, one is a type of Gillette razor and the other is a rather pointless pastime. But when it comes to football, everyone is a fully paid-up member of the pundit's union.

During Italia 1990 I was at a dinner party. Some of the guests had 'really got into football during this world cup'. One chap was lucky enough to have become an expert on the offside rule and we were fortunate enough to be the recipients of his newly gained knowledge. He moved the salt and pepper pots around to demonstrate why the olive oil was clearly in an offside position. The women in the party swooned at his immense wisdom.

The offside rule as he explained it was correct when he was at school, but it had changed in the meantime. You no longer needed to have two players 'between' you and the goal. Now 'level' was OK. It had been ratified by FIFA and Italia 1990 was the first World Cup where the new law was used. This meant that the olive oil was in fact onside, because it was being played on by the balsamic vinegar. It was quite a posh do.

When he rebuffed my notion of a law change, citing his three weeks' experience of football watching as evidence, I had to ask him his occupation. He was an accountant, so you don't need me to tell you he was an interesting character, but his facts didn't add up. I don't suffer fools gladly, especially arrogant, pompous fools. We mix about as well as oil and vinegar.

He was one of those people who spend more time transmitting than receiving. He didn't think to ask what I did for a job. Only the hostess knew that I was a football commentator for BBC local radio at the time. We exchanged smiles and continued with our starters, mains and puds. It wasn't until coffee and mints that the hostess let slip my true vocation.

Then the charmless accountant conceded that perhaps there had been a rule change, but it hadn't been given much publicity. He made that face that people sometimes do, when they look into the distance with their head on one side and say things like, 'I was sure...' They think if they continue to believe an incorrect fact is true, it will somehow miraculously change. Plonkers!

One thing I have learnt in life is everyone likes to talk about themselves. If you sit next to someone you don't know and ask them questions, you will be able to have a conversation with almost anyone in the world. If they are a good person they will ask you questions back. If they are a self-obsessed fool full of their own importance they will continue to spout on about themselves and not ask anything in return.

For your information, if you find yourself sitting next to me at a dinner in the future, I know a bit about sport in general and football in particular. I can hold informed conversations about movies and sitcoms. I've a broad knowledge of comedy and music and a much narrower knowledge of science, history and religion. I don't know much about geography or nature, so if you ever play me at Trivial Pursuit those are the questions to ask me when I reach the middle.

The number of times I've been stuck at weddings, wondering how on earth I am going to survive in a roomful of strangers, when a love of football has given me a bond with a fellow guest. Of course, everyone really wants to talk about their own team. My mate Dave and I have lots of chats about football. He talks about Hull and I talk about West Ham. Occasionally we stop and listen to what the other one is saying, but we mainly talk about our own teams. Who knows anything about Hull?

Football, as they say, is a funny old game, and there's nothing better than talking about it. The actual event isn't always the best entertainment, but the after-match drinks and chat can't be beaten. I love banter with my mates who support Spurs and Arsenal and other minor London teams. As long as it doesn't spill over into anything physical, it's great. I can't understand people who want to fight about football, but banter is great. I've the misfortune that all three of my sisters have married outside the faith. I have two Gooner brothers-in-law and a Red Devil. I'll say all sorts of stuff to them and so does my dad. But when I'm on the microphone it's completely different, I have my sensible head on.

People who don't quite get football are the ones who expect it's going to be fun all the time. It's not; it's far more likely to break your heart. When you look at it against other forms of entertainment, it's a wonder so many of us spend our weekends watching it, and the rest of the week talking about it.

If you go to a movie you might love it or be a bit disappointed, but in the end you will have had a fairly good evening. You'll have been warm and dry with some interesting images to look at. A director will have told you a story, with a beginning, a middle and an end. Beforehand you'll have known whether to expect a fish out of water comedy, a bodice-ripping romance or an historical drama. The story might have been rubbish, but chances are the dustbin-sized bucket of popcorn will have left you with a warm contented feeling. The only emptiness will be in your wallet, those dustbins don't come cheap.

When you go to a football match you are not guaranteed a good time. You don't know what sort of story you are going to get. It might be a true-life drama, it might be a screwball comedy or a horror story. You might be cold, your team might lose and you could well come away feeling worse than when you arrived. At the cinema you might be annoyed by fools who sit munching their popcorn loudly. The smell of their nachos with melted cheese might waft annoyingly in front of your nose. But the moviegoer is unlikely to stand up and start shouting at the screen.

If you are watching a courtroom drama and the case isn't going the way you'd like, chances are no one will start singing 'the district attorney's a wanker'. At football matches this is not the case. The person who sits in front of you is likely to do a lot of shouting. Similar to the dinner party guest, there is a law of nature which states that the less a person knows about football, the louder their voice is.

THE GINKS FACTOR

I have to be really careful what I say on the microphone before a match. A lot of people think I have a mystic ability to affect the course of a game. If I talk about our unbeaten record, it is like waving a red rag at the bull of destiny. I've been known to single-handedly lose games, because of my ill-thought-out comments on the mike pre-match. I've also caused defeats by playing the wrong tunes, reading out results from early kick-offs and walking on the cracks in the pavement.

Football fans are incredibly superstitious. They'll wear the same pair of socks all season if they think they are lucky. If the people in the adjacent seats are fortunate, they'll wash them between matches.

When I started playing *The Great Escape* theme tune in the second half of the 2002/03 season, one supporter emailed to say I should stop playing it immediately. In his words it would 'ginks the team's chances of avoiding relegation'.

Of course he meant 'jinx', but to this day we use the word 'ginks' (with a hard 'g') at the pre-match meeting. We use it as a way of assessing whether or not to mention something. There is a school of thought amongst fans that if I mention something good before kick-off it will 'ginks' the chances of it happening.

The 'ginks' theory goes like this. If I play 'The Great Escape' we'll definitely go down. If I welcome people to 'Fortress Upton Park' our defences will crumble. If I quote any statistic, the odds gods will hear me and make bad things happen. If I say we haven't let in a goal in three games, we'll let in a handful.

If I name the player of the month, he'll get injured. If I welcome back a former player, he'll score a hat-trick. If I say it's a lovely day, it will rain. If I read out the name of the Grand National winner, he'll be shot in the paddock. That's the sort of thing that supporters believe will happen. I'm flattered that they think I have this power, but I don't.

Footballers are just as bad as fans, when it comes to superstitions. Lots of players have pre-match rituals that they have to go through to bring them luck. Actually it's not about bringing them luck, it's about avoiding bad luck. They think if they do something different it will jinx them. Some like to walk out behind the captain or ahead of the goalkeeper. Others have to wear a particular shirt number.

When Paulo Futre arrived at West Ham he had it written into his contract that he had to wear the number ten shirt, except nobody seemed to spot this might be a problem. We already had a number ten, John Moncur. Futre was a former AC Milan and Portugal midfielder, but he now had dodgy knees and a bad attitude, so he came to West Ham. Dodgy knees and bad attitudes would put other clubs off, but Harry Redknapp saw them as attributes. He loved buying damaged goods because it knocked the price down.

Paulo should have made his debut for West Ham at Arsenal, but when he walked into the dressing room he saw the shirt hanging on his peg was number sixteen. He stormed off in a huff and didn't play. His heroes were Pele and Eusebio. They'd both worn number ten, and so did he. At that point I would have sent him packing and pointed out that he wasn't in the same league as Pele or Eusebio. He was lucky to be in the same league as John Moncur, given his dodgy knees. But Paulo pointed out that the number was in his contract, so West Ham were a bit stuffed. It always pays to read the small print on players' contracts, as we were to find out a few years later to our cost. In the end Paulo Futre bribed John Moncur with the offer of a free holiday at his villa in the Algarve, if they could swap numbers. Moncur accepted and Futre wore the number ten shirt for the rest of his time at West Ham. It turned out that ten wasn't his lucky number after all. He made ten appearances and then left.

The Ginks Factor is a real phenomenon. Even if I don't believe in it, the very fact that the players are superstitious and so are the fans, means it can become a self-fulfilling prophesy. Anything that makes people nervous is a bad thing. So I make sure I never say or do anything that is likely to anger Lady Luck or whichever gods are in charge of our destiny.

I lost faith in Lady Luck after I was driving to the game one Saturday and went past Lambeth Palace. The Archbishop of Canterbury was crossing on the zebra in front of me. I figured that if a black cat crossing your path was meant to be lucky, the most powerful churchman in England was likely to be even more lucky. He wasn't. We lost 1–0.

STAND UP IF YOU LOVE WEST HAM

You don't have to be a comedian to follow West Ham but it helps. Friends have always very kindly told me I'm funny and I should have a go at stand-up. I've written sketches for light entertainment shows for Radio 4 and I've devised and presented comedy panel games but I've never seen myself as a comic. Quite rightly as it turns out, but back in 2002 I decided to have a go.

I always like to try out something new after a break-up. In the late 1980s I split up with my girlfriend Helen and spent the next fourteen years as a vegetarian. When Charlotte and I finally admitted defeat, I took up golf. Catherine's departure heralded my venture into the world of comedy. It was an itch that needed scratching, so I enrolled on a course at the Amused Moose comedy club.

So it was that I found myself in a basement beneath a gay bar on Archer Street in Soho, just round the corner from the famous Windmill Theatre. It was a Saturday afternoon in April. Sixteen hopefuls had come to learn from comedian Logan Murray.

It was every Saturday for three months and some Sundays. I had to miss a few sessions because of West Ham games, but there was usually something to laugh at, whether I was at the Amused Moose or the Boleyn.

I kept waiting for the week when we actually learnt how to write jokes, but it never happened. It was all about work-shopping emotions and seeing what humour developed.

Logan taught us all sorts of improvisational games. We

spent the first two weeks experimenting with high and low status. One minute we were high and mighty, the next minute down in the gutter. It was a bit like watching West Ham under Glenn Roeder.

Eventually we started to try our hands at actual stand-up. Not joke telling, more like story telling.

It was nerve-racking standing up in front of the rest of the group and performing. We played gag tag, where you sat on a bar stool and had to say something funny about a subject shouted from the audience. If someone else wanted to take over, they would tag you.

It all led up to a showcase evening, where we would each perform ten minutes of material to a live audience. Before any of us were really ready, the evening was upon us.

It was 3 June 2002, the Golden Jubilee Bank Holiday. Everyone was in happy spirits because of the Queen being in charge for so long. A few drinks had been taken in celebration by the audience when the time came for me to make my way to the stage.

For reasons best known to myself, I'd decided to wear a Cameroon football shirt with the name 'Geremi' on the back. I did football-related material in my act, as it was a World Cup year. Cameroon had become the first country to wear vests for football matches and I'd bought one, as one of their players shared my name. Sadly FIFA wouldn't let them wear them at the World Cup, so they had to have short sleeves stitched on to them. Even worse, the other Geremi signed for Chelsea later, so I couldn't ever wear the shirt again.

I wore a T-shirt under the Cameroon vest onstage. It was one layer too many. I was boiling under the lights and perspiring freely. Not just because of the lights but because, as always with anything new, I was nervous. A lot of Imodium had been consumed and my Bobby Moore statue was tucked away in my bag backstage.

Every precaution had been taken. The only thing now was to remember the routine. I'd seen a lot of comics write bullet points for their act on the back of their hands. This would be the answer for me. I scribbled down eight keywords on the back of my hand in felt pen. This was a huge mistake, I should have used biro.

Each act came on and did their piece, with mixed levels of success. No one was booed off, because the audience was made up of fellow performers and their families. But it was obvious that some people were doing better than others.

Eventually my time came. I had a good opening section and it went down well. I did a World Cup reference and got a laugh when I turned round to show them 'Geremi' on the back of my shirt. I glanced down at my hand to see what was next, but I couldn't read anything. My hand was a sea of blue. I was so nervous my hands had become very sweaty, washing away the felt pen.

I stood for what seemed like ages, thinking what to do.

What comes next? Oh my god, what comes next?

One thing I'd learnt from performing in front of my classmates was if something goes wrong, try and use it to your advantage. I looked into the audience to see if there was anything I could feed off, any expression, anybody wearing something odd. But with the stage lights shining directly into my eyes I couldn't see a thing. I could barely make out the shape of the first row and then it was just blackness. They'd also gone quiet, not unreasonably expecting the funny man on the stage to make them laugh and maybe spend a little less time staring at his hand.

At that moment I was possessed by the spirit of the great Roy Walker, star of the TV show *Catchphrase*, which is strange because he's not dead.

'Say what you see, see what you say,' Roy seemed to be saying. It was hard to tell with the lights, the sweat and his strong Northern Ireland accent.

I showed the audience my hand. 'Look at that,' I said. 'I wrote my routine on my hand, but it's melted.' They laughed heartily. Look at the funny man, he doesn't even know what sort of pen to use to cheat. Thinking about it now, 'melted' wasn't the right word at all. The ink hadn't melted, it had been lifted off the skin and was now swimming around in a pool of perspiration.

Audiences, like West Ham crowds, love it when something goes wrong. Even the spirit of Roy was laughing, presumably relieved at not being dead.

Nobody died that night. Everyone was competitive and supportive all at once. I met some lovely people. Logan had said at the start of the course only one person from the group was likely to make it in the competitive world of comedy. We must have been a good group, because quite a few made it. My best mates in the group were Marek Larwood and Chris Corcoran. Marek has the ability to pull the oddest of faces, even for a Norwich City fan. He went on to star in *We Are Klang* on the BBC. I went to see Chris in his own Edinburgh Festival show. He's better known to yummy mummies as the presenter of D*oodle Do* on the CBeebies Channel. Another in our group was Tom Wrigglesworth, who's on Radio 4 a lot and always makes me laugh.

Logan's previous group had included Greg Davies and Rhod Gilbert who both went on to great things. Perhaps I should have stuck at it. After the course we were encouraged to put our names down for open spots at clubs. Typically an open spot is ten minutes long. You don't get paid; you're there to pad out a show, between the established acts.

The whole business was incredibly frightening. First you had to ring up the promoter of the club and ask for a spot on the bill. Most of them were great, but some treated newbies with contempt. We were the lowest of the low.

I performed twenty-six open spots at comedy clubs across London in the six months after the course. I died three times. The other twenty-three went well, but it's the three that didn't that I'll always remember. It was horrible.

One scary night in Wimbledon I followed Nina Conti onto the stage. She's a very funny ventriloquist, so she really should have been top of the bill, but I think she was trying out new material and had another gig to go to. She likes to keep her hand in. Boom, boom. Yes, sitting here writing this I am hilarious but that night in Wimbledon I died on my arse.

After five minutes of material that had gone down well in other clubs, I'd had a few chuckles, but no real laughs. Then someone shouted out, 'Say something funny, mate.'

The only thing I could think to say was, 'You paid to get in.'

But I didn't think of that until a long time afterwards, when I was driving home. It was too late by then as the heckler had gone home by tube.

I decided that stand-up comedy was not for me. I'm quite funny for a radio presenter, probably a bit too funny for a TV reporter, but I'm not funny enough to be a comedian. When your sole purpose is to make people laugh, you'd better be good at it. My skill is to make information entertaining, often by adding humour. It's the icing on the cake, not the cake itself. I've done a few stand-up gigs since, but I mainly work now as an after-dinner speaker. I love the art of telling stories. If people laugh it's a bonus, but if not there's still the story to enjoy.

I have the utmost respect for comedians because I know it's the hardest, scariest thing I've ever done. Anything since has seemed easy by comparison.

I learnt an incredible amount about thinking on your feet. When things go wrong at West Ham or during live TV outside broadcasts, I often dig deep into what I learnt from Logan and the other Amused Moosers.

JOE COLE

One of the most gifted young players ever to come through the ranks at West Ham was Joe Cole. He was a child prodigy, the most talked about schoolboy footballer in the country. Manchester United were always interested in him. A ball-carrying midfielder with incredible dribbling skills, he once scored seven of England's eight goals in a youth international against Spain. He starred in West Ham's FA Youth Cup-winning side that thrashed Coventry 9–0 in the 1999 final.

Joe Cole was made captain in the 2002/03 season at the age of just twenty-one. I was delighted, we'd been hearing for years that Joe was the chosen one, the Boy Wonder who would lead us to glory.

On his seventeenth birthday, Joe graduated from our academy and signed professional forms on the pitch at half-time during a game. I went a bit over the top on the microphone. I know, it doesn't sound like me! I told the watching crowd that they would be able to tell their grandchildren they were there the day Joe Cole signed for West Ham. I was slaughtered in the papers for putting too much pressure on the young player. Listening to a phone-in on the radio, I heard Jonathan Pearce say 'the announcer hadn't thought it through'.

The pundits had a point, but I was excited. The crowd were excited. It was something to cheer about at last.

Joe, so self-controlled and calm when in possession of a football, looked scared stiff standing in the tunnel, waiting to go out and sign the forms. He kept checking with me that he didn't have to say anything on the microphone. I wouldn't ask him anything, would I? There was no need to speak, I assured him. I would do all that, he just had to wave. He dutifully acknowledged all four grandstands and I spoke, perhaps a bit too much. Yes, I went over the top, but this was Joe Cole. It is still one of my treasured memories.

Joe typifies all that I love about West Ham. He's skilful, determined and home-grown. We didn't buy him; he was developed at our academy by Tony Carr and his team. Any club with a rich benefactor can buy the best players in the world, but there's nothing more satisfying than building your own team from scratch.

As kids my sisters and I spent a lot of time with our Nanna. On one visit my sisters gave Nan a dressing table set. I'm not sure what the technical term is, but it was made of lace and you laid your hairbrushes out on it. The girls had spent ages making this, something they were keen to stress. Now Nanna had a reputation for the understatement. She never really got excited about anything of material value, she was just glad to see us. If we'd turned up with jewel-encrusted Fabergé eggs, she'd have thanked us in just the same manner as if they'd been Easter eggs full of chocolate drops.

The girls were a little disappointed to the reaction the lace hairbrush mat thing received. 'We didn't buy it,' they stressed. 'Never mind,' said Nan, 'I like it just the same.'

She thought they were worried about not having paid for it, but just the opposite was true. They were proud that it was homemade. That's how I feel about Joe Cole and the others like Rio and Frank. They're special, like the lace hairbrush mat thing, although they're worth a little bit more.

I'M FOREVER BLOWING BUBBLES

One of the most important jobs as announcer at West Ham is making sure 'I'm Forever Blowing Bubbles' is played at the right time. It's not rocket salad; you just need to start it about thirty seconds before the team line-ups start moving. This means having a chat with the referee to see when he's going to walk them on. If it's a live TV match, the floor manager from the broadcaster is more likely to call it, so it's worth befriending them. If it's a Sky game they always run exactly to time, so you know where you are. The BBC are also very good, although you'd expect me to say that. Ideally I want 'I'm Forever Blowing Bubbles' to be reaching a crescendo as the team emerge from the tunnel.

My team have played this song before kick-off for as long as I can remember. It's been sung on the terraces at the Boleyn Ground since the 1920s. So what's it all about? What is the link between an East London football club and a music hall song?

Cue American style TV voiceover: 'This is the story of a football-mad headmaster, a curly-haired young footballer, a poster featuring a future head of Naval intelligence and an American lyricist who was really three people. Confused? You won't be, after this week's episode of *Soap*.'

'I'm Forever Blowing Bubbles' was first heard in a Broadway musical, *The Passing Show of 1918*. The song proved popular and was registered in 1919 with music by John Kellette and lyrics by Jaan Kenbrovin. If Jaan Kenbrovin looks like a strange name, even by American standards, there's a very good reason. It's a composite of the first names and surnames of the three men who wrote the lyrics. They all had contracts with different publishers. Jaan Kenbrovin was actually James Kendis, James Brockman and Nat Vincent. So that's the first weird thing. Other hit songs from *The Passing Show of 1918* were 'Smiles', 'Twit, Twit, Twit' and 'My Vampire Girl'. So perhaps we got off lightly.

'Bubbles' was certainly a catchy song, but it had no link with sport of any kind. In fact it's a song about failure. It includes the lines:

'Then like my dreams they fade and die. Fortune's always hiding, I've looked everywhere. I'm forever blowing bubbles. Pretty bubbles in the air.'

Not the sort of thing you'd pick as an anthem to inspire the team onto the pitch. But hey, we're West Ham, we're a bit different. At the end we sing 'United', (clap, clap, clap) 'United', (clap, clap, clap).

The first sporting connection with 'Bubbles' came after the Black Sox incident that rocked baseball in 1919. Eight of the Chicago White Sox, including the legendary Shoeless Joe Jackson, took bribes to throw the World Series against the Cincinnati Reds. A jazz song of the day parodied 'Bubbles' with the altered lyrics, 'I'm forever blowing ballgames'. You'll hear the song in the 1988 movie *Eight Men Out*.

By the n1920s 'Bubbles' had crossed the Atlantic. The first English version of the sheet music with Dorothy Ward on the cover in a rather fetching hat was displayed for a time in the West Ham United club museum. It became a favourite in the music halls, a pop song of its time. Dorothy Ward was the Madonna of her day, described as a 'handsome and striking woman, with auburn hair, wonderful carriage and a fine figure'.

It was important in those days to have a wonderful

carriage, as not many people had their own transport. Especially as Dorothy was from Birmingham and the big bucks were to be made in London. As far as I know, Dorothy never came to a West Ham match. She was probably a Villa or Blues fan. So we can't blame her for the arrival of our defeatist anthem. The blame for that is put at the door of Cornelius Beal.

He may sound like somebody who'd teach Harry Potter how to cast spells at Hogwarts, but he was actually the head of Park School, near West Ham Park. According to club historian, John Helliar, the singing of 'Bubbles' at West Ham games was down to Beal.

This is where it turns into a bit of a soap opera. I need to introduce two kids at this point, both with curly hair, both called William and both nicknamed 'Bubbles'. One was a gifted young footballer called Billy Murray who played for Park School. The other was William Milbourne James, the grandson of the painter Sir John Everett Millais.

William featured on an advertising poster for Pears soap, from a painting by his granddad. It was a classic poster of its time, depicting a curly-haired kid with a bowl of soapy water, a pipe in his hand, looking wistfully up at a bubble which is hovering somewhere between the 'e' and 'a' of Pears. It's a lovely picture and it was all over the tube and buses in the 1920s.

Because of his resemblance to the other William, Billy Murray was nicknamed 'Bubbles' by everyone at Park School, whether they used Pears soap or not. He was a decent player and played for West Ham district in the early 1920s.

Cornelius Beal liked to make up his own lyrics to songs. He wasn't as good as Jaan Kenbrovin, because there was only one of him. Cornelius would change the words to fit players in his team. Park School had some top talent; the legendary West Ham striker Syd Puddefoot was a Park boy and so was 'Big Jim' Barrett. They probably had songs sung about them, but it was the song about Billy 'Bubbles' Murray that is most remembered. 'I'm Forever Blowing Bubbles' was heard whenever Park School or West Ham Boys were playing. They swept the board in the early 1920s in front of large crowds. Many of the people who watched school football on a Saturday morning would make their way to the Boleyn Ground in the afternoon and the song went with them.

Sadly Billy's dreams of professional football faded and died like the bubbles in his song. Jim Barrett and Syd Puddefoot went on to be West Ham United legends. Billy Murray never signed for the club, yet his song has outlived them all. It doesn't sound very likely, does it? Yet I've learnt never to apply logic to football songs. Notts County fans sing about the problems of owning a wheelbarrow with a wheel that keeps falling off. Chelsea fans are always singing about mowing meadows and doing unhygienic things with sticks of celery. And the most famous of them all, Liverpool's 'You'll Never Walk Alone', is a song from the Rodgers and Hammerstein musical *Carousel*, sung by the heroine's friend, to help her through the death of her husband in a bank robbery.

Over the years our song has evolved. It's usually sung fairly fast these days. Back in the 1960s it was a lot slower paced. The fans in the Chicken Run, the long terracing in the lower tier of the East Stand, used to sway from side to side as they belted out the slower version. I'd love to see that slow swaying again one day.

'I'm Forever Blowing Bubbles' has been recorded by a number of artists over the years. The version we play before kick-off was recorded by the FA Cup Final squad of 1975. I've played the recording by East Ham-born Vera Lynn a few times too. The Cockney Rejects' punk version is often requested as an atmosphere builder, although I don't think it adds much. I used to like pogoing to it as a teenager, but it's virtually impossible to sing along to.

The original picture in the Pears' poster was called 'A Child's World' and was painted by Sir John Everett Millais in 1886. He sold the canvas for £2,200 to the Pears' soap people along with copyright over the image. When it appeared as an advert for soap, Sir John was criticised by the art world for 'selling out'. He did have doubts, especially as the child in the picture was his grandson. But artists have to pay the bills like the rest of us, so he agreed.

The kid in the picture, William Milbourne James, was known to everyone for the rest of his life as 'Bubbles', whether he liked it or not. Bubbles always rise to the top in water and he reached the rank of admiral in the Royal Navy and served in naval intelligence in both World Wars. They still called him Bubbles; he must have been quite a character to be able to command respect.

After leaving the navy, after a spell as an MP for Portsmouth, he retired. But he still couldn't shake off the nickname. He moved to Scotland, to Fife, where he kept up his link with the sea by supporting the Elie and Earlsferry Sailing Club. In return they named a dinghy in his honour. It was called, you've guessed it, 'Bubbles'.

In my first season at West Ham, we set a new world record at Upton Park. Before the Middlesbrough game on 16 May little claret bubble makers were handed out to every fan. 23,680 fans blew bubbles for a minute, to seal our place in the *Guinness Book of World Records*.

If you'd like to see the original painting of Bubbles, it is still in the hands of soap people. Pears sold out to Lever Brothers and the picture is now in the Lady Lever Art Gallery at Port Sunlight on Merseyside.

The background is very dark, but if you look closely you can see a plant in a pot on one side of the boy, with a broken flowerpot on the other. I'm told that one represents life, the other death. In the middle the boy looks up at the delicate floating bubble, which represents beauty amidst the fragile nature of life.

Sorry to go all Sister Wendy on you, it's a habit I must get out of. Let me put it in football terms. I like to think the floating bubble, beautiful yet strong, symbolises the West Ham ideal of playing entertaining football. The plant and the broken pot represent triumph and relegation.

So that's why we sing 'Bubbles'. It's a long, complicated tale. The next time you hear the West Ham faithful belt it out you'll have more of an insight. It won't stop the majority getting the words wrong though.

I'm a bit pedantic, as you might have noted. I like tradition and I like things to be right. However, I'm also aware that things evolve and also that the people who sing their hearts out for West Ham should be applauded and not ticked off by me. So I'll say my piece and then shut up.

It's 'nearly reach the sky', not, 'they reach the sky'. If the bubble ever reached the sky, the whole song wouldn't make sense. It's a song about unrealised dreams. It may not be suitable for a sporting anthem, because of its inherent sense of failure, but I wouldn't have it any other way. If you sing 'they' instead of 'nearly' you are wrong. It doesn't scan and it doesn't make any sense. Why do you do it? I know it's not going to change by me banging on about it, but at least I've drawn a line in the sand. If you choose to overstep that line, it's up to you. I'll love you just the same whatever you sing, but there it is. I've said my piece, and let's not mention it again.

Apart from to say there must have been somebody with a loud voice who once got it wrong, and everyone else followed. But that's it, let's leave it now. Wrong or not, when that song is sung at volume it makes my hair stand on end. And if you've seen the shiny top of my head, you'll know that's no mean feat.

Perhaps my greatest innovation as the West Ham announcer was the fading of 'Bubbles' after 'fade and die'. I'd noticed that the song builds and builds. It gets really loud on the line 'fortune's always hiding'. Some people I think only join in on that line. Others pick that line to really give it some oomph.

My cunning plan was conceived shortly after the building of the new West Stand. I decided to fade the music down completely after 'fade and die'. The crowd carried on singing unaccompanied from 'fortune's always hiding' until the end. It sounded awesome. We've done it to this day, except it's not me who physically fades it down now. That responsibility now lies with my assistant announcer Russell Budden. To ease the pressure slightly, he's dubbed a version which stops dead at 'fade and die'. That's because he's a coward.

'I'm Forever Blowing Bubbles' is our song, and we will sing it forever. In the season before I was unceremoniously sacked there was a suggestion from above that we should stop playing it before games. I made it clear that I would not continue if that was the case.

I've only ever made two demands of the club: that we always play 'Bubbles' and we never play music after goals. My intransigence was not well received. After I was given the Spanish archer, the club did experiment with dropping 'Bubbles'. It was a PR disaster. The fans hated the change. From my seat watching in the stands, people would ask me why I wasn't the announcer any more and why we'd stopped playing 'Bubbles'. I didn't know the answer to either question. After a few games, Bubbles was revived, not always at the right time or at the right volume, but it was back. We've run out to it ever since. I hope we always do.

WHO ARE YA?

As you've probably guessed, I'm a traditionalist when it comes to football. I like the old ways, the singing and the chanting. I'm not a fan of the modern 'sit on your arse until something happens and then cheer' approach. Yet at odds with that, I'm always happier sitting down at football. If terraces ever came back, I would still choose to sit. I've never enjoyed standing up at games for three reasons. I'm a short arse, so I can't see over the heads. I have a lower-back problem that I'd much rather aggravate on the golf course. And thirdly I was at Hillsborough and it's hard to forget that stuff.

But I know lots of people who would like to see a return to standing at games. I would support that, as long as it's done properly. On the continent there are magnificent stadiums that can accommodate safe standing for domestic fixtures and be converted to all-seater for European games. It's something that we should look at.

In the days of terraces the atmosphere at grounds across the country was a lot better. People would arrive a lot earlier, so they could get the best positions. It meant the noise level built up in the ground a lot earlier. You could also stand near your mates. People are much more likely to sing if they're surrounded by their friends. If you wanted to sing, you could move to the area of the ground where the noisy lot congregated. Years ago you could even change stands if you wanted to, by just walking around the ground.

Nowadays the turnstiles open ninety minutes before kick-off, but most seats are still empty twenty minutes before the game starts. Of course some people arrive early, wait for the turnstiles to open and come into the ground straight away. They watch the warm-ups and everything.

We have entertainment on the big screens as soon as the turnstiles open. There're music videos on the screens and I'll welcome everyone and trail ahead to the pre-match and half-time guests. I'll give a shout out to any touring parties that are with us for the day, like the Dublin Hammers or the Belgian Irons.

I sometimes wish we could return to the old days, when the atmosphere was solely generated by the two rival sets of fans. Of course it was taken too far in the 1970s and 80s when the singing was marred by violence. But there's nothing like an intimidating, hostile atmosphere to scare the willies out of the opposition. The crowd noise at West Ham was always fantastic.

I loved the tribal nature of it. Frankie says, 'When two tribes go to war, a point is all that you can score.' Our war cry was worth a goal start, which is lucky, because we'd often need a goal start just to get a draw.

Protocol demanded a certain number of songs be sung, some challenges laid down and some standard responses expected from the rivals. Failure to live up to the challenge would result in a loss of face.

It's a common thing amongst football fans to enquire of the opposition supporters who they are. The chant goes something like, 'Who are ya? Who are ya? Who are ya?' That's the gist of it. I think I've remembered all the words correctly. The tune is, well, there's not really much of a tune, but there is a lot of pointing at the people in question.

It's a strange question to ask because the name of the opposition will have been in the morning papers. It will also feature on the match ticket. There may even be a few clues gleaned by reading the matchday programme or glancing at the scoreboard.

How you answer it is up to you. Presumably you will know who you are, so perhaps just saying that is enough. It's a bit like the first question in the general knowledge round on *Mastermind*. It's easy enough to answer, and the only way you are going to get it wrong is if you panic under pressure.

The traditional response to this easy question is for the opposition to start singing a song. It won't necessarily be phrased as an answer. It's not like a French lesson where *'ou est le ballon?'* is followed by *'le ballon est dans l'arbre'*. However, it should leave the questioner in no doubt as to who the opposition are. Occasionally you will get a reply along the lines of 'We are Leeds, We are Leeds, We are Leeds', but this tends to be mainly when you are playing Leeds.

TAKING THE MIKE

Most clubs now have an announcer with a broadcasting background. In London the daddy of them all is 'Diddy' David Hamilton. I used to listen to his afternoon show on Radio One in the 1970s. He's been the announcer at Fulham since 1996, two years before I started at West Ham.

Diddy, who earned his nickname from his time spent working with Ken Dodd, was a director of Fulham at one point and has even survived a sacking as the announcer. He may be one of the shortest matchday presenters in the game, but his standing is high, especially amongst the Fulham faithful. A fan's campaign led to his reinstatement, with Mohamed 'Call me Al' Fayed telling him he has a job for life and bizarrely presenting him with a bottle of whisky and some Viagra. Since then Diddy's standing has grown enormously.

It's common enough for a football announcer to be sacked; as a breed we are always overstepping the mark and getting into trouble.

Preston pitchside announcer Adam Catterall wasn't impressed with the referee, so as North End and Crystal Palace took the field after the interval, he welcomed supporters to the 'second half of the Uriah Rennie show'. Adam survived that one, but quit a couple of years later after fan protests, ironically about reading out the away team too quickly. His fast talking had meant the PNE fans didn't have the chance to applaud returning favourite Graham Alexander, who was now with rivals Burnley.

Reading announcer Jonathan Richards lost his job after a rant about former manager Mark McGhee, when they played Millwall.

Charlton announcer Brian Cole at a South London derby kept referring to the opposition as Crystal Palarse. Of course it was popular with the home fans, but it was unforgiveable and he was given the boot.

The Bristol Rovers announcer also lost his job after a derby game. His announcement of a substitution went like this, 'Coming on, number eight, Junior Bent...and I bet he is.'

Swindon's Peter Lewis described a red card against player-manager Steve McMahon as one of the worst decisions he'd seen. He was also red-carded by the club.

Then there was the time when Manchester United were playing in London and the man on the mike, I won't say who it was, decided to take the mick out of the high number of Cockney Reds. Historically there have always been four well-supported teams in London: Arsenal, Spurs, West Ham and Manchester United. Over the public address system, aimed at the Manchester United fans, came the following: 'Message for the travelling supporters. All roads to Surrey and Kent are running normally.' There were huge cheers from the home crowd. Now that sort of comment is funny as banter between fans, but saying it over the PA is another thing completely. It shows a lack of respect for the travelling support. They've made the effort to come to the game. They're not fair-weather fans, they're the real deal and it's not up to the announcer to ridicule them. That sort of announcement can lead to crowd trouble.

Who do these people think they are? I know announcers are also fans, but all of the above incidents show a complete lack of professionalism. I've often wanted to shout at the ref, particularly Graham Poll, but I'll not give my opinion until I've taken my claret and blue tie off and I'm sitting down with a pint. We do things properly at West Ham.

INTERNATIONAL MATCH IN DUBLIN

This brings us to the 2002/03 season, which contains scenes some readers may find disturbing. It was an awful time for the West Ham leg of the stool, but other things were going well. I finally met my princess and I represented my country at full international level.

The first half of the season was so awful, I can't bring myself to mention it. By the New Year we still hadn't won at home. We were bottom of the table, not surprisingly. When our first home win did come it was in the FA Cup against Nottingham Forest. And I wasn't there to see it.

I was in Dublin for another big match. My ex-girlfriend Helen from local radio days was getting married. She did get a brief mention earlier, so don't be getting her mixed up with Charlotte who looked like Catherine Zeta Jones.

Here are Helen's matchday statistics: Born in Dublin, she'd transferred to England and was a regular fixture in my life between 1988 and 1990, plus a few friendlies in 1991.

Helen's a lovely blonde Irish woman with a gorgeous accent and cute freckles. In a movie of the book, she'd be played by Julianne Moore, with Dervla Kirwan as her voice coach. Helen and I had worked together in Nottingham. I was at the BBC and she worked as a news reporter for Radio Trent.

We lived together for a bit and parted on good terms as we both moved to London, where she became an editor with ITV and I stumbled around between various jobs in TV and radio. We kept in touch, and she became something of an analyst of my relationship break-ups and topsy-turvy career. So it was that I found myself in Dublin on the first weekend of January 2003, for her wedding to Ed. It was an international match; he was Scottish Presbyterian and she was Irish Catholic and the wedding took place in Clontarf on a freezing cold day.

Meanwhile back at the Boleyn, West Ham were taking on Nottingham Forest in the third round of the FA Cup, but I'd opted to go to the wedding. Helen was not only my ex, she was my triple ex. She chucked me three times in the late 1980s, usually around Christmas. I'm not sure if she wanted to save on presents. After the third occasion I got the message and we became firm friends.

If I was in a movie and someone had stolen my identity and fitted me up for a crime, and the mob was after me, as well as the cops, I'd ring Helen. I've watched enough films to know you mustn't ring your family or colleagues, because they'll have the phones tapped. You always need an old friend, who'll believe in you and bring a change of clothing and some money to a roadside diner. Helen is my phone-a-friend if that ever happens, so let's hope the feds and the bad guys don't read this.

We kicked off at 2:45 in Dublin, fifteen minutes ahead of the other match. As the fair Helen swept down the aisle on her brother's arm, I imagined Joe Cole leading the players off the pitch after the warm-up, ready for Glenn Roeder's team talk.

I had a tiny in-ear radio with me, from a vodka promotion event I'd worked at. I kept it switched off during the service, but as soon as we finished I popped round the back to find we were 2–1 down. I kept my composure, returned to the front of the church and gave the bride a quick hug. As soon as she saw me she burst into tears. How had she heard the score, I wondered?

Half-time in both events happened simultaneously. As they changed ends at Upton Park, we changed venues, moving on to the Royal Dublin Society. On the specially commissioned double-decker bus I listened hoping for news from West Ham. In Dublin the big English teams to follow are Arsenal, Liverpool and Manchester United and the fellow on the radio didn't seem to be mentioning the West Ham game much. Cork is the place to go if you want to meet Happy Hammers. There's a huge following for the club, dating back to the 1950s when Cork boy Noel Cantwell came across the Irish Sea to play for us.

With no news on the second half, I tried retuning to other stations, but the vodka radio would only pick up RTE. Seeing my furrowed brow and not knowing about the hidden radio, the family of the bride comforted me, thinking I must be suffering with the emotion of my ex's wedding.

As we arrived at the reception, Joe Cole equalised for West Ham. Actually it happened slightly earlier, but RTE radio didn't think fit to interrupt a studio discussion about Mick McCarthy's successor as Irish manager. In fact the RTE flash was beaten by a text from my dad, who knew I would be eager for news. I was clapping my hands with glee as I left the bus. Good, thought the bride's sisters, he's pleased with the venue. He's obviously over the worst of it!

With ice on the ground outside and alcohol flowing freely inside, there were raised eyebrows at my decision to wander up and down the courtyard for the next fifteen minutes. My tiny radio discreetly hidden from view, I must have looked a cold and lonely figure. Sure, the little fellow is having a relapse, they thought, we'll leave him to it.

By the time I finally entered the hall I was an emotional wreck. Jermain Defoe had scored again, David Johnson had missed a penalty for Forest, Marlon Harewood had seen a goal disallowed and I'd nearly lost two toes to frostbite.

With the victory achieved, I could start to enjoy myself. Helen's sisters performed an amazing 'Riverdance' type spectacle. There wasn't a dry eye in the house. My ex was safely married and she'd still be my first phone call if the mob and the cops were after me. Safe in that knowledge I could now head back to London and concentrate on a great cup run. Maybe this was going to be West Ham's year.

We were drawn away to Manchester United in the next round and lost 6–0.

MEETING MY MATCH

So Helen was married and Charlotte was with someone she'd met at Ceroc. All around me people were paired up, but I was young, free and single again. Well, free and single anyway. When Catherine moved out, because she 'needed time to think', I sat and waited for her to come back, even though it was apparent to all my friends that she wasn't going to. Like all West Ham fans I'm fiercely loyal and I never give up, even when it's clearly a lost cause. My family were used to my serial monogamy. At Mum and Dad's ruby wedding, my big sister, the other Kathryn, had organised two group photos, one with Cath and one without. She said she was fed up with me splitting up with girlfriends before family photos had even been developed. It seemed harsh at the time, but she had a point.

My problem was I always went for beautiful women who worked in the media and looked like film stars. What I needed was a plain girl with an ordinary job. A year on I hadn't met any, I'm not sure my heart was in it. I kept hoping Cath would come back, having decided she would like short chubby children after all. This is pretty much what happens to Ricky Gervais and Jennifer Garner in *The Invention of Lying*. But Ricky wrote that film and this wasn't the movies, this was real life. Eventually I heard a rumour that Catherine had met someone. Then she popped up on *Ready Steady Cook* telling Ainsley Harriott she was engaged. It wasn't the best way to find out, but it spurred me into action and that night I joined dating website Match.com. They promised if you hadn't found anyone in six months, you could have another six months free. It didn't sound much of a guarantee, but I signed up for a year, as it was cheaper than doing it monthly. I like a bit of romance, but there's nothing like a deal. Nobody on the site advertised themselves as a plain girl with an ordinary job, but I was sure I'd find one somewhere.

Having taken the one-year package, I wanted to get my money's worth and dated lots of different women. It was great fun. I'd heartily recommend it to anyone. I started at the 2002 Commonwealth Games which were held in Manchester. Dating wasn't an official sport, but I was part of the BBC's Nations and Regions team, so that's how I remember when it was. I had dinner with a Derbyshire woman who drove across the dales to meet me in Manchester one evening. She was great, but not for me. Over the next few months I met some lovely women. It turns out that when you reach forty as a single male, you suddenly become very eligible. None of them were plain and they had all sorts of jobs. One was mysterious and wouldn't tell me her profession until we met. I thought she might be a spy, but she was a tube driver. I had a few months with the director of a ski tour firm. We started well, but went downhill very quickly. I moved on to a musical theatre actress and part-time masseuse. While we dated she was massaging Sean Bean. Not actually during our dates, because I wouldn't stand for that. He was playing Macbeth in the West End and she confirmed that he has a tattoo that says '100 per cent Blade', to show his allegiance to Sheffield United.

I split up with the musical masseuse before she manipulated me and continued the quest to meet my princess. It was tough work, but someone had to do it. I was scoring more often than anyone in the West Ham attack, but I really needed to settle down, because I was worn out. Things were looking good when I met a South African called Jeanette on assignment to IBM in the UK. I lost my way en-route to her flat in East Twickenham. Very tired after a week of breakfast shows on Mean Country, I cut up a police car on the Richmond one-way system. The copper pulled me over, but let me off with a warning, after hearing I was a country music presenter on a blind date. It sounded such a tragic combination, he must have felt sorry for me, but I took it as a sign. I was right, when the door opened there stood a beautiful blonde Afrikaner. Jeanette had sounded friendly on the phone, but I'd grown up in the apartheid era, when villains in movies always had South African accents. I hadn't expected her to be as lovely as this. I hadn't learnt my lesson, I'd still gone for a beauty, but I somehow knew that this time my quest was over. In the movie of this book, Cameron Diaz, Kim Basinger, and Michelle Pfeiffer would all be considered for the role, but they'd be rejected for not being gorgeous enough. Even Charlize Theron with her South African roots wouldn't get a call back.

CALLED UP FOR ENGLAND

In February 2003 England were scheduled to play their first ever full international at West Ham, a friendly against Australia. Wembley Stadium was being redeveloped, so England were playing their games at grounds around the country.

As soon as the fixture was arranged, I wrote to the Football Association and offered my services as the announcer at the match. I was very excited that the national side were going to play at my team's home.

I received a polite but rather snooty reply thanking me for my interest, but they had their own announcer that they would be using. Maybe they thought I had ideas above my station. I'd heard the England announcer and he was good. He was a bit too happy all the time for my liking and he played rather too many 'Rocking All over the World' type anthems. But he was a decent announcer.

I'd already announced a few internationals at various levels, but never for the senior team.

My first game had been in my very first season, when England faced Bulgaria in an under-21 international. The names were a bit tricky, so I sought out the press officer from the Bulgarian FA and asked him for help with pronunciation. I spelt out the Bulgarian names phonetically. Names like Iordan, Ivan and Petar, I wrote out as Yordan, Eevan and Pettar. As I wrote the names out, he would nod his head at my pronunciation, but shake his head in disbelief at my spelling. I think he dealt mainly with the written press.

My other concern was the hair-raising business of the national anthems. At under-21 level, there's no live singer just the anthems played from a CD. The Football Association provided a disc featuring national anthems of the world. The Bulgarian anthem was track two and 'God Save the Queen' was track ten.

The teams ran out and once they were in position I pressed play on track two. The Bulgarian anthem blared out. At least I assume it was the Bulgarian anthem. They seemed to know the words anyway, the fans and players all joined in.

Next came the nerve-racking bit. I had to manually click past tracks 3, 4, 5, 6, 7, 8 and 9 to reach our anthem. Having safely arrived at track ten, I checked it was track ten, checked again and then once more for luck. It seemed like minutes had passed, but it was probably just a few seconds. If this went wrong it was going to be awful. I pressed play, held my breath and was relieved to hear the familiar sound of 'our tune'. If I'd stuffed up and pressed play too early, on track nine, the crowd would have been treated to 'Deutschland, Deutschland, Uber Alles'. I would have been completely mortified as my mistake was transmitted to TV audiences around the world.

After getting through the names and then the anthems, the game itself was a breeze. The night was rounded off perfectly with an England win, the only goal of the game scored by West Ham's Frank Lampard.

After that I was a regular for all internationals played at West Ham. A few months before the visit of Australia I announced an under-20 game against Switzerland. West Ham's Glen Johnson looked at home in the number five shirt but we lost. Twelve thousand turned up on a chilly night. I played the correct national anthems and nobody booed the Swiss anthem, which was good. Mind you, the Swiss don't have any natural enemies. Such is their reputation for neutrality in global conflicts, the Swiss army only carry penknives.

I was working on behalf of the Football Association that night. I really hoped I was in with a shout of announcing at the England v Australia full international that was coming up in February. It turns out my chances of getting the call were as remote as Switzerland invading Austria.

A couple of weeks before the game, I contacted the Football Association again and pointed out that I would be there on the night. If they needed any help, they only had to ask. I received another polite and slightly less snooty letter of thanks. They were sure they'd be fine, but thanks for the offer.

On the night I arrived at the ground as normal. There was no sign in the box of Steve the England announcer. Maybe he hadn't turned up. Maybe I was going to the ball after all.

I wasn't. My golden carriage turned into a pumpkin when I looked out of the window onto the pitch below. They'd built a little sound desk in the front of the Dr Martens Stand. He was going to be announcing from a seat at the front of the stand. I was very jealous. I'd always wished I could work outside on a regular match day. I'd love to be out there, instead of up in the box, where the crowd noise came through a speaker that you could turn up or down.

This chap was making his debut at the Boleyn and he was working outside. It wasn't fair.

My bottom lip touching the ground in front of me, I went down for a word with the England announcer. He was very pleased to see me. He'd been looking all over the place he said. Not in the announcer's box apparently, but he'd had a good old search of other less likely places.

The long and the short of it was he was looking to leave early. It was his sister's party that night and he wanted to attend. How would I fancy announcing the second half?

Two things came to mind. Firstly, what a plonker, leaving an England game to go to a party! I'd give my right arm to be the England announcer and this fellow just wasn't bothered. Now I'm big on family myself, so I could see why he'd want to go, but when your country calls I think you step up and your family has to understand.

The second emotion was much bigger. I was going to be the England announcer in the second half. Hurrah!

Natasha, who helped out with the birthday dedications in the box, took my photograph. It was documentary proof of me standing with a microphone in front of the stand with all the England branding everywhere. I was very small in it, with the Dr Martens Stand huge behind me, looking spectacular under the floodlights. When Tash gave me that photo at the next West Ham game, I knew that I would treasure it forever.

England lost the game 3–1. The only time England ever played a full international at West Ham, we lost 3–1. To Australia! You'd expect to lose to them at cricket or rugby, but at football?

The Aussies have a great sense of humour. There was a banner that night that read, 'If we win this, then you suck at EVERYTHING!' I don't believe even the person that made that banner actually believed the Socceroos would win. But they did.

England were 2–0 down at half-time when Steve left for his sister's party. I hope she was happy to see him. Sven-Göran Eriksson wasn't happy with England. He made eleven changes in the second half. I announced them all, including the arrival of a young lad by the name of Wayne Rooney. Great things were expected from him. The seventeen-year-old was the youngest player ever to be capped by his country.

I've never known a game like it for substitutions. No wonder Steve left. The fourth official was holding up his electronic board virtually continuously. I was like a bingo caller.

'One little duck, number two, Gary Neville. Cup of tea, number three, Ashley Cole. Lucky for some, number seven, David Beckham. Legs Eleven, Kieron Dyer. Two fat ladies, the St John Ambulance helpers.'

The crowd marked them off on their programmes with their bingo dabbers.

'Leaving the field Man Alive, number five, Rio Ferdinand. Coming on Sweet Sixteen, Ledley King.'

I was announcing at an England game. I was nervous, but exhilarated. There was a producer sitting next to me and he handed me bits of paper telling me what to say. Of course I didn't really do the bingo numbers. That was just in my head. It was so much easier than being the West Ham announcer, where I had to think about what I was doing. It's something I've found in the broadcasting world, the higher you get the easier it becomes. Not because you get any better, but because there are people who do half your work for you. People in local radio are all heroes. They work twice as hard, for half the money that the national people get.

That night I was floating on air. I was at the top of my game. I pronounced every name clearly and loudly. Luckily we were playing Australia and not Latvia or Morocco, where the surnames can be tricky. Surely I would be spotted and that England job would soon be my own. Today my club, tomorrow my country and one day the world!

In reality I announced for forty-five minutes and that was it. England drew 1–1 in the second half. They lost overall, but they drew in my half. It surely meant I was the better of the two announcers. The atmosphere had certainly picked up once I took over on the mike. Maybe I did do the bingo numbers out loud! But it probably had more to do with England playing better. After fielding a strong team in the first half, Sven had opted for young guns in the second. They were all keen to impress. It was obvious that Rooney was going to be quite a player once he grew up. Actually he never did grow up, but he certainly improved as a player as he got older.

The atmosphere improved even more thanks to a goal from 'Key of the Door, number twenty-one, Francis Jeffers' that gave England a chance of a comeback. I remember exactly what I announced. 'Goal for England scored by Francis Jeffers!' It was simple but effective and it was followed by a massive cheer, the crowd appreciating the succinct form of my announcement.

It couldn't get much better than this. It didn't. The Aussies scored a third. I remember exactly what I said. 'Goal for Australia scored by Brett Emerton.' I'd found a winning formula and I was sticking to it. There was a massive cheer from the Aussies in the crowd and there were loads of them. The whole of London's Australian community seemed to have turned out. I don't know who was serving the drinks in the pubs that night.

The creator of the 'If we win this, then you suck at EVERYTHING' banner was presumably hailed as a latter-day Nostradamus by his mates.

I was the only England fan that left the game that night walking on air. We'd been rubbish. England invented football, rugby and cricket and now the Aussies had beaten us at all of them.

There was much wringing of hands by the newspaper journalists that night, which made writing their columns very difficult. I was on the laptop too, writing to the Football Association to say how much I'd enjoyed being the announcer, even if it was only for one half. I reminded them that I was always available and would love to represent my country again.

I received a polite and very snotty reply, pointing out

that they had their own announcer. Thank you very much for the offer, you grubby little oik, now please go back under whichever stone you came from.

They may not be the exact words.

Oh well, I'd tried. There's only so much you can do. Maybe the England announcer was from a large family and there'd be lots of parties for him to attend, paving the way for me.

To be fair to Steve he did send me a cheque with half his fee. At least he said it was half his fee. If it was half, he didn't have a very good agent. I suspect it was a quarter.

Oh well, never mind, he packed in being the England announcer shortly afterwards anyway. England played most of their games at Old Trafford after that, using the Manchester United announcer Alan Keegan. Now he is very good and even in my wildest dreams I didn't imagine they'd pay for me to travel up to Manchester, when they had a perfectly good announcer on their doorstep.

There's no career progression in the announcing world. I can't move to Arsenal in a big-money transfer, because I'm not an Arsenal fan. Besides, I have a loud voice and might wake somebody up. Leyton Orient did once ask me to fill in when their announcer was ill, but I said no. It wasn't for me, even though West Ham gave me permission. Loaning out strikers to lower division clubs to give them confidence is one thing, but I would not feel comfortable enthusiastically announcing goals for a rival club. Even if they are very friendly rivals like the 'O's.

When Wembley was built I fancied my chances of being the announcer there. Being the England announcer would have dovetailed perfectly with being the West Ham announcer, because West Ham and England can never play a match on the same day. It's the law.

My agent was in talks with Wembley about who would announce at England internationals when they returned to their grand new stadium. There was talk of a shortlist and auditions, but at the last minute I was told the responsibility had been passed from Wembley to the Football Association. The selection process was scrapped as the FA opted to continue with Alan Keegan, the Manchester United announcer.

I've never announced for England since. I've done a few internationals at under-21 and under-19 level and a few finals like the FA Vase and the Women's FA Cup, but I've not won any more full England caps. You don't actually get a cap, except in your own head. I didn't mind, I knew I'd represented my country and I had that picture of me in front of the West Stand holding the microphone. Or did I?

At the time of my England debut I'd just started dating Jeanette. She was very taken with the photo of me on the pitch. She liked it so much she cut me out and put me in a small frame by her bed. The West Stand was completely cut out. The picture could have been taken anywhere. I wasn't best pleased.

ROEDER HELL

OK, there's no avoiding it any further. Let's take a look at that awful relegation season. Twenty-four games into the league season and we still hadn't won at home. Our first league win at the Boleyn came on 29 January against Blackburn. The previous season Upton Park had been a fortress. People were using a different 'f' word now. Glenn Roeder had lost the support of senior professionals like Paolo Di Canio and we were in freefall.

I started getting emails from people asking for me to play the music from the film *The Great Escape* as the team ran out. I was reluctant to do this as we always run out to 'I'm Forever Blowing Bubbles'. Some things should never change. However, the message boards on the interweb also started claiming it would inspire the players. It's dangerous to take too much notice of message boards, but something clearly needed to be done. I'm not sure if the forum posters had ever seen the film though; only three of the allied prisoners escape and lots of the rest are shot.

However, it's a stirring tune, if a little corny, so I decided to give it a play. Not when the teams ran out, but just before kick-off. The crowd joined in clapping along, and it did make for a terrific atmosphere at the start to the game, certainly better than the team deserved. I'm not a fan of that kind of choreographed clapping, but we were in dire need of something.

I first played it against Fulham and then Newcastle. We drew them both, before winning the home game against

Blackburn. On the message boards 'The Great Escape' received mixed reviews. The ones who'd asked for it obviously loved it and the improved atmosphere it brought. Some felt it wasn't the West Ham way. Others thought it embarrassing that we had to artificially create an atmosphere.

There were also those who believed in the 'ginks' theory. By playing 'The Great Escape', I was in fact sealing our destiny. The very mention of the word 'escape', would ensure that we wouldn't. One forum poster on the web by the name of Skunk Pussy said he would break my nose. He sounded very angry. I imagine it can't have been easy growing up with a name like that. What were his parents thinking?

When we were eventually relegated on the last day of the season at Birmingham, their fears were realised. They'd been right all along, if only I'd listened. The supporters of 'The Great Escape' melted quietly into the background. To this day, you'll hardly find anyone who thinks it was a good idea, yet on match days it improved the atmosphere at kick-off by 100 per cent and I can't remember many people not clapping along.

Success has many fathers, failure has only one. I received so much abuse that season from fellow supporters, never in real life, but usually via email or the message forums. It's amazing how brave cyber-warriors are.

We didn't escape, that was my real crime. Surely it's only right that I should be taken into a clearing and shot. But let's imagine for a moment this is not wartime justice. We've heard the lies and the damned lies, what about the statistics?

I played 'The Great Escape' for our last nine home league games. In those games we had five wins: against Blackburn, Spurs, Sunderland, Middlesbrough and Chelsea. There were three draws: Fulham, Newcastle and

Aston Villa. We only lost one game when 'The Great Escape' was played before kick-off and that was against Liverpool.

So that rousing wartime tune earned us eighteen points from a possible twenty-seven. In the previous ten home league games, how many points do you think we earned?

Four points! That's how many we earned from a possible thirty points. We drew four games and lost the other six. We did not win a home game until I started playing 'The Great Escape'.

So did I 'ginks' us? Was it all my fault? Did I really deserve all the horrendous abuse I received via email, from so-called fans? No, I did not deserve to get shot. We nearly got out of it. 'The Great Escape' gave us hope right up until the last game of the season. At worst I should have been locked in the slammer for a week, with nothing more than a baseball and mitt for company.

We so nearly pulled off the great escape. We only lost once in our last eleven games, but I was still given a ridiculous amount of stick from fans. Never in real life, not once did anyone say anything bad to me at a game, it was always on web forums and via email. Maybe it was because I had a column in the matchday programme with my email address at the bottom. With no other email address listed in the whole publication, it seemed to become the email of choice for letting off steam.

Do I sound angry about it? Well I was at the time, but my therapist says I'm nearly over it. That Skunk Pussy business left a nasty taste in the mouth.

We went down with forty-two points, a magical number for any fan of sci-fi based comedy, but also the highest ever total for a relegated team. Forty-two! It felt awful, even worse than being made to listen to Vogon poetry, which I'm sure you know is the third worst poetry in the universe.

Growing up as a kid, I used to love the classic BBC radio

serial, *The Hitchhikers Guide to the Galaxy*. I used to tape it and listen to it over and over again. When it was made into a TV series I already knew all the stories and would regale my friends at school with tales of Arthur Dent and Zaphod Beeblebrox. My favourite character was Slartibartfast the planet designer who specialised in crinkly edges, and was very proud of the fjords he'd created for Norway.

In the programme a giant computer is built to calculate the answer to life, the universe and everything. After seven and a half million years of thinking, it finally comes up with the answer: forty-two. Just that, the number forty-two, the number of points that we were relegated with.

This was a disastrous season. Paolo Di Canio, our inspirational Italian, fell out with Glenn Roeder. Much as I love Paolo he must have been a nightmare to manage. He always knew better than the boss. Now he probably did, but he should have at least given Glenn the impression that he was still in charge. Besides, Glenn, to be fair to him, did travel to big games in the north. Paolo had a nosebleed every time he travelled further than Watford. If jabs had been available for 'northern flu' back then, we'd have had a much better season.

I didn't dislike Glenn Roeder, he just seemed out of his depth. The fans were against him, but nobody would have wished on him what happened on Easter Monday. We'd beaten Middlesbrough and Glenn was relaxing in his office with his coaching staff when he collapsed. It was originally thought to be a heart attack, later reports said a stroke. In fact it was a brain tumour. Luckily for Glenn, the club doctor Ges Steinberg was still in the ground. He looked after Glenn until the ambulance arrived.

At times like this, football isn't the most important thing in the world. The legendary Bill Shankly was wrong about it being more important than life and death.

West Ham did what we do in a crisis: we called in Trevor

Brooking. He took us down with dignity, taking seven points from the last nine. On the last day of the season we drew at Birmingham, but we weren't in control of our own destiny. Bolton's victory over Middlesbrough sent us down. We'd taken nineteen points from the last ten games, but we still hadn't managed to beat the hoodoo of the bottom team at Christmas always being relegated. West Brom would become the only team to buck that trend, when they survived two years later.

At that point West Ham should have sacked Glenn Roeder, but we didn't. We did the decent thing and didn't kick a man when he was down.

We were relegated from the top division, despite having a squad that reads like a *Who's Who* of future England internationals. We went down with Joe Cole, Jermain Defoe, Glen Johnson and Michael Carrick in the team, plus the England keeper David James. We had so much flair in the squad, with Trevor Sinclair and Paolo Di Canio regularly taking the breath away.

On Sky Sports Saturday morning show *Soccer AM*, they have a feature called 'Showboat', where the best bits of skill from the previous week are showcased. West Ham dominated that feature that season. Joe Cole, Trevor Sinclair and Paolo Di Canio were Showboat stars, but we still went down.

I still don't really understand how we did it. It shows attacking flair is not enough if you don't score goals, and you let lots in at the other end. Joe Cole was made captain at the age of just twenty-one. When we were relegated he had to leave to pursue his career with Chelsea. That wasn't fair to a player of his quality.

It was widely accepted that we were too good to go down. Everyone said it. Look at all that attacking talent, those incredible young players. The most annoying aspect of that season was losing our crop of talented youngsters.

In gardening terms we ran a brilliant nursery, our young talent had been nurtured and was now ready to bloom. But we had a dry season and they were uprooted and sold. The seeds that we had lovingly sowed would be reaped by someone else. Eventually they would flower in England white, but not in the claret and blue.

Forty-two at the time of writing is still the highest total that any team has been relegated with. Once you have that number in your head, it's amazing how many times you notice it. Most streets have a number forty-two, apart from short ones.

It is also one of the most mentioned multiples of seven in popular culture. It originally cropped up a lot in the writing of Lewis Carroll, the *Alice in Wonderland* chap. That's where Douglas Adams picked it up. He thought it was the funniest of the two-digit numbers. I'm not sure he's right; I think fifty-five just has the edge.

Douglas Adams is such a hero to so many people and the number features in episodes of *Stargate Atlantis* and *Dr Who*. The band Level 42 take their name from it and TV family The Kumars don't live at number forty-two by accident. Kumars creator Sanjeev Bhaskar is a *Hitchhikers* fan.

I love everything Douglas Adams ever wrote, but when I see the number forty-two, all I think about is that wretched season when we were relegated with forty-two points. It wasn't the answer to life, the universe and everything. It was a horrible end to a dreadful season that saw us drop out of the top flight. So long and thanks for all the fish, as the dolphins said when they left the earth, seconds before it was demolished by the Vogons to make way for a hyper-space bypass.

Still, at least my radio career was back on track or so it seemed. The ratings were flying up at Mean Country, especially my breakfast show. The second Gulf War was in full flow and in depressing times there's nothing like country music to cheer you up. Surely I would come to the attention of a network station again?

As the station's stock rose, all the presenters were called in one Friday afternoon and told that from Monday, the station would be operating on a digital jukebox format. That sounds very lovely, but actually means there's no presenters, so we were actually sacked. I left the building that day for the last time, with a huge box of pens. They had the station logo on them and it was changing its name, so it wasn't stealing. But just in case God thought it was technically stealing, I spent the next year leaving them in public places for poor people to find.

Season in a Nutshell 2002/03

We lost 4–0 at Newcastle on the opening day, setting the tone for the season. We spent most of it in the bottom three and were relegated.

Highlight – There may have been one, but I can't think of it.

Lowlight – It was all rubbish. Glenn Roeder lost the dressing room and Paolo Di Canio didn't travel to big away games, especially in the north. We lost to Iain Dowie's Oldham in the Worthington Cup and were bottom of the league at Christmas. The atmosphere at Upton Park was awful and we didn't win a home league game until late January. We were relegated on the last day of the season.

Team news – We had some great players like Di Canio, Jermain Defoe, Joe Cole, Les Ferdinand and Freddie Kanoute, although it's fair to say most of our talent was up front. How a manager could get relegated with a side as talented as that is beyond me.

Villain – We needed some fight in the team, so Roeder signed Lee Bowyer who loved fighting. He would fight with team-mates, on evenings out and sometimes on the pitch. Despite being a West Ham fan, Bowyer should never have been allowed to wear the claret and blue. I gave him the least enthusiastic welcome I could on the microphone, without losing my job.

Worst moment – The mood was so ugly The Hammerettes were booed against Leeds as they walked onto the pitch. The fans didn't even wait to see how they danced, that's how bad it was. I felt sorry for the girls.

More important than football moment – Manager Glenn Roeder collapsed with a brain tumour after a game. We held our breath and wished him well.

Hero – Club doctor Ges Steinberg kept Glenn alive until the ambulance arrived.

New this season – The Hammers Grand Draw replaced the 50/50 Draw at half-time. It meant a guaranteed prize of a thousand pounds. The Hammerettes were given a new portable pitch speaker, which meant they could hear the music without everyone's ears bleeding in the stands.

International highlight – Announcing England under-20s against Switzerland, followed by my first full cap for England against Australia, where I announced Wayne Rooney's arrival on the international scene.

It shouldn't happen to an announcer – West Ham fan Nik Turner proposed to his partner Cat Presley on the pitch. She said yes as the crowd sang, 'You don't know what you're doing!' I played 'The Great Escape' before kick-off for the second half of the season, but we didn't escape. Some people felt it was my fault.

Missed games – Just one, for Helen's wedding.

Did we win at Anfield? – What do you think? We lost 2–0.

My bald patch – The size of a beermat (a round one, not a square one)

Three-Legged Stool Review

Job leg – After working for BBC TV as a reporter at the Commonwealth Games in Manchester, I returned to my first love, radio, presenting the breakfast show on Mean Country 1035AM in Wembley. It was great to be back at Wembley again. I hoped it wouldn't be too long before I returned there with West Ham.

Relationship leg – It took a TV cookery show to convince me that Catherine wasn't coming back. I'd been simmering on a low heat for too long. Now I was cooking with gas again as I plunged headlong into online dating. I met lots of interesting women and finally a very special lady.

West Ham leg – It fell off the stool. We were relegated.

OUT OF AFRICA

I spent the summer visiting South Africa to meet Jeanette's family. The Krugers are lovely people, very much like my own family. Her Ma was treasurer at the church and her Pa had helped set up the university. Jeanette is the great-great-great-granddaughter of President Kruger, who was the leader of the Afrikaners in the Boer War against the British. He's the man who gives his name to Kruger National Park and the Krugerrand gold coins. I don't have any relatives with their faces on money, but I liked the Krugers straight away.

Shortly after we arrived Pa took me on a tour of their home town, Potchefstroom, two hours' drive west of Johannesburg. Potch is lovely, but there was something he really wanted to show me that I wasn't expecting. We visited the Potch concentration camp memorial. The British used concentration camps during the Second Boer War to house the women and children of the Boer fighters. They didn't give them enough food and the conditions were shameful. Twenty-eight thousand women, children and elderly Afrikaners died in British camps. They didn't teach us about that in history at school, did they? I felt awful reading all the names on the memorial. I'd expected to have the moral high ground on a visit to white South Africans, having boycotted all goods during the apartheid era. Now it turned out my country was responsible for these awful atrocities. Lord Kitchener, that fellow with the huge moustache on the 'Your Country Needs You' poster, is reviled as a war criminal by Afrikaners.

Jeanette and I holidayed in South Africa, visiting the cell on Robben Island where Nelson Mandela was kept prisoner. A former inmate took us round, regaling us with stories of the football league that the political prisoners organised themselves, played to FIFA rules. Nelson himself wasn't allowed to take part, but the current South African President Jacob Zuma was a keen player for a team called Rangers. It put West Ham's problems into perspective. We vowed that we would return to South Africa in 2010 for the World Cup.

I'm always fascinated by people telling their own stories. All the guides at Robben Island are former prisoners. Ours was a splendid fellow who acted out his stories with relish. At one point when we were in a dining room, he dramatically slammed the door closed, trapping us all inside. He would only release us if he was asked some good questions. A small boy burst into tears.

THREE BOBBYS

Bobby – what a brilliant name, just hearing it makes me happy. I think of Bobby Moore, Bobby Charlton and Bobby Chocolate.

Bobby Moore

When I was a kid the biggest name in football was Bobby Moore. He was the England captain when we won the World Cup in 1966. I don't remember much about it as I was three. My middle sister Melanie was only a few days old, so Dad watched the game with the baby on his lap. I'm not sure where I was, but Mel says it was a good game and we won it 4–2. Either she has a great memory, or she's watched it back on DVD.

No trip to the Boleyn Ground is complete without a visit to the World Cup Heroes statue on the corner of Green Street and Barking Road, with Bobby held aloft holding the trophy. The best thing about Bobby Moore was that he was also the captain of West Ham. By the time the 1970 World Cup came round, I was fully up to speed about football. I had wall charts, the lot. Mel says the pictures from Mexico were a bit fuzzy, but it gave it a certain quality. She was only four, but already had a keen eye.

I took my little statue of Bobby Moore to my first day at the BBC, my first day at Channel Five and it even went on holiday with me to Morocco for the 1984 Olympics. The games weren't held in Morocco, but it's where I went on holiday. Bobby stood on top of the hotel TV for good luck as Daley Thompson won the decathlon in Los Angeles. He tilted slightly to one side because I left him on a radiator and his base melted. That's Bobby not Daley.

I only met Bobby Moore twice in real life, apart from cheering him on from the crowd at West Ham. The first time was in 1975. We were moving house and Nanna took me and my big sister Kathryn to the movies, to keep us out of the way of the removal men. We saw *Towering Inferno* with Steve McQueen and Paul Newman.

In those days, you had to queue outside a cinema for a popular film. We queued along the side of the Gants Hill Odeon. I had a bit of restless leg syndrome and danced about with excitement at the thought of seeing a skyscraper go up in flames. My forefathers are from the low-lying fens of Cambridgeshire, so any tall building is exciting. I still have cousins who point when they see an aeroplane in the sky.

So I was dancing around like Nijinsky, the racehorse not the ballet dancer, and accidentally trod on the toes of the man behind us. He was tall and I looked up to say sorry. It was Bobby Moore. I mumbled an apology and went bright red. After that I don't remember anything, the film is a complete blur.

Kathryn apparently did strike up a conversation with him. She went to Miss Brill's dance classes with Bobby's daughter Roberta, who was the same age. The way Kathryn tells it, she was on first-name terms with Bobby, but I don't believe a word of it, I think the story has been embellished over the years, I mean whoever heard of the surname Brill? I remember being told the following weekend Bobby Moore missed a penalty and it was all because I trod on his toe. Well I know that's rubbish, because Bobby didn't take penalties. So you can forget that one, Kathryn!

The other time I met Bobby was at Villa Park the day West Ham lost the FA Cup semi-final, 4–0 to Nottingham

Forest. The other semi-final between Spurs and Arsenal, the first at Wembley, was live on TV in the press room beforehand. There were plenty of places to sit, but I deliberately sat right next to Bob and we chatted all through the game. I can't remember what we said, it was all about the match, but I was talking to Bobby Moore. Spurs won, setting up the mouth-watering prospect of a West Ham/ Spurs final.

As the press room emptied I went to the loo. Bobby Moore was emerging from a cubicle. As he washed his hands I wished him good luck with his radio commentary and then I went into the cubicle he'd just left. Now I'm a bit of a stickler when it comes to hygiene, a bit like Niles from *Frasier*, but for the first time ever, I didn't wipe the toilet seat down before taking my seat. Bobby Moore was the greatest ever captain of West Ham and England, his germs could not be harmful. On reflection it is odd behaviour and I'm not sure I should be mentioning it in a book. But, better out than in.

I took my seat in the stand, still grinning, and ready to watch West Ham fight for a place in an all-London cup final. The West Ham fans were magnificent that day, the best I've ever known, even better in my view than that legendary play-off semi-final against Ipswich in the Pardew era, when we didn't stop singing 'Billy Bonds Claret and Blue Army' all day.

We lost 4–0.

When Bobby died in 1993 I was working at BBC Greater London Radio. It came up as just a few words on the wires: England's World Cup-winning captain Bobby Moore has died of bowel cancer. Working in broadcasting you develop immunity to bad news stories, otherwise you'd never be able to cope with live situations. However, when it's one of your heroes from childhood it's tough. My little statue of Bobby that sat on my bedside locker as a kid had come with me to my interview at GLR and he'd been there for my first show. Now I had to read the newsflash.

With tears streaming down my face, I ripped off the script from the printer and walked into the studio. The news editor intercepted me and asked if I wanted somebody else to read it, but I said I would be all right. I put my head down and read it, just exactly what it said on the script, and then walked out again without talking to the presenter.

Bobby Moore played 108 times for England, a record at the time. Peter Shilton and David Beckham have since overtaken that total. Shilts played on longer because he was a keeper and Becks made a lot of his appearances as a sub, but Bobby played every single minute of every one of his 108 appearances.

The Bobby Moore Fund does brilliant work in his memory, raising awareness of bowel cancer. I've been inspired every time I've met Stephanie Moore at events where I've supported them as a speaker or auctioneer. If you are ever looking for a charity to support they are lovely people to work with. Each year I stand out at the London Marathon cheering on every Bobby Moore Fund runner wearing the red shirts with a number six on the back. I'd love to run it one year for the BMF, but my osteopath won't let me.

The first game after Bobby's death was against Wolves. A giant number six shirt made out of claret and blue flowers was carried into the centre circle by Geoff Hurst and Martin Peters. Like many around me I was struggling to hold back the tears. Then two Wolves fans ran onto the pitch with a tribute of their own. They obviously hadn't cleared it with anyone, but the stewards were brilliant and didn't overreact, allowing them to place their tribute, I think it was a cross in Wolves colours, alongside the official tributes in the centre circle. They were warmly applauded all the way back to their seats. We won the game 3–1, which was fitting. At the end my heart was in my mouth as a West Ham skinhead ran onto the pitch. He ran to the Wolves end, applauded them, they clapped him back and he ran off. I'm with Brian Clough when it comes to pitch invasions, nobody should ever enter the field of play. But those two mini-invasions were special moments and were a fitting tribute to England's greatest ever captain.

Bobby Charlton

I've been in trouble a few times with announcements I've made. In my first season I upset a knight of the realm. Sir Bobby Charlton is a legendary figure in the game, famed throughout the land for his ferocious shot. He inspired England to a World Cup triumph, won a European Cup for Manchester United and invented a hairstyle.

During the half-time interval of a game against Manchester United, I announced the scores at other games across the country. There was a huge cheer from the crowd when I said, 'The good news is Spurs are losing'. At this point Bobby Charlton turned to one of the West Ham directors and said, 'He shouldn't have said that. It's not right to say that.'

This was later relayed to me by a board member, but with the proviso that I should definitely keep on doing it, because they liked it. After all, we are West Ham United not the BBC, and we don't have to be impartial. While I'm big on respecting the opposition fans, it's another matter entirely to have a bit of banter over the PA about other teams. Their fans can't feel threatened as they're not at the match. However, since Bobby's comment I've not said anything like that again, I do it all with the intonation in my voice.

Not only was Bobby Charlton a member of England's World Cup-winning side in 1966, he also invented the comb-over hairstyle. To be fair, Ralph Coates of Spurs and Burnley did a lot to develop the style, but it was Charlton who gave his name to the comb-over. For younger readers who have only seen footage of Charlton as one of those people on the pitch who thought it was all over, or seen him with a Russian hat in the Manchester United directors box, let me fill you in on the missing years. In the 1970s, Bobby's career was still in full flow, but his hairline had retired. Well, not so much retired as retreated to the back of his head. Bobby came up with a cunning plan. It was so cunning it completely fooled football fans the world over.

His hair had fallen out in the classic male baldness style favoured by monks. He now sported a perfectly smooth top of the head, with good strong hair all around the edges on three sides, but with nothing at the front. It was a bit like a very circular green on a golf course with only one approach route if you wanted to avoid the rough. In a moment of genius Charlton devised the comb-over, which did exactly what it says on the tin. He deliberately cultivated the hair on one side of his head, so it was six or seven inches long. He would then comb it over to join the hair on the other side of his head. Now here comes the cunning bit. The combed-over hair would lie on top of the bald head and create the illusion of growing hair.

On close inspection you would wonder why all the hair was lying left to right and why you could see skin through the strands. But from a distance it gave a passable imitation of realistic hair, like Action Man but without the gripping hands or the eagle eyes. Bobby would walk out proudly sporting his trademark hair at the start of the game. The illusion worked brilliantly until the game started. Then as he ran about the flap of combed-over hair would start to lift up. Bobby was a brilliant player with a cracking shot. When you look back on old footage from the

1970s he always seems to be scoring against West Ham, unless he's wearing the white shirt of England.

In those days a goal celebration involved your team lifting you in the air while you held one alarm aloft. It was this lifting motion that often caused the combed flap to rise up. His hair mirrored his one-armed salute. It was man and hair in perfect harmony. The irony was that Harmony was a brand of hair spray which might well have solved the problem.

Tragically Bobby failed to patent the comb-over, leaving the door wide open for Ralph Coates to get in on the flap action. If anything Coates' comb-over was even more impressive, but he didn't have a World Cup Winner's medal so he lost out in the naming rights. If Ralph had gone in front of the *Dragons' Den* team they would have rejected his request for investment in hair styling products needed to perfect the look.

Duncan Bannatyne would have been a youngster in Scotland still dreaming of building his network of gyms, but if he had been alive he would have shaken his head and pushed his chair back. 'It's a stylish look, Ralph, but you haven't invented it, you've only developed it to the next level. You can't patent it, because everyone knows it as "the Bobby Charlton". And you play for Spurs. So for that reason I'm out.'

With that Ralph would have scuttled down the spiral staircase without looking presenter Evan Davis straight in the eye, pausing only to pat down his flap of hair as he exited the building.

Bobby Chocolate

You're probably wondering who Bobby Chocolate is? When West Ham were relegated in 1992 I went on a holiday to Cyprus with a girl called Alyson. After a few days of pacing up and down the beach listening to The Smiths' *Hatful of Hollow* cassette on my Sony Walkman, I felt ready to talk to people again. I was testing Alyson's knowledge of football, to see if she'd be a suitable life partner. She failed miserably. In her defence she was Welsh, but she hadn't heard of Bobby Moore and that clinched it for me. When I gave her a clue to his surname by saying, 'Please, sir, I want some...' she answered 'Chocolate?'

After that we always talked about a mythical footballer called Bobby Chocolate. It wasn't as funny as it sounds and Alyson wasn't invited to the Boleyn on our return.

HAMMERS OR IRONS?

OK, fingers on buzzers and no conferring. You're in a pub quiz and you're asked the nickname of West Ham United. What do you say? Well, you don't say anything, because it's no conferring, but the chances are you'd write down 'The Hammers'.

Hang on, what's the buzzer for, if we're writing things down?

I don't know but everyone knows 'The Hammers' is the correct answer. The papers always call us 'The Hammers'. Except it's not the only answer; amongst the family of West Ham fans it's much more likely that we'll call ourselves 'The Irons'.

On a match day you'll always hear, 'Come on you Irons!' It's very rare to hear, 'Up the Hammers' outside of an episode of alleged TV sitcom *Till Death Us Do Part*. I didn't much care for the show about Alf Garnett, the racist West Ham fan. He was played by Warren Mitchell, a Jewish Spurs fan, so not exactly made for the part of an East London bigot. The show was meant to poke fun at intolerance, but many people who watched it were cheering for Alf rather than laughing at his ridiculous views. Alf Garnett was a disgrace to the claret and blue scarf he wore.

I appear to have climbed on a soapbox. I'm not sure who left it there. The point is the nickname we're given, isn't the one that we tend to use ourselves. It's like the royal family calling someone Bertie, when they're really called George, or because they've forgotten their name, but know it has a number at the end.

Lots of teams have more than one nickname. Bolton are known the world over as Wanderers, but their own fans call them the Trotters. West Bromwich Albion might officially be the Throstles, but they're more commonly the Baggies, after the baggy trousers worn by their supporters coming straight from the factories. Gooners used to be a derisory term used for Arsenal instead of the Gunners. Now the term Gooners is used by their own fans as a nickname. Older football fans always call them The Arsenal from the days when they were the works team for the Royal Arsenal at Woolwich.

So why are we 'The Hammers' as well as 'The Irons'?

The neutral fan often thinks the name Hammers comes from the Ham of West Ham, but it's from the riveting hammers used at Thames Ironworks, as featured on the club badge. The shipbuilding firm is also the source of The Irons name. The big old hammers were used to whack the rivets into the iron cladding on the ships. After a hard week of whacking it was great to relax by watching your football team. It was the most natural thing in the world to support them with songs about your favourite tool. The same principle applies today when Manchester United fans sing about Wayne Rooney.

I suspect the more common usage of Hammers by the press in particular is down to its suitability in headlines. If we win big the headline is likely to be 'A Right Hammering'. When we lose it's often 'Hammered'.

'A Right Ironing' doesn't have the same ring to it. 'West Ham Well and Truly Ironed!' A big result in football has little in common with starching your shirt collars.

The club itself also leans towards Hammers rather than Irons. The club matchday programme has been called Hammer and more recently Hammers.

There's perhaps another reason why we've been branded as Hammers rather than Irons. In cockney rhyming slang 'Iron' is used as a term for homosexual; Iron hoof meaning poof. It shouldn't be a problem in these liberal times, but there's always been a bit of a time lag between football supporters and the rest of the world. Just ask Brighton fans, many of whom are probably not gay, yet they are continually subjected to chants of 'Does your boyfriend know you're here?' It's all because they come from a town with a larger than average gay population. It really is the last resort.

There's another naming question that splits West Ham fans, and it crops up in a dream that I've had many times. I'm a guest on the quiz show *Who Wants to Be a Millionaire?* It's more of a nightmare really, because I end up losing a million pounds.

The million-pound question is 'What's the name of West Ham United's home ground?'

'The Boleyn Ground,' I say, quickly adding, 'Final answer.'

Chris Tarrant says that's the wrong answer, looks sad and the lights come on and the crowd groan. Chris reveals the correct answer is 'Upton Park' and then I wake up screaming. Sometimes I argue with him for a bit that Boleyn Ground is the true name of the ground, but he never hands over the cheque. Once I yelled at him that Upton Park is a tube station, but he was already on the fastest-finger-first round to find the next contestant.

Of course there are a number of inaccuracies in the dream, not least the fact that Boleyn Ground would presumably not be one of the four displayed options if Upton Park was also there. Also the dream bears more than a passing resemblance to an episode of *Only Fools and Horses*. Rodney is Del's 'phone a friend' on a quiz show, correctly answers 'Ravel' to a classical music question, but is incorrectly told the answer is wrong. Del chastises him with the line, 'Everyone knows Ravel make shoes!'

In real life I don't have a problem with calling the ground Upton Park, in the same way as I interchange 'The Hammers' with 'The Irons'. I prefer Boleyn Ground if I'm honest, as that is the ground's actual name. Upton Park is the area, but because of common usage it's perfectly acceptable as well.

The one thing I am a bit picky about is the dropping of the 'the'. I don't like it when people say Hammers have taken the lead. We're not called Hammers, we're 'The Hammers'. However, I've no problem with the dropping of the 'H'. I realise I'm one of the few supporters who pronounce it in our nickname or proper name, but I wouldn't 'ave 'ad much work on the BBC if I'd started dropping my 'H's now would I? Oh, and while we're at it, there's no 'H' in the pronunciation of 'H'. It's 'aitch' not 'haitch'.

Right, let's get out of here before I fall over, there's soap-boxes springing up everywhere.

MOORE THAN I COULD BEAR

Relegation costs a fortune. The TV money, in what was then called Nationwide League Division One, is rubbish compared to the Premier League. West Ham have always had high average attendances, but it's harder to sell hospitality packages in the lower division. The corporate boxes in the Bobby Moore Stand were closed down. Lots of the full-time staff were laid off. People who I'd worked with for five years lost their jobs. They hadn't performed any worse in the last year, but they were out of work now. The players who had underperformed spectacularly kept their jobs, unless they were out of contract.

All non-playing staff had to take a 10 per cent pay cut. The club obviously had to make savings, to cope with the cost of relegation, but the people who were hit were the low earners. The players didn't take pay cuts; there were no relegation clauses in their contracts, thanks to good agents and fear of the 'ginks' effect. (Put a relegation clause in your contract and it's more likely to happen.)

Four games into the season Glenn Roeder was sacked. It's hard not to feel sorry for Glenn. On the day we were relegated at Birmingham, he was watching on television in hospital, waiting to have a brain tumour removed. I remember how stressed I was that day, I can only imagine how he felt.

The call went out for brave Sir Trevor again. He hadn't actually been knighted at that point, but he was beginning to look comfortable in the caretaker's coat. There were calls for him to be given the job full time. He'd nearly managed to keep us up, and he had the air of a manager that could inspire and be loved by the fans at the same time.

But Trevor distanced himself from the permanent role. Who can blame him? When you've achieved a near godlike status, why jeopardise it. The talk was of Alan Pardew, the Reading manager, taking over. After a while Pardew left Reading and then spent a long time on gardening leave. When I finally met him he didn't seem like a man who would enjoy something as sedate as gardening.

In the meantime brave Sir Trevor rallied his knights and we started getting some results. Thirteen games into the season we were unbeaten at home and lying fifth in the table.

The man who became universally known as 'Pards' was unveiled before kick-off at the Burnley match. I said something like 'We've waited a long time to get our man, please give a West Ham welcome to Alan Pardew.'

Pards was clearly taken aback by the warmth of the reception. He needn't have been. Every West Ham manager is greeted as a new member of the family. All families have arguments, and they often leave with their tails between their legs, but every new boss starts with a welcome.

It must have difficult for Pards to take over from Trevor. He'd done great things at Reading, and was tipped as a manager to watch, but he was succeeding a legend. Trevor had played his entire career for West Ham, apart from two games for Cork City right at the end. He'd won an FA Cup Final with a rare headed goal. He'd represented his country forty-seven times.

In two spells as caretaker manager, he'd lost only one game out of fourteen, wining nine of them. Everyone loves Trevor. He has such a charming manner. He inspires confidence in all around him. When he played the game he had such an elegance about him, his team-mates nicknamed him 'Hadleigh', after the squire in the TV show, not the town in Suffolk.

Pards was big on creating an atmosphere. He spoke a lot about building a 'positive stadium'. A lot of this fell on my shoulders. For this reason Alan Pardew's time at West Ham has a special place in my heart. He made the announcer's role a lot more important. However, he also criticised me more than any other manager before or since, and often in public. I'm in two minds about where he rates in my all-time West Ham managers' list. He was inspiring and committed, but he was also arrogant and cruel.

MOVING TO THE DUGOUT

Alan Pardew was manager number three for me, and although he was a bit of a control freak, he had some good ideas. I just wish he trusted me to know what I was doing. I didn't tell him how his team should play, well not to his face anyway.

Pards 'positive stadium at all costs' policy was the opposite of Harry Redknapp and his policy of not getting the crowd going, in case it put pressure on the players. It was a lot more proactive than Glenn Roeder and his 'carry on as before' approach.

Pards told me he wanted me to have a cup of tea with him in his office before every game. We'd have a chat about how to get the fans buzzing. It all sounded very exciting as I do like a nice cup of tea. The other innovation was he wanted me to sit at pitch level, not up in the announcer's box. He was amazed that I was a two and a half minutes' walk away, up on the third level. Pards wanted me close to the dugout, so I could be straight onto the pitch at half-time, to keep the atmosphere going.

I liked the idea of this; until I saw the seat I'd been allocated. It was in the back row of the lower tier of the West Stand, right amongst the fans. This wasn't such a good idea and only lasted one game. I had a walkie-talkie and a microphone, plus a clipboard with the team sheet. I was easily noticeable as the announcer, so of course everyone would talk to me. It made keeping an eye on the game virtually impossible as people kept asking for details of substitutes, scores at other games, last-minute birthday requests. It hadn't been thought through at all. Every time I had to make an announcement, people around me would shout out. You've no idea what a magnet a live microphone can be to people with loud voices.

While I like to think most of my announcements are well thought out, the amateur announcers around me didn't seem to have put much thought into them at all. Think of the group of people you've been to watch football with. Now think of the one who is the most likely to shout out inappropriate things. Well imagine that each group has sent its loudest member forward for a special contest of 'loud members'. The contest is to be staged in the last few rows at the centre of the Lower West Stand. That's how that day felt to me. I lived in constant fear of the microphone being grabbed. It was all good-natured banter, and some of it was very funny, but it wasn't the sort of material you'd want broadcasting over the public address system.

After the game I asked the stadium manager for a seat in the dugout. If I'd been dressed as Oliver Twist asking Mr Bumble for more gruel, he couldn't have pulled a sterner face. He let it be known that this would not be happening.

Now early on in my career, I would have just accepted this, but I was now in my sixth season at the club and I felt I had something to add. The benefits of being at pitch level would be enormous. It would be so much easier to see the substitutions and find out how many added minutes there would be. So I held firm.

One thing I've found at West Ham is that everybody is good at their own job and they see things from the viewpoint of that job. Everybody has different ideas about what makes a successful day.

The groundsman wants his grass to look pitch perfect before the game. So if we've arranged for dancers or musicians pre-match, that doesn't go down well. From my point of view as stadium announcer, I don't care what the pitch looks like; I'm more concerned that the sprinklers don't go off while the Help For Heroes representatives are still on the pitch. We have different successful outcomes. His is a lush, fast playing surface; mine is that our guests don't get damp.

There's always a compromise to be had. One time Dougie the groundsman asked me to walk out onto the pitch only on the light-green strips of grass, and walk back only on the dark strips. Initially it seemed like the most pointless, pedantic nonsense I'd ever heard. However, when he explained the reason, it made sense. The grass is, of course, the same colour all over the pitch. It just looks light and dark depending on which way it's been mown and rolled. Grass lying flat towards you looks dark, while grass lying facing away from you looks light. By walking onto the pitch on the light ones I would leave no footprints. Walking on the dark ones scuffed them the other way and left light footprints.

To this day, I only ever walk out onto the pitch on the light grass and back on the dark. I also don't walk on the white lines. The dancers and anyone who comes onto the pitch are asked not to walk on the lines either. They sometimes forget, which makes it a bad day for Dougie.

When I'd started the job I was in my mid-thirties and still quite volatile. I'd despair at what I perceived as some of the daft decisions made by people around me. Now I'd turned forty and I had a much more mature approach to life. I'd started doing after-dinner speaking and corporate hosting, which meant I dealt a lot with business people. I'd only worked in the 'meeja' world before that. While still a 'luvvy' myself, I began to see how the business world operated.

I decided to approach the stadium manager from his own point of view. His successful outcome would be a safe stadium, so I pointed out that having a live microphone amongst supporters was not helpful in maintaining crowd safety. It would affect my ability to put out calm, clear messages in an emergency. It might even provoke a disturbance if someone tried to grab the microphone.

It was a cunning plan and I argued it well. It still didn't look as though I was going to get my way though. So, I pulled out my trump card. The manager wanted me down at pitch level. The next game when I arrived I was told there was a seat in the dugout with my name on it. I've sat there ever since.

The going for a cup of tea in Alan's office before the game wasn't such a success. I went twice, but only sat down once. The first time he had somebody with him, so he asked me to come back in ten minutes. I did, but he'd gone.

He saw me later in the tunnel. 'What's your patter for today?' he asked, clearly mistaking me for a shopping channel presenter trying to shift some dodgy vegetable chopping invention. I told him the various messages I was planning to make. He nodded his head sagely, clearly rubber stamping them. For a fan like me it was great to be working closely with the manager of West Ham, but announcing details of tickets on sale for upcoming games didn't really need his approval.

Pards went into the dressing room still nodding. Clearly our meeting was over. It hadn't taken long, it achieved nothing and I didn't get a brew. Still, the next week I knocked on the door of his office again. He looked a bit surprised to see me, but invited me in. We sat down, me on a chair and him on the edge of his desk. It meant I had to look up at him, which was a bit odd. He had a mug of tea in his hand, but I wasn't offered one. I felt a bit like a kid who'd been called to the headmaster's office, except I hadn't done anything wrong. Then he asked me what he could do for me. I reminded him that he'd asked me to come and see him in his office before every game.

'That's right,' he said nodding thoughtfully, his lips pursed. He reminded me a bit of a *Thunderbirds* puppet, maybe Scott or Virgil, but definitely not Brains. 'I want you to get the crowd rocking today. I want them 100 per cent behind the team. What I want you to do is to play 'I'm Forever Blowing Bubbles' just as the team are running out!'

So that was his brilliant plan. He wanted me to play 'Bubbles' as the team ran out. What an incredible idea. If only we'd thought of it ourselves! Thank goodness a former glazier had arrived at the Academy of Football to give us the benefit of his knowledge of East London and its traditions.

I sat in my seat looking up at him, wondering how to break to him the news that we'd been running out to this particular tune for as long as I could remember. His hair was virtually white, apart from a little bit of greying black at the front. He has an intense way of looking at you that suggests that you will agree with him. He was completely still, a bit like the *Thunderbirds* pictures on the wall at Tracy Island. When the brothers contacted base, the eyes on their picture would flash on and off. Actually thinking about it, there was an Alan in *Thunderbirds* and he had white hair. He was the astronaut, or was it space cadet?

The real Alan's eyes showed no signs of flashing, so I had to think quickly. I didn't want to make our new manager feel uncomfortable, so I replied that it was a great idea. I would ensure that we played 'Bubbles' every week as the team ran out. He nodded his approval, slid off the desk and opened the door. It appeared that this meeting was over, either he was leaving the room or I was. It turned out it was me. I never did get a cup of tea from Alan, so I popped into the press lounge for a brew. I wrote on my clipboard 'Bubbles' in big letters, just in case I forgot.

The next two matches I knocked on Alan's door and he wasn't there either time. After that I stopped going. Any more memos from the Department of the Bleeding Obvious would have to be delivered to me at impromptu meetings in the tunnel. There weren't any more memos, just the same one, over and over again. Every time Alan saw me pre-match, he'd say, 'Get them going today, remember Bubbles really loud before kick-off.'

It was like he had a pre-match checklist. 1. Have a mug of tea on my own in my office. 2. Find a place for Hayden Mullins in the team, any position will do. 3. Tell Jeremy to play 'Bubbles' before kick-off. 4. Check in with Tracy Island that there's no mission today. 5. Take seat in dugout briefly, before pacing about shouting. 6. Stand up at the press conference, so the reporters look smaller.

It took a while for Alan to make his mark at West Ham. He'd been a journeyman footballer, who'd started late in life after working as a glazier. He famously fitted the glass in the windows on the Nat West Tower in the City, but his career as a player never reached such heights. He'd never managed in the top flight, yet now he was trying to inspire players who had played at the top level. David James was the England goalie. Rob Lee and Michael Carrick had also represented England. There were international captains like Christian Dailly and Steve Lomas. Under-21 star Little Jermain may have handed in his transfer request on the day after we were relegated, but he was still playing for us, even though he kept getting sent off.

Pards not only bent my ear about having a positive atmosphere in the stadium, he also made the training ground a positive place to go to work. He had pictures of Bobby Moore taken down at Chadwell Heath, because he felt the club lived in the past a bit. They were replaced with motivational messages. Nothing wrong with that, psychology is a big part of the modern game. But then he sanctioned a range of West Ham T-shirts in the club shop which read 'Moore than just a football team'. Now in my book, if you are going to start wrapping yourself in the name of Bobby Moore, you'd better be very special indeed. Maybe 'I've bitten off Moore than I can chew', would have been more appropriate.

Defoe and James were sold as the board balanced the books. The football we were playing had little to do with the traditions of Bobby Moore, maybe the shirts were about Dudley Moore? But, dire as it was to watch, Pards did start to grind out some results. We crept up the table and eventually finished fourth, earning a play-off semifinal against Ipswich.

I was summoned to a meeting at the training ground to discuss the pre-match build-up. Ipswich had won the first leg by a goal to nil. The atmosphere at Portman Road had been electric. Pards wanted to make sure we dug deep and gave the Tractor Boys a rough ride. A positive stadium was called for, he told me. Brilliant plan, Alan, I never would have thought of that.

Surprise, surprise, he wanted me to play 'Bubbles' before the game. Even more surprising I was offered a cup of tea, but he didn't make it. Still, I nearly fell off my chair in excitement. Other plans included the playing of the 'Post Horn Gallop' as the teams emerged from the tunnel. This is a fox hunting fanfare played on a long straight instrument called a post horn. West Ham used to run out to it in the 1950s and Pards had been promised by his coach Roger Cross that it would generate a terrific atmosphere.

I couldn't quite see the relevance of a fox hunting tune in the East End, but it's hard to argue against tradition. My mission was to create a wall of sound. Alan wanted it loud.

On the walls at Chadwell Heath were lots of these motivational messages that he loved so much. This time there were new posters about the Ipswich game. They were all about the number of 'golden crosses' that Pards wanted to see flying in on the night. We were clearly going for an attacking policy, with crosses in the box the key to winning the contest.

Pards told me on no account was I to mention to anyone the 'night of the golden crosses' plan. Even though I was a lifelong West Ham fan, who'd been charged with creating a game-winning atmosphere, he still felt it necessary to tell me not to give the tactics away. On the day of the game Pards contacted me via press officer Peter Stewart, asking for a certain song to be played that night. I told you he was hands on! The tune was 'Luck Be A Lady' by Frank Sinatra. So, with all his talk of a positive stadium and how it was all about belief, he had panicked at the last minute and decided to throw himself at the feet of Lady Luck. It meant I had to make a detour into the West End to try and find it. You wouldn't believe how many Frank Sinatra compilation albums don't have 'Luck Be A Lady' on them. I rushed from shop to shop on Oxford Street and then Piccadilly Circus, looking for this one song. I'm not a great shopper at the best of times, but this was like last-minute panic shopping on Christmas Eve. It wasn't ideal preparation for a big game. It's not like I have a pre-match warm-up to go through, but I do like to have a few minutes to sit and think and get into the zone. I'd rather not rush out of the tunnel, out of breath, trying to read out the team sheets. Eventually I found Frank singing a live version with the Rat Pack that would have to do, and set off for the stadium just in time for the pre-match meeting.

That night under floodlights at West Ham was the best atmosphere I've ever experienced at the ground in my time as announcer, and probably as a fan too. The pre-match build-up was awesome. I'll give Pards his due, his ideas all paid off. He gave instructions for the stewards to switch off all the plasma TVs in the concourses in the run-up to kick-off.

Some fans weren't happy about that, but it worked beautifully. It forced everyone into their seats earlier to see what all the noise was about. It was like a pressure cooker in the ground, with the noise levels going up and up. I've never known anything like it. We played Frank's request for luck to be a lady tonight, and she was.

We had a man with a hunting horn, who ran out ahead of the teams playing the 'Post Horn Gallop'. It wasn't really a tune, he just blew and blew. Personally it didn't stir anything in me, but I think the older fans liked it. We played 'Bubbles', faded it on 'fortune's always hiding' and I've never heard the rest of the words sung with such emotion.

By kick-off I thought the ground was going to burst. It was a memorable night and we won 2–0 with goals from Matthew Etherington and Christian Dailly. The second goal was from a corner, the ball hit Dailly in the knackers, but he overcame the pain and managed to score. Our captain had balls of steel and our manager in his white slogan T-shirt jumped into the crowd.

Christian always gave 100 per cent and was one of my favourite players. He was a terrific skipper who fully deserved his own song. To the tune of 'Pretty Baby', the fans would sing, 'Oh Christian Dailly, you are the love of my life, Oh Christian Dailly, I'd let you shag my wife!' It's one of those songs that is still heard at West Ham, years after his departure, like those for Paolo Di Canio and Ludek Miklosko.

That night lives long in the memory; the final at Cardiff sadly does not. It was a disaster, I don't know what happened to all the positivity, but it evaporated in Cardiff. I've no idea why, it was the same team and the same fans; I can only think it was the announcer's fault. Not me, guvnor, I was sitting with the fans, having a day off from the microphone at a neutral venue.

People still remember Pards with fondness, because he took us to the Millennium Stadium three years in a row, with two play-off finals and then an FA Cup Final. That's fair enough, but I'd argue that with the squad we had we should have won automatic promotion, and we only needed to go back the following year because we messed up the first time.

We played Iain Dowie's Crystal Palace in the 2004 final. Jeanette by now had moved into my Docklands flat and travelled with me on the specially chartered train to Cardiff. She was enjoying watching football now, although I don't think she fully understood the rules. Netta had grown up watching the Springboks and the Blue Bulls but was enjoying watching what they call soccer. On the train she sent her mum a text to say she was going to see West Ham in the football final. A text came back in Afrikaans saying 'enjoy the rugby'.

Jeanette was most impressed with the cooked breakfast served on our table as it was bedecked with claret and blue flowers. The club paid for a train ticket and a match ticket for staff members and we could buy another one for each of our partners. It was a lovely way of saying thank you. I really felt part of the team.

Pards had a new slogan T-shirt for the final, something about us being the original academy. In his mind he was Stephen Fry, but in reality he came across as Barry Fry. Having ridden the Bobby Moore wave, he'd now gone back even further in time. But, Malcolm Allison never plotted tactics like these with the salt and pepper pots at Cassettari's Café. We didn't pass mustard; in fact we hardly passed the ball. It was a shocking performance and Crystal Palace were worthy winners by a goal to nil.

Hayden Mullins played out of position at left back. Pards loved Hayden and though he was a good determined midfielder, he was no full back. The other thing I've never understood about that game was Pardew's decision to take off his three strikers: Marlon Harewood, Bobby Zamora and David Connolly. We were a goal down, needing to score to get back into the final and he took off the three men most likely to score.

We came home from Cardiff deflated. The food on the train was great though, and by the time we rolled back into London,we were all looking forward to the next season. Jeanette sent Ma a text saying 'we lost the soccer!' Maybe next time we'd win automatic promotion. We certainly had a squad that should have finished higher than fourth. Surely we could do better than that?

We couldn't.

SEASON IN A NUTSHELL 2003/04

Not wanting to kick a man when he was down, West Ham didn't sack Glenn Roeder. After his illness he returned to work and was sacked four games into the season, making it much harder for his replacement, with no pre-season. Even worse, it took ages for Alan Pardew to be released by Reading, so by the time he'd finished his gardening leave we were way behind the rest in the race for promotion.

Highlight – We travelled to the Millennium Stadium to take on Crystal Palace in the play-off final.

Lowlight – We travelled to the Millennium Stadium to take on Crystal Palace in the play-off final and lost in a terrible performance.

Another lowlight – The players opting to change in their hotel rooms on a trip to Rotherham, rather than in the small dressing room. It showed a lack of respect to our Yorkshire hosts. We needed to accept we weren't in the Premier League any more. After that Billy Big Boots attitude, we lost 1–0.

Golden moment – The atmosphere in the play-off semi-final at home to Ipswich. We rocked the stadium that night. It makes me shiver just thinking about it.

Hero – Christian Dailly a true captain who inspired his team. During a moment of intense personal pain, he still had the presence of mind to score the goal that booked a place in the play-off final.

Villain – Glenn Roeder. I felt sorry for him because of his illness, but most problems that currently affect West Ham can be traced back to his time in charge. He was presented with a golden generation of young talent and he took us down.

Team news – Relegation meant we lost our best players. Glen Johnson and Joe Cole went to Chelsea bankrolled by their new billionaire owner Roman Abramovich. Trevor

Sinclair took his incredible skills to Manchester City. Superman John Moncur was released and the mercurial genius Paolo Di Canio went to Charlton. In return David Connolly arrived, who wasn't a great success. Matthew Etherington joined from White Hart Lane, claiming West Ham were a bigger club than Spurs. Even I didn't believe that, but I enjoyed hearing it.

It shouldn't happen to an announcer – I moved to a new announcing position in the dugout. It meant I could liaise with the fourth official and tunnel stewards about added time and substitutions. It was much better from a work point of view, and much more exciting as a fan.

Missed games – None.

Did we win at Anfield? – No, but for once we didn't lose. We didn't play them as we were in a lower division.

My bald patch – The size of the bottom of a grande decaff skinny vanilla latte at Starbucks. Actually the mug can have anything in it as long as it's grande, but that's what I'd have.

Three-Legged Stool Review

Job leg – I did a lot of TV news reporting, mainly the 'And Finally' end of the news bulletin. After years of being freelance, I took up a six-month contract to cover a reporter on maternity leave. It was good to be back in the BBC family and they sent me on a course to learn how to use a camera and edit. I love learning new stuff and set off enthusiastically to cover a story in La Manga in Spain. When I looked at them later in an edit suite, my pictures were rubbish.

Relationship leg – I went to South Africa for the first time to meet Jeanette's family. They are lovely people and all called me Jim instead of Jem. I asked if they knew my name was really Jem and they said 'yis'.

West Ham leg – Despite having one of the strongest squads in the division, we failed to win promotion at the first attempt.

CHILD'S PLAY

Pregnant Pause

West Ham fans are remarkable. They're passionate and vocal. They sing whether they're winning, losing or drawing. They sing on the way to games and on the way home from games. Some of them even sing in the shower, I know I do. I mainly sing 'Delilah', which might be a Stoke City song, but I've been singing it since the good old days when it was just a jolly number about a chap who stabs his girlfriend to death.

West Ham fans follow their team through thin and thin with never a word of complaint. Well maybe a few words, but usually short words beginning with letters from the early part of the alphabet.

However, there is one feature of West Ham fans that sets them apart. They have a unique ability that no other group of sporting fans in the world can match. They are nearly always born on a Saturday afternoon. It's an amazing thing, what are the chances of that I wonder? Is it something in the water?

In recent years there has been a slight shift in the figures. The data is still grouped predominantly around Saturday afternoons, but there is a trend towards baby Hammers also being released from captivity on Sunday afternoons and Monday evenings. How can we explain this statistical anomaly?

In my first season as announcer I noticed at most games there would be a message for an expectant father to ring home, as his wife had just gone into labour. The content of the message would never vary. There would never be any mention of a hospital, even though going straight there could save a vital few minutes. It was always 'wife' and never 'partner', and it was always to ring home, never somewhere more suitable for going into labour. It was as if they were all written by the same person.

I suspect it had been going on for years. A chap would ring the club claiming another chap's wife had gone into labour. A well-meaning receptionist would take the message and pass it on to the announcer who would read it out. This would explain the cheers I would occasionally hear that bore little relation to the game and were usually preceded by a muffled announcement from the speaker high up in the old West Stand.

Now I was the announcer and it was down to me to read the messages out, but it was obvious to me that they were hoaxes. Especially as there would be three times as many phantom pregnancies when the match was being screened live on television. This explained why the trend shifted to Sundays and Mondays too.

I resolved not to announce any of them, which didn't go down well. You would have thought I'd decided to kill the babies myself. There was outrage from the receptionists; I might as well have changed my name to King Herod. Supposing his wife really has gone into labour, they would say. Can you live with yourself if you've caused a man to miss the birth of his child?

Now and again I would bow to the pressure and read one of the messages out. It was harmless. I didn't believe there was a baby, but at least it generated a cheer. Some games, when the team weren't playing well, it was the only cheer of the afternoon. The less I announced them, the fewer calls we received. After a few years in the job I stopped doing them completely. As mobile phones became more prevalent, I had the perfect excuse. What man would go to a game without his phone if his wife was expecting?

Birthdays

One of my jobs that I greatly enjoy is reading out the birthday messages at half-time. There can be no greater thrill in a young supporter's life than to hear their name read out over the PA. Over the seasons I've started to recognise the same names coming round again and again. I don't think the Saunders family of Loughton have ever had a birthday without it being announced at West Ham. I suppose there might be a member of the Saunders clan who has a birthday in the summer months who must feel very left out.

There's no need. If you have a family member unlucky enough to have been born during the months when the beautiful game is on holiday, there is a back-up plan. Just write in asking for a welcome to the match. It doesn't have to be your birthday. It's highly unlikely the Birthday Police are going to come round your house demanding to see your birth certificate.

The most popular birthdays I read out are between the ages of seven and twelve. After twelve it tails off a bit. Teenagers are too busy sulking or being cool to be bovvered about birthday requests. Six-year-olds are the most likely to be welcomed to their first ever game. I did once welcome a woman in her sixties who'd been a supporter all her life, but this was her first ever game. As she was from East London, I did think it a bit feeble that she couldn't have made it a bit earlier, but we all worship in our own way. Maybe she couldn't afford the time or the ticket, maybe she didn't like crowds, or maybe she was from East London in South Africa. Who knows and frankly who cares?

There seems to be an unwritten convention with adults that only the big birthdays are requested. After eighteen and twenty-one, you don't get a mention until you are thirty. After that it's forty, fifty, sixty, seventy and eighty. I did a ninety once, but I've never had a century. There have also been a few 85- and 95-year-olds as well. When you get to that age, some families think it's best to get the halfway birthdays in as well, just in case you don't make it to the next big one.

I love reading out the birthday greetings for really old people, proper old Irons, who are a bit rusty, but still haven't seized up. If someone is eighty-five, they must have gone through so many hard times. I'm not talking about wartime, rationing and rickets but the traumatic times following the Irons. How many relegations and cup defeats to small teams must those poor old-timers remember? Their faces are lined with the worry.

Compare and contrast them with an 85-year-old just across London. Arsenal have only been relegated once, back in 1913. Even then they were miraculously back in the top flight in 1919 despite not winning promotion. They benefited from Division One being enlarged, although why they were chosen ahead of the teams who finished above them in Division Two is a bit shady. Tottenham, who finished bottom and were relegated, also had a case for staying put – no wonder Tottenham and Arsenal fans don't get on.

I'd like to compare the lines on the face of an old Iron and an old Gooner and see if we can trace the generations of worry.

The really sad thing about dedications for senior West Ham fans is that they nearly always seem to sit in the East Stand. They have the worst view of the pitch, a legacy of building the new West Stand behind the old West Stand and sliding the pitch over. Plans to redevelop the East Stand were shelved when we were relegated, so the pitch remains a cab ride away for the old boys in the East, who can't have the best of eyesight. Why they don't relocate I don't know, but I suppose when you've grown up with the people around you, it would be a wrench.

I love reading out the half-time messages, especially for kids at their first ever game. They are so excited to hear their name read out, with no idea of the years of heartache and misery ahead.

The youngsters probably won't hear their message because they'll be in the queue for a hot dog. I know the older guys might miss their greeting as they're in the loo, especially if it's a cold day. And I know the really old ones probably can't hear their message anyway, even though they're the most likely to ask for the speakers to be turned down, because of all the loud music. But it's the thought that counts and that's the West Ham way.

A Missing Child

I'm not a fan of announcements during the game. Some stadiums you hear all sorts of weird messages over the PA system. To be honest, I think a lot of it is people wanting to hear their names read out during matches. Half-time is not enough for these people; they want to make sure everyone hears their name being read out. They don't want to risk people being in the queue for a pie or in the loo. In support of this theory, I've noticed we have a lot more lost children during live television games. Is there something in the satellite signal that makes children lose their bearings or have I been watching too many episodes of *The X Files*? (For younger readers this was bit like *X Factor*, but all the competitors were aliens. The first series was won by Catatonia with a song about Mulder and Scully.)

We were playing Everton once and I was given a message about a lost child. I was told this young lad had been separated from his parents, who were very worried. I

didn't want to announce it, but I was told I had to by the
stadium manager. I queried it again, because I suspected
it was a ruse for a child's name to be read out over the PA,
so he and his friends could all hear it.

I was told I definitely had to do the announcement. The
Everton supporter who'd spoken to a steward had apparently seemed genuine and there was real concern about
this lost little boy. To be honest if there's a chance that a
child is missing, it's a no-brainer. I'll always read it out. I
wouldn't want it on my conscience if anything happened
to a young fan. So I read it out. 'We have a lost little boy
who has been separated from his family. Would Michael
Shields contact the nearest steward?'

There was a cheer from the Everton fans. I know scousers like a laugh, but it seemed strange to cheer a lost child
announcement. I didn't announce it again, as I sensed
something was wrong. The stadium manager insisted
I repeat it, but this time I held my ground. It didn't feel
right. He wasn't happy about it, but my mind wasn't going
to be changed. There was something familiar about that
kid's name, but I couldn't think what it was.

I wish I'd gone with my original instinct because a
member of the Everton media team came along and tapped
me on the shoulder. He pointed out that Michael Shields
was a Liverpool fan who had been detained in Bulgaria
charged with the attempted murder of a barman after a
European match. He told me that Everton fans had asked
for the message to be read out at all their away games in
the season so far. Each time a 'concerned' fan would ask a
steward who'd contact the PA announcer.

I asked the Everton media officer if he'd considered
making clubs across the country aware of this, as it was
in very bad taste. He said he hadn't thought of that, but
maybe they should. He grinned through his beard, clearly
amused at my 'mistake'. Except it wasn't a mistake was it?

I'd acted in the best of faith under pressure from an official of my team concerned for a child. Terrace humour is always cruel. There's not much clubs can do about it, but the messages being read out is something Everton could easily have stopped.

I didn't like the way he smiled, so I rolled my eyeballs upwards and walked away from him. The Liverpool fan being held in a Bulgarian prison deserved better than having his plight ridiculed at grounds up and down the country. The following season against Everton the 'Michael Shields' missing boy announcement was again requested and again Everton hadn't contacted West Ham to warn us about it. I was disappointed at that, but of course I remembered and this time I didn't read it out.

Michael Shields continued to protest his innocence to the attempted murder charge and served four years in prison. After a high-profile campaign he was granted a royal pardon in 2009.

Kids for a Quid

It's so important that children are brought to the Boleyn Ground at an early age. They needed to be blooded before they are drawn over to the dark side. I'm talking about Manchester United and Chelsea, by the way, not Satan or Lord Voldemort. Worshipping the Red Devils is bad enough.

Often a youngster's first trip to West Ham is at a Kids for a Quid game. This is a great idea and I always like to welcome those people who are at their very first West Ham United game. It's a special moment.

However a Kids for a Quid night presents a few extra challenges for the announcer to keep the atmosphere alive. While most youngsters look forward to the game for weeks and really go for it, there's a number who are only bothered about autographs and hot dogs. They have the attention span of gnats and they'd rather be at home playing on their PlayStation. Having grown up with central heating, they don't like the cold. Their voices are too high to sing properly and they don't know the songs anyway.

Aside from the bored, hungry gamers, there are the kids that don't cheer until we are winning. They don't appreciate how important cheering is on the road to winning. Cheers can lead to winning, but tiny humans aren't proactive. They're so used to consuming and watching things, they've forgotten how to take part. So if you're reading this and have a younger sibling or child, please remind them that you don't go to a game to be a spectator. While watching West Ham can loosely be described as entertainment, you don't go to the Boleyn to enjoy yourself; you go to worship at the cathedral of football where generations of East Londoners have worshipped before you. Once you've done a bit of worshipping, by all means have a hotdog. We are a broad church and don't mind a bit of mustard in the aisles.

I've been to pantomimes in theatres over the Christmas holidays and hardly been able to hear myself think. Children are whipped into a frenzy cheering for the hero and booing the villain. It's the same at wrestling, but at a proper sport like football, they'll happily sit and watch and occasionally pester for food, because no one is directing them. Now you might think that is my job, and I certainly do everything I can to make a young fan's trip enjoyable, but I can't be shouting out over the PA once the game has started. Where would we be then? America, that's where, and nobody wants that.

THE GOSPEL OF JUDAS

Since the departure of Harry Redknapp I've resumed the noble tradition of welcoming back old players. To read the papers you'd think West Ham fans are often hostile to former players, but nothing could be further from the truth. Most old boys are greeted with warm applause, however there are a few who are not accorded such respect. This is because they have either left under a cloud or have bad-mouthed us in the media. There are a number of ways to upset us, the most serious of which will lead to the person qualifying for the Judas Award. There's no trophy actually presented, but the winner is entitled to a chant of 'Judas' every time he touches the ball. This will last until we get fed up or he starts crying.

There are a number of ways to be nominated for a Judas Award. Putting in a transfer request the day after relegation would be the way a small person might do it. Gesturing to our fans out of the blue during a game would be a weightier example. Wearing another team's colours in a newspaper article, while on our books, would be the most serious offence. This was the crime committed by Paul Ince, the original Judas.

I say the original, of course there was one before him, but that was two thousand years ago, when Thames Ironworks were still making coracles. In the bible, Judas Iscariot is the chap who betrayed Jesus to the Romans. He was rewarded with thirty pieces of silver for his trouble, which would be a lot in today's money. Jesus was crucified and Judas, filled with remorse, hanged himself.

What Paul Ince did wasn't quite as bad as that, but it was still pretty bad. In football terms it was about the worst thing a player can do. He was photographed in a Manchester United shirt!

The only excuse for that kind of behaviour is being a Manchester United player. Paul Ince wasn't. He played for West Ham.

Ince was our best young player for ages and he broke our hearts. A West Ham fan as a kid, he'd come up through the youth team and was making a name for himself in the first team in the late 1980s.

When West Ham were relegated in 1989 we knew it would be hard to hold on to our talented midfielder. His strong tackling, accurate passing and an engine that kept going forever made him the target for Manchester United. The deal was nearly done when Paul went on holiday. He allowed himself to be photographed in a Manchester United shirt so he didn't have to come back from holiday for a photo when the deal went through.

When you think about it, Manchester United are the biggest club side in English football and probably the world. It doesn't get much bigger for a player than to sign for them. Much as it breaks my heart to say it, we'd have been sad to see him go, but we'd have understood. We're football fans, so we only care about one club, but for him football was his career. Who were we to stand in the way of him playing on a bigger stage?

I love the BBC but if Sky Sports come knocking, I'm out of here. That's how careers go. However, I'd like to think if Sky did call me up, I'd be bothered enough to return from holiday to have my picture taken with Jeff Stelling.

Paul Ince didn't want to have his break disturbed. He'd probably got a lot of reading to catch up on. He made a cunning plan, which could only fail if he was let down by the newspapers. So it was virtually foolproof.

The picture was taken by the *Daily Star* and tucked away in their archive with instructions not to use it until the deal was completed. Sadly for him, Ince failed his medical, so the transfer was held up. The *Daily Express* shared offices with the *Daily Star* and when they were looking for a picture to use for an Ince story they came across the one of him wearing the Man Utd shirt. The *Express* published it and all hell broke loose.

It was tough for Ince as it appeared that he was putting himself in the shop window. As West Ham fans we know that players will leave for bigger clubs and we accept that. But we hate it when they start making noises about moving on.

Rio Ferdinand always gets a great reception when he returns. So does Michael Carrick.

Paul Ince joined Manchester United shortly afterwards, but not until he'd played again for West Ham. The fans have never forgiven him. Nor has my Dad. Despite being a former treasurer of the local church, when he mentions Judas there's no doubt who he's talking about.

Of course there are two sides to every story. Ince will argue that he was badly advised by his agent. As a young kid looking forward to his holiday he just did what he was told.

As I'm sure you'll remember from Sunday School, Judas Iscariot gets a bad press. But that's only because we don't get to hear his side of the story. Like Paul Ince, I'm sure he wasn't a bad person really.

The approved version of the bible doesn't contain the Book of Judas, but it does exist as one of the so-called Gnostic gospels. In the book Judas gets a much better write up, as you'd expect from a book with his name on the cover. It claims he was the one disciple who fully understood his master's teachings. The other eleven are portrayed as knuckleheads who took things far too literally and went about sacrificing animals all the time. Judas must have felt like a Barcelona player on loan at Stoke.

The book goes on to claim Judas was given orders by Christ himself to betray him. He was in on the whole plan. He had to do the 'kissing in the garden' business to set in motion the sequence that would lead to the crucifixion and ultimately resurrection.

The Book of Judas doesn't end well though. Unlike the other accounts he doesn't hang himself, but is stoned to death by the other eleven disciples, who were understandably not best pleased with him. As they were knuckleheads, they hadn't been in on the plan, as they'd probably have given the game away.

I don't know which account is true, because I wasn't there. We have to rely on accounts from the time. History is written by the victors or those left behind. The Book of Judas isn't believed by the church, so he's been reviled for the last two thousand years, when in fact he might have been a good bloke. If Jesus ever does come back he might be really annoyed about the way his mate was treated.

Paul Ince must be a bit fed up with the way he's treated by West Ham fans, but he could always say sorry. How hard would that be? He grew up as a West Ham fan and if he'd just apologised he could have defused the situation. But he never did.

When Harry was manager he talked about bringing Paul Ince back as a player. Incey was towards the end of a sparkling career that had seen him enjoy success with Manchester United and Liverpool. Now old and knackered, he was looking for somewhere to see out his days. Harry mentioned to the papers that he thought Paul could do a job for us. It provoked outrage from West Ham fans.

I asked Harry who he would get to introduce Ince onto the pitch. I told him I couldn't bring myself to do it. Harry thought I was joking and just laughed. But I wasn't joking.

Not a very Christian attitude, you might think, from someone who knows so much about the bible, but I mainly read
it for the stories.

I like to think at West Ham we have a brilliant reputation for welcoming back old players. Those we loved, who
put their heart and soul into the club, are warmly greeted
no matter what shirt they now wear. As long as they didn't
disrespect West Ham as they left.

We don't mind them walking out of the door as long as
they do it in the proper manner.

Jermain Defoe was another great young footballer who
came up through our youth team. The day after we were
relegated he put in a transfer request. He says it was his
agent, which has a familiar ring to it. However, players
are accountable for their own actions and the West Ham
faithful never let him forget the day he kicked us when we
were down.

Defoe is greeted with chants of Judas whenever he
returns. Along with some other songs that I can't repeat
there's also the very humorous 'You're just a small Paul
Ince' chant.

Frank Lampard has a similar song which goes, 'You're
just a fat Paul Ince.'

Ince has become the benchmark on the Judas scale.
I wondered what song the fans would sing about him
when we drew Milton Keynes in the cup. MK Dons are
a franchise which the football authorities to their shame
allowed, betraying the loyal football fans of Wimbledon. It
was perhaps fitting that 'Judas' should be their manager.

As he walked out sporting a little moustache and looking a little pudgier than I remembered, I held my breath
and waited. After the horrible Judas chant we needed
something witty.

A Paul Ince-based song like the ones for Fat Frank
and Little Jermain wouldn't work, because this was

Paul Ince. Besides 'You're just Paul Ince', wouldn't have scanned. Instead the crowd came up with: 'You're just a fat Eddie Murphy, Fat Eddie Murrrr Feeee, you're just a fat Eddie Murphy.'

On the Judas Scale Paul Ince will always be ten. If he ever says sorry, he could slide down that scale to as low as a seven. All he has to do is apologise for being shirty. But he can't be bothered. He's probably too busy having holidays.

RAG AND BONE MEN

In November 2004 I received a call from the announcer at Cardiff City. Ali has a reputation as one of the 'livelier' announcers in the football world. He has cult status with Bluebirds fans, while other supporters would spell it only slightly differently.

He's a decent bloke, though, who loves his team but he can be a bit of a nutter when it comes to the opposition. He gets away with it because Sam Hammam, the Cardiff chairman at the time, used to love that kind of banter.

'I'm just ringing to say I'm sorry about the other night,' he said. 'The papers have got it all out of proportion. I was only having a laugh.'

I'd no idea what he was on about. West Ham had played at Cardiff two nights before, losing 4–1. I hadn't gone to the game as I'd mislaid my passport.

It sounded as though Ali might have let his heart rule his head, and not for the first time.

I adopted the role of a senior announcer in the world of football, put my head on one side and asked him to tell me all about it. He couldn't tell I had my head on one side, as we were on the phone, but he told me the whole story.

'What it is, right,' he said. 'I likes to have a laugh, see. So when your lot ran out, I played the theme tune from *Steptoe and Son*.' I could hear the laughter in his Welsh accent.

'Why did you do that?' I enquired.

'Well, because of you being cockneys, see. Rag and bone men and that,' he explained.

I was none the wiser. It appeared that he thought that East London was populated largely with people who earn their living from reselling scrap. I pointed out that *Steptoe and Son* was set in Shepherd's Bush, which is in West London. I can't remember whether football was ever mentioned in the show, but surely Harold and his dad would have been QPR fans or Manchester United.

I told Ali that it didn't sound too bad and I was sure West Ham fans would see the funny side of it.

'But that's not all,' he said. 'I did this announcement about someone having left their shire horse and rag and bone cart on double yellow lines and could they move it.'

I didn't like the sound of that so much. I don't like stereo-typing; it's a lazy form of humour. It's also racist and a bit backward; just the sort of thing you'd expect from the Welsh. Did you see what I did there?

When an English team play a Welsh team, you expect a few choice songs. English fans would always make suggestions about the inappropriate use of sheep in the valleys. I'm not sure what the Welsh sing about us, but it will definitely be very tuneful.

But I wouldn't expect the announcer to adopt the same tone. I can't imagine me making any jokes about the Welsh visitors to our stadium. It's just not the done thing.

However, Ali likes that kind of banter. He told me that when they play Swansea, he always plays 'Gipsys, Tramps and Thieves' by Cher, as the Swans run onto the pitch. Apparently the Cardiff fans love it.

I wondered what would happen if Cardiff ever played a team managed by Gordon Strachan. Ali would be lucky to escape. Talking to him on the phone it's clear it was only banter, but it's a dangerous game to play. You only need a few hard nuts taking offence and it can all kick off.

Fortunately for Ali the seven hundred travelling fans didn't cause any trouble. If anything people I spoke to thought it was funny.

Later that season West Ham played Cardiff at the Boleyn Ground. During the first half our fans started singing 'Swing Low, Sweet Chariot', the anthem adopted by fans of the England rugby team. Our egg chasers had just won the World Cup, beating Australia with that fantastic Jonny Wilkinson drop goal at the end of the final. With rugby being the Welsh national sport, the whole of the West Ham crowd joined in. We were world champions in their sport.

At half-time, I decided to play a CD of 'Swing Low, Sweet Chariot'. It was brilliant, really atmospheric, and the fans all joined in with vigour. Well, not the Cardiff fans obviously.

I don't think I did too much wrong by playing a song that's associated with the national team. I didn't say anything, I just played a tune. I think it would be a shame if we couldn't play an England anthem in England, but there were implications for the police who were having a difficult time with the Cardiff fans. Afterwards one of the senior coppers collared me. 'Bloody 'ell, Jeremy,' he said. 'We were just about holding them, then you put on that bloody song and they went nuts.'

He looked like he'd had quite a day of it as there were a few marks on his uniform.

'Sorry about that,' I said, genuinely concerned that I'd caused him trouble.

'Yeah, don't do it again,' he said. 'Mind you, it was bloody funny. We were all laughing.'

We had a bit of a review of music after that. At one big game I was told I couldn't play 'Two Tribes' by Frankie Goes to Hollywood, because it contains the line 'When two tribes go to war, a point is all that you can score.' Another on the banned list was 'I Predict a Riot' by the Kaiser Chiefs, which was fair enough.

There's nothing better than a bit of banter between rival supporters, but when you are the man on the microphone you have to be very careful. I try and run a filter on everything I say, wondering how it could be wrongly interpreted. Will it offend anybody, will it cause crowd problems and can the press make any mischief by quoting it out of context? Could it be misheard or wrongly interpreted? If it passes all those filters I'll say it out loud, but if not it's edited out in the cutting room in my head. As announcers we only get a few seconds to make these judgements and that's why so many have been sacked over the years.

UPSETTING EVERYBODY

In January 2005 we lost 2–0 at home to a Sheffield United team in bright orange shirts which were far too loud to be worn in a built-up area. It was like losing to a team of stewards. If you're serious about promotion you can't be losing home games to your rivals at the top. I was disappointed and for the FA Cup tie with Norwich I wrote what was perceived by Pards as a negative column in the programme. It pretty much echoed what he'd said after the Sheffield United game, but I'd forgotten that I was chief cheerleader. Pards was allowed to moan, but my job was propaganda not free thinking. I was told my column was being rested for the next three games. The offence must have been more serious than I first thought, because I never returned to writing for the programme, which is a real shame.

Another time I was publicly criticised by the manager at a press conference. After a bad run of results we were winning a game when the stadium manager asked me to do an announcement about problems on the District Line. It meant people would have trouble getting home, so he felt it would be best to give them a chance to leave early. I queried this, saying that it would lead to a mass exodus which would kill the atmosphere, just when we needed a boost. However, he was adamant and I'm duty-bound to follow his instructions. Pards went nuts. He glared at me as he left the pitch, but didn't say anything. He saved that until he was in front of journalists in a packed press lounge. He ranted about how his team had just had a great result, but hardly anyone was left to applaud them off the pitch, because the announcer was more interested in giving out train times. I sat quietly at the back thinking that was a bit harsh. A few journalists asked me for comments but I just smiled and left. I'll always back the manager of my team. I think Pards did some great things at West Ham, but I found his style of belittling people in public rather cruel and unnecessary.

Do I need to mention it was not the West Ham way? No, I thought not.

The phrase being 'sent to Coventry' is used when no one will talk to you, because you've upset everyone. In April 2005, when Coventry were sent to us, I managed to upset a lot of people. I fell out with Coventry, West Ham and some of our fans.

With six games to go, we were seventh in the table, two points outside the play-off positions. We were playing Coventry that day, and I did my best to get the crowd going, but I made another big mistake according to Pards.

Championship leaders Sunderland were playing fifth-placed Reading in the day's early kick-off. Visitors Reading were the surprise winners and I announced the score before our game. It seemed perfectly reasonable to do so, as Reading, previously managed by Pards, were one of the teams we were chasing. My mistake, according to Alan, was to completely kill the atmosphere. By announcing bad news, I had destroyed all positivity within a ten-mile radius of Upton Park; never mind that most of the fans had watched the closing minutes of the Sunderland/Reading game on the plasma screens in the concourses before taking their seats. I had actually verbalised the bad news and that meant we would surely lose.

In fact we won 3–0, our third win in a week, but I was still in the doghouse. Pardew thought the fans' sole purpose in life was to cheer his team on, they weren't allowed to have any thoughts of their own. They weren't to be fed any information, just good news or no news. It was all a bit *1984* for my liking. I was waiting for Pards to invite me to room 101 and not serve me a cup of tea. I can't help thinking that having won 3–0 he might have created a more positive atmosphere himself by praising his team in his post-match interviews, rather than laying into the poor old announcer, who was just doing his job. Instead Pards slaughtered me in public, not for the first time, and then moaned about a fan protest after the game, which was aimed at the board not him. Why mention it? Come on, Alan, let's keep it positive!

The game itself was memorable for one of the most spectacular own goals you will ever see. There were fifteen minutes left and the game was goalless when Coventry defender Richard Shaw headed the ball like a bullet past his keeper. It was a stunning goal that would have been a contender for goal of the month, if it wasn't in his own net. It was such a good goal that I announced it with glee. 'Goal for West Ham scored by Richard Shawwwww.'

Many people still come up to me and say that is one of their funniest West Ham moments. Not only did they enjoy the comedy of the goal, but also the sheer exuberance of my announcement. Sadly the Coventry officials didn't see it that way and made a complaint. Apparently it's not the done thing to sound happy about an own goal. The correct protocol is to shuffle embarrassedly on your heels and whisper an almost apologetic announcement. It's the equivalent of winning a point in a tennis match by the ball hitting the top of the net and dropping just over. You are meant to put your hand up to your opponent, tip your head to one side and adopt a facial expression that suggests this is not the way you wanted to win.

Shouting Richard Shawwwww was not the English way, damnit. I was being reminded of this by Coventry City, the club whose manager had once pinned me up against a wall in the Chairman's Lounge to give me a lesson in manners. The Youth Cup Final win was a distant memory and Gordon Strachan was long gone. He'd been succeeded by Roland Nilsson, followed by Trevor Peake, Gary McAllister, Eric Black, Steve Ogrizovic, Peter Reid, Adrian Heath and Micky Adams. For a club with such impeccable manners they'd gone through a lot of managers in six seasons.

Teddy Sheringham and Bobby Zamora added late goals and I announced them with almost as much relish as the Rick Shaw rocket. West Ham won the game 3–0, but supporters frustrated in a lack of investment from the board had planned a protest at the end of the game. After the whistle lots of people stayed in their seats, particularly in the West Stand Lower and the Bobby Moore Lower. There was chanting at the board. 'Brown Out, Brown Out.'

I received instructions from Paul Aldridge, the managing director, to drown out the protests by playing loud music. I felt uneasy about doing this, but if I hadn't I probably wouldn't have been the announcer for much longer. So I played loud music, which upset the fans. I wasn't popular on the message boards that night. I sat in the announcer's room feeling bad about drowning out a valid protest. But like a waiter in the Gestapo restaurant, I was just taking orders.

I'd upset Coventry's board and our own fans, but at least my employers were happy with me. At this point someone from the control room next door walked in.

'Turn that music down,' he said. 'My stewards can't hear my instructions over their walkie-talkies.'

I pointed out that Paul Aldridge had told me to turn up the music.

'I don't care,' said the control room man 'it's a safety matter and I need my stewards to be able to hear me.'

I couldn't see why it was a safety matter. From my position I could see the two sets of supporters in neighbouring stands trying to link up with each other in one large group. The stewards were trying to keep them apart. I'm not sure why. It's not as if the Bobby Moore Lower were going to start a fight with the West Stand Lower. We've had some grim times at West Ham over the years, but I can't recall a civil war between rival stands.

But again, obeying orders, I turned the music down. The supporters cheered as though they'd won a victory. After a while they left the ground having made their point. I think that protest may have led to the club agreeing to fan representation at board meetings.

I left the Boleyn that night thinking I'd upset my manager, our fans, the control room and the opposition, all on the same day. In most jobs that would have been a bad day at the office. But, we'd won 3–0 and I was a happy Hammer. Besides, I was still smiling at that extraordinary own goal scored by Richard Shawwwwwwwwwwwwwwwwwwwwww.

ALL QUIET ON THE PRESTON FRONT

We limped on to the end of the 2004/05 season, just managing to finish sixth in the table. It wasn't a great position for the team considering the squad we had, but at least we were in the play-offs again. Once more we faced Ipswich, with the first leg at Upton Park this time.

It was an early kick-off which dampened the atmosphere a bit. We had the guy who was playing Dean Martin in the West End show *The Rat Pack* sing 'That's Zamora' to the tune of 'That's Amore'. It was beautifully sung but it was a cabaret song not a rousing anthem. The West Ham fans prepared to sing 'Zamora, wooooah, Zamora. He came from White Hart Lane. He's better than Jermain. Zamora, wooooah, Zamora.'

It wasn't the firecracker atmosphere of the previous season, but I'd done my job of delivering a positive stadium. It certainly paid off; we started well and went 2–0 up in thirteen minutes, with goals from Harewood and Zamora.

But I can't do much about a positive stadium once the game is under way. It's up to the players after that and with the manager getting increasingly anxious in the technical area, we threw away the lead to finish two-all. Pards had an argument with Ipswich boss Joe Royle on the touchline as the pressure began to tell. Fortunately two Zamora goals at Portman Road in the second leg booked our place in the final. This time Alan Pardew knew he had to win promotion or his job was on the line.

So, we ended the 2004/05 season with another trip to

Wales and this time I was let down by the fashion sense of my fellow travellers. Having lost the previous season we were back in the play-off final at Cardiff as Wembley was still being rebuilt. How long does it take to build a ground? This time we faced Preston North End. We travelled up on the train again, but this time the journey home seemed a lot shorter – we won, ending our two-year stay in the second tier of football.

Before the kick-off I was asked to go onto the pitch and warm up the crowd, or at least half of it. I didn't address the North End, just the East End.

I strode confidently out onto the pitch with our large West Ham mascots, Herbie the Hammer and Bubbles the Bear. The Cardiff turf was in magnificent condition, and it was going to stay that way, because a burly Welsh steward didn't like the look of my furry friends and wouldn't let them on the grass.

Well, Bubbles is furry, Herbie is made of a shinier metallic-looking material. It's unusual for a mascot to be an inanimate object rather than a living breathing creature, but when your team is called The Hammers it makes sense. Herbie is a bit scary for the younger children. Not every child is fully comfortable shaking hands with a large hammer, so for this reason Bubbles was introduced a few years after his scary chum. Bubbles, as you'd expect, is very round and every kid knows bears are friendly. Who doesn't like Pudsey, Sooty or Paddington?

I like to think that Bubbles is the acceptable face of the footballing mascot, beloved by the tiny fans, while Herbie is the more dangerous mascot that appeals to the older rebel kids. Ironically, away from the football ground, you'd be more likely to survive a hammer attack than a mauling by a bear.

On that lovely day in Cardiff the only mauling was from an over-officious steward, who was clearly under the impression that this was God's grass and we were the spawn of the devil sent from England to trample on it.

'You can come on,' he cried in an Uncle Bryn accent, 'but they can't, not with those big feet!' When I protested he told me that they wanted to keep the pitch in tip-top condition for the start of the game. Bearing in mind there were three play-off games to be played on the pitch that weekend, I think one extra hammer and a bear wouldn't have made much difference. But he didn't look like a man that was about to change his mind. Or indeed have much of a mind.

Herbie and Bubbles traipsed back to the touchline, with their heads bowed, swinging their arms, looking for sympathy. You know what mascots are like, they can't talk but they have very flamboyant gestures. It was a sad sight, a cute cuddly bear and a not so cute, not so cuddly hammer being ordered from the field of play. They'd woken that morning expecting to realise their dreams, to reach a pinnacle in the furry mascot world. They'd be the envy of Rammie the Ram and the other championship fur balls. Now their dream was in the gutter, they'd been humiliated by a jobsworth Welshman who didn't want them to touch the green, green grass of home.

The wronged hammer and bear milked it for all it was worth, conveying so much emotion without speaking. It's hard to know how hammers behave in the wild, but Herbie really nailed his performance. As for Bubbles, she was brilliant. If Andy Serkis had spent a year living with bears to learn their mannerisms, he couldn't have topped her performance.

The West Ham supporters stood as one to boo the steward. The solidarity with those cartoon creatures was amazing. If the steward had arrested Nelson Mandela, Bob Geldof and Felicity Kendall, he couldn't have received a more hostile reception. There was talk of a 'George Davis is

Innocent' type protest; with buckets of white paint already being ordered.

Despite losing my mute companions I did my bit, welcoming the fans and starting the singing of 'I'm Forever Blowing Bubbles'. I had the advantage as the regular Preston announcer wasn't there.

Being the stadium announcer can be a bit restrictive. It means you can only take a holiday during the close season. If you are clever you can fit in a sneaky two weeks around an international break weekend. There's always the chance of fixtures moving to Sundays or Mondays for television or a cup replay. I usually play safe and go for the close season. It means we go to South Africa in winter, and everyone asks why we didn't come when it was warmer. The Preston announcer had booked a holiday abroad, not expecting his team's season to last into the play-offs. I felt sorry for him, missing out on his team's chance to return to the top division for the first time in forty-four years. The once great Preston had been relegated the year before I was born. In his place they had a rather nervous stand-in, who seemed overawed at the prospect of not only announcing, but actually going onto the pitch at the Millennium Stadium in front of just over seventy thousand fans.

Deepdale Duck was there though, proudly resplendent in his mascot costume. The stadium held no fear for him; it was like water off a duck's back. Inside Deepdale was a man with a shaved head apart from the letters PNE carved into the back. Carved is the wrong word, because PNE was spelt out by the bits of hair left behind. I don't know what the correct term is, but his friends kept telling him it spelt PEN. He kept checking in the mirror, but I could tell he wasn't quite sure, what with it being backwards in the reflection.

It was 0–0 at half-time as I made my way down to the pitch again. I'd been invited to commentate on a penalty shootout between Herbie the Hammer and Deepdale Duck. For some reason the mascot's large feet were now deemed OK, yet they were exactly the same feet. I once interviewed a Paralympic runner who changed his feet depending on what he was doing. When I arrived at his house, he was wearing his general-use feet, but when we went outside to film him training, he put on his running feet.

Herbie and Bubbles are not international competitors. Trying to get a bear and a hammer onto an aeroplane would be a nightmare in the current climate. They are, however, very gifted entertainers and they waltzed onto the pitch with me at half-time. Deepdale Duck also waddled past security. 'Uncle Bryn' was nowhere to be seen, probably having an omelette.

The Preston stand-in announcer let me take charge of the commentary on the penalty shootout. He was still looking scared. Nobody said I had to be unbiased and with me roaring him on, Herbie easily won the shootout. I like to think I helped rescue his mascot dream. He was a Happy Hammer and so was his mum, who was down on the pitch to watch it. I'm not sure if I mentioned it, but in real life Bubbles is Herbie's mum. It used to be the other way around, but then he got too big to fit in the Bubbles costume, so they swapped. The Herbie outfit is much roomier or so I'm led to believe. I've never tried it on; it tends to be a bit sweaty in those costumes. I once spent a day as Pudsey Bear for Children in Need. I lost a pound in sweat for every pound we raised. Whoever wore it the next day will have suffered.

I climbed back up to my seat in the grandstand in time to see Bobby Zamora score the only goal of the game. Jeanette and I celebrated with the travelling fans. It was a lovely, lovely day. It was like going on a road trip with all your mates and finding out your syndicate has won the lottery. After two years in the wilderness, we were back. Goodbye Ceefax page 325, hello page 324.

We had won promotion back into the Premier League. I had my access all areas pass from the pre-match announcing, so I went into the changing room and congratulated the players. Pards asked me if I could man the PA at the celebrations at the ground the following evening. It seemed I wasn't the most useless announcer in the world any more.

Well, not until this point, because I was already booked to work elsewhere the next day. If I'd known the plan, I would of course have left the day free, but no one had mentioned this might be an option. The previous season a promotion celebration had been mapped out but we lost to Palace. That old football superstition reared its head again. If we planned a celebration we would 'ginks' it.

So we'd won, but now there was no plan. The hastily arranged celebration didn't fit in with my schedule, which turned out to be just as well. The next day I was working at the BBC, watching live pictures from West Ham on Sky Sports News. They showed lots of shots of crowds and balconies and microphones that didn't work. The crowd couldn't hear what was going on, so it was just a lot of people waving. The Mayor was greeted with chants of 'Who are ya?' which is only to be expected if there's no audible introduction. All sense of occasion was lost and my team looked like a two-bob outfit, when they should have been basking in the glory of promotion in front of a national audience. It was a shambles.

But never mind that. We'd won promotion. We were back in the top flight with a team of great youngsters. I'd had my day of celebration at Cardiff, at long last finding a girlfriend who enjoyed coming to games. My old sparring partner Alan Pardew had brought some pride back into West Ham. Now we would be competing on the big stage again. Who knows, we might even win a trophy, maybe the FA Cup. The next final was due to be played at Wembley for the first time since the old stadium was dismantled.

We'd appeared at the first final at the Empire Stadium in 1923, it would be fitting if we were back at the first final at the new Wembley.

I celebrated promotion by asking Jeanette to marry me. It was during the Live 8 concert, which we turned down as it was only on the television. Having agreed that she would say yes, I decided a more glamorous proposal was called for, so we set off for Tower Bridge. My family had a tradition of bridge proposals as my Dad asked my Mum to marry him on Clare College Bridge in Cambridge. They headed originally for the more famous King's College Bridge, but that was too busy for such a special moment, so they headed for neighbouring Clare. Years later, on the even busier Tower Bridge with Jeanette, I knelt down and asked for her hand. I was slightly worried that I would drop the ring, as a kid I was always worried that bridge would open up as we drove over it, but it never did. After a slightly longer pause for thought than I was expecting, she said yes.

We hoped to get married later that year, but it's more complicated to marry a foreigner than you think. Too many people have watched the film *Green Card*, so to prevent marriages of convenience your partner now has to have indefinite leave to remain before you can get hitched. That would take a while longer.

SEASON IN A NUTSHELL 2004/05

After a poor start we came good at the end. Just one defeat in our last ten games saw us sneak into the play-offs by clinching sixth spot. It all came good in Cardiff where we beat Preston to earn a return to the Premier League.

Highlight – We celebrated a hundred years at the Boleyn Ground. The best win was 5–0 at home to Plymouth.

Lowlight – Herbie and Bubbles being kicked off the pitch in Cardiff by an overzealous steward.

International highlight – London made it onto a shortlist of five cities to host the Olympics in 2012. I proudly stuck an 'I'm backing the bid' sticker in my car.

Worst moment – Being told off for announcing an own goal scored by Coventry's Richard Shaw with too much excitement.

Hero – Trevor Brooking was knighted by Prince Charles. Arise, Sir Trevor!

Villain – Alan Pardew for trying to do everyone's job at the club rather than concentrating on his own and for being instrumental in me losing my column in the matchday programme.

Team news – Teddy Sheringham was a great signing, even though he was in his late thirties, because he famously had 'an extra yard in his head'. Sergei Rebrov also joined, but didn't have an extra yard anywhere.

It shouldn't happen to an announcer – We hosted the National Bubble Gum Blowing Contest Finals at the stadium. The biggest bubble blown in two minutes won three thousand pounds and a chance to take on the American champion on television show *Ministry of Mayhem*.

New this season – A 1:48 scale replica of HMS *Warrior* was installed into the main reception in the West Stand. It was rumoured to cost a quarter of a million pounds, almost as much as the original, the first ever iron-clad warship built by Thames Ironworks in 1860. I'd rather the money had been spent on the team.

Missed games – None.

Did we win at Anfield? – No, they still wouldn't let us play Liverpool, because of that 'being in a different division' rule.

My bald patch – The size of a Snow Patrol CD. Probably *Final Straw*. But any CD would give you an idea.

Three-Legged Stool Review

Job leg – Lots of really interesting reporting work, including sailing round the Isle of Wight with Ellen MacArthur for a TV feature before she set off for a shot at the round the world solo record. Ellen proved to be a better camera operator than me, filming all my pieces to camera perfectly.

Relationship leg – Jeanette had now moved in and everything was going really well. It looks as though I may finally have cracked this leg, but not in a bad way that's going to cause it to snap off.

West Ham leg – We won promotion back to the Premier League. Back of the net!

WHATEVER HAPPENED TO THE HAMMERETTES?

They haven't danced for ages at West Ham, but the Hammerettes are still talked about a lot by supporters. For many youngsters the highlight of many games came at half-time, when the girls came on to the pitch and danced to the latest tunes from the hit parade. I haven't watched *Top of the Pops* in years, they could take it off and I wouldn't notice, but the girls dancing would keep me up to date with the latest grooves that the kids were shaking down. Or at least they used to. Suddenly one week they were gone.

I had a chat with Carl Bailey, their manager, to find out what they've been up to in the meantime. Carl, you'll remember, is the Australian former rugby league player with the London Broncos, who played the CDs from the shed in my early days as the announcer. The girls still dance all over the world, but not at West Ham any more.

The name Hammerettes goes back years at West Ham, as it was the name of the women who sold the matchday programmes, wearing very daring for the day claret and blue uniforms. The current generation began dancing at West Ham in the 96/97 season, a couple of seasons before I started as announcer. They lasted until the end of the 03/04 season.

In some of our darkest hours at West Ham the only entertainment we had was at half-time. The girls often showed better footwork than the players. I know a lot of people didn't like the loud music at the break because they wanted to discuss the game with their friends. It had to be loud for the girls to be able to hear it and keep in time with the beat. For them to be able to hear it at pitch level, it was deafening in the stands. Eventually to solve the problem a portable speaker was wheeled to the edge of the pitch.

The girls would also sell the half-time draw tickets. They preferred selling in the corporate areas, their little tops and shorts might have been ideal for dancing, but they offered little protection against the bawdiest of fans. Mostly it was good-natured though, I don't think we ever lost a Hammerette to the crowd! As reporter Brian Hanrahan used to say in the Falklands, 'I counted them all out, and I counted them all back.'

The one person who wasn't keen on the Hammerettes was the groundsman. Dougie worried that the girls would damage his pitch. Bearing in mind they were mere slips of girls and wore trainers, it's hard to see how much damage they could cause, compared to the twelve-stone footballers with their studs on. Quite often the sprinklers to water the pitch came on during the girls' dancing. They were true professionals and would always continue. Sometimes during the half-time interval there would be a rain storm, but they'd still dance regardless. Some people felt they performed better when they were a little wet. You see that's the trouble. Just thinking about the dancers has led to a smutty 'Carry On' bit of innuendo.

So where did they go? I've kept in touch with Carl over the years. I've been his guest at Harlequins and Twickenham, as the girls also dance at rugby. He says at the last count there were eight different groups of dancers who call themselves 'Hammerettes'. It's like pop bands which split up producing lots of splinter groups who all want to use the original name when they tour.

Carl's girls are called The AllStarzz and there's a core of twenty-six of them, who dance all around the world. At the end of their last season as Hammerettes, team captain Claire Dawson swapped shirts with Teddy Sheringham, before setting off for a round the world trip with Carl and a handpicked group of dancers. They performed at the IRB international rugby sevens tournament in Hong Kong and then Australia.

When they came back after six weeks ready for the new season, Bailey contacted West Ham and found they were no longer needed. One of the dancers who'd been left out of the tour had formed her own group, charmed West Ham's Scott Duxbury and set up a new deal with the club to use her girls instead. The two troupes were at loggerheads for a while, as Carl had trademarked the name 'Hammerettes'. However, it never came to a battle as West Ham decided it would be easier to dispense with the dancers altogether. There was never any announcement; they just weren't there at the start of the new season.

Bailey says he would have fought harder to keep the West Ham gig but he'd just been diagnosed with testicular cancer, so the last thing he needed was conflict. Fortunately he won the more important battle and beat his cancer. He felt his girls had a brilliant first six seasons at West Ham, but after seasons seven and eight, he felt they got a bit stale and needed freshening up a bit. He's frustrated that they never had the chance.

In the early days the dancers were largely from in and around Romford. Today he has girls from much further afield, but says there's still a West Ham-supporting core to the team and they'd love to return to the Boleyn Ground. You'll still see them dancing at sports arenas across the world, but they've only been back to dance at West Ham once. In 2010 two rival teams were offered the chance to dance again, after a fan's campaign. Both groups danced and were well received, but the club decided not to make it permanent.

I've mixed views about the Hammerettes. On the one hand the idea of dancing girls seems a bit dated and doesn't really fit in with the family club image we are trying to promote, but as dancers go, they were better than most and I enjoyed watching them. On balance I'd like to see them back again, if not full time, maybe just at Kids for a Quid games, as they certainly add something to the matchday experience.

I always found them very professional to deal with. Carl had rigid rules prohibiting drinking, smoking and drugs. His girls weren't allowed to socialise with players, unless it was an official club event where the players were also guests.

Two of the most striking dancers from the old days were Carly and Dee, the blonde Harrop twins. They were incredible acrobats who'd do all sorts of flips and tricks while we waited for the teams to emerge for the second half. Taking time out from the Hammerettes the twins went on to work as stunt doubles in the movies, appearing in *Lara Croft – Tomb Raider*, *Charlie and the Chocolate Factory* and *Thunderbirds*. When you see Rachel Weisz doing back flips in *The Mummy Returns* it's really Dee from Dagenham.

As for team captain Claire who swapped shirts with Teddy in their last match, well she married the manager; Claire Dawson is now Claire Bailey and they run the group together.

FINDING FRODO

One match I was announcing from my position up in the box when some club officials came in at the back. They were with two people from the film world. I recognised one with a scar across his face. I'd last seen him in the background in *Braveheart* or was it *Gladiator*? They were doing research for a film they were making. It was going to be filmed at West Ham and was about an American who came to live in London and fell in love with football. It was to be called *The Yank* and it sounded great. They asked a lot of questions about how the build-up works on a match day. What songs do the fans sing and what announcements do I make?

They were going to be filming at a future home match and they might need to film me doing a bit of announcing. It sounded great, I'd been on TV and radio all my working life, but the idea of being in a movie was very exciting.

It didn't happen. The film was made, but it wasn't called *The Yank*. It was called *Green Street* in the UK, but in other countries it was released as *Green Street Hooligans*, which should give you some idea to its theme. It wasn't about football at all, it was about football violence. The star of the film was Elijah Wood, best known for his lead role as Frodo Baggins in the *Lord of the Rings* trilogy. Elijah played an American student kicked out of Harvard for a crime he didn't commit. He came to live in London with his sister and fell in love with English soccerball.

He was soon sucked into the murky world of football

violence, becoming a member of the 'Green Street Elite', a thinly veiled version of the real life 'Inter City Firm'. One of the characters was played by Geordie actor Charlie Hunnam, with one of the worst cockney accents in movie history. It was second only to the legendary Dick Van Dyke. Nowadays Dick plays a doctor in *Diagnosis Murder*, but even he couldn't have brought this movie back to life – it was shocking.

The final scene depicts a huge fight between West Ham and Millwall firms. How anyone at the club could think that would be a good idea for our club's reputation is beyond me! A few years later West Ham and Millwall fans played out a real version of the violence at a Carling Cup tie at the Boleyn. I've never been so frightened in my life.

When I put the question to the man at the club who brokered the deal, he couldn't see what my problem was. The club had been paid £25,000 as a facilitation fee. He actually thought we'd done well out of the deal. Not only had we been paid, but we'd also generated a lot of free publicity. Twenty-five grand is a lot of money to you and me. It's a new car or an extension to the house, but to a football club it's peanuts. It's less than a single week's wages for a lot of players. For the sake of a measly £25,000 every time someone rents that dreadful movie, my club's name is dragged through the dirt. It's the sort of free publicity we could do without. It may have seemed like a free advert, but I would have paid £25,000 to distance us from the movie.

Fortunately everyone involved in that dreadful decision has left the club now, and it certainly wouldn't be allowed to happen again. It makes me so angry when I think of the damage it has done. West Ham is famous throughout the world. When I've been in America or South Africa and I've been wearing a West Ham hat, people come up to me and talk about Bobby Moore and Trevor Brooking. They always mention our reputation for playing entertaining football and there's the old chestnut about winning the World Cup.

Now people talk to me about *Green Street*. Am I meant to be proud of it? I deplore violence at football and I deplore bad films. As movies go it is a shocker. I like films where there's someone to cheer for, where there's a chance of right overcoming wrong. I can't cheer for anyone in *Green Street*, it's just one set of yobbos bashing another set. Just because one 'firm' are wearing my team's colours doesn't mean I have any affinity with them.

I always watch films like *ID*, *The Football Factory* and both versions of *The Firm* with interest. They're set in my world, even if I hate the mindless violence. The crucial difference with *Green Street* is the club allowed cameras to film in the ground, which appears to endorse the movie.

Maybe I'm overreacting, *The Arsenal Stadium Mystery* of 1939 was filmed at Highbury and no one batted an eyelid. One of the opposition's star players was murdered in the first few minutes of the film, yet Arsenal Football Club clearly didn't endorse killings at games. As long as it didn't wake anyone in the crowd, no one at Highbury the Library seemed to mind.

One game I arrived at West Ham and was told a big secret. This was the day they were going to be filming the crowd scenes for *The Yank*. Somewhere in the crowd was Elijah Wood and some other unnamed actors. It was very hush-hush. No one would tell me exactly where they were sitting. I was told that under no circumstances was I to announce that the actors and film crew were in the ground. Quite what circumstances would entail me revealing the whereabouts of a hairy little hobbit, I don't know, but I took it onboard.

My assistant Russell spent the whole of the first half scouring the stadium with a pair of binoculars, from our vantage point in the announcer's box on the third tier. I don't know if you are familiar with the literary genre of *Where's Wally?* books. It's an entertaining premise, where children are encouraged to scour through pictures looking for a gentleman in a red and white hooped shirt with a stripy hat and glasses. I imagine Wally probably follows Doncaster Rovers.

Our version was 'Find Frodo'. It was a lot more difficult. Elijah would not be wearing red and white. He'd probably be wearing claret and blue, which was going to make finding him a lot more difficult in the West Ham crowd. Just before half-time, Russell found him. He'd make a good detective and in fact his dad was a copper. Russ spotted a few extra cameras in some of the dugouts. You might not have noticed, but there are trenches strategically placed around the ground where camera crews can be positioned. For live TV games they are all used, but for other games most are covered over, with just a few used by snappers from the papers. The extra cameras didn't look like the usual TV cameras and for a long time they were all trained on the Bobby Moore end of the ground.

Russ noticed a section of the front row of the Bobby Moore Lower cheering for no apparent reason. The Bobby Moore Lower is always pretty vocal. They sing a lot, but they don't spontaneously cheer without reason. It happened again when the ball was in the middle of the pitch, with neither goal under threat. The same people in the front row were jumping up and down and slapping each other on the backs. The binoculars revealed it was Elijah Wood and some others we didn't recognise. We were excited in the box. I loved the *Lord of the Rings* films. Now Frodo had left the Shire and had come to the Academy of Football.

I would have loved to welcome him, but I remembered that 'under no circumstances' rule and kept quiet. Even if the Dark Riders had galloped onto the pitch from the Chicken Run, hell-bent on getting the ring back I wouldn't have warned Frodo. He'd have been on his own. The trick where he puts on the ring and goes invisible would fool those around him, but the Dark Riders would have sniffed him out no trouble.

Elijah Wood claims to be a West Ham fan since shooting the movie. Yes, I bet he is! He probably stood on the north bank as a kid. It's amazing how many celebrities claim a link with West Ham. They come over here, these Hollywood stars, looking for a bit of East End glamour! They're nothing but glory hunters. It's the same with players who have had no connection at all with the club, but as soon as they put pen to paper on a contract they suddenly claim they're West Ham through and through. Elijah has been to two matches to my knowledge, but it could be as many as three.

When the filming was completed the tiny little hobbit joined me on the pitch at half-time during a later match with Gillingham. His enormous hairy feet made a right mess of the grass. I was delighted to have a big-name Hollywood star to interview on the pitch. I'd followed his adventures over the years and had admired his determination to overcome Christopher Lee, who had scared the life out of me when I interviewed him on my afternoon radio show on GLR in the 1990s. Elijah has massive eyes and although I knew he wasn't Frodo, he looked just like him. This was the brave little chap who'd sorted out the evil Sauron, taken the one ring back to Mount Doom and now was going to star in a film about the Happy Hammers – remember I still thought it was going to be an anti-violence film called *The Yank*. If you've seen the film, you'll know that is not the case. Elijah told the crowd that he loved West Ham and said 'awesome' a lot. Way to go, Hammers! I suppose he's been busy in the intervening years, but as far as I know he's not been back. If he has, I haven't seen him, but maybe he had that ring on!

ALAN PARDEW'S CLARET AND BLUE ARMY

A simple measure of a West Ham manager's popularity is by listening to the crowd. Do they sing his name in front of the words 'claret and blue army'? Johnny Lyall's claret and blue army and Billy Bonds' claret and blue army were sung over and over again. Harry Redknapp made the grade, but Glenn Roeder never did. If West Ham fans are disgruntled with the manager they will sing 'We are West Ham's Claret and Blue Army'.

It took Pards a while to win over the fans, but promotion clinched it for him and in his third season, with us back in the top flight, it was regularly sung home and away. We'd been one of the favourites for relegation, but we were much better than anyone expected as we climbed to a creditable ninth place on the last day of the 2005/06 season against Spurs.

Tottenham at home is always eagerly anticipated, but this year there was nothing to play for, apart from the fun of denying our closest rivals a place in the money-spinning Champions League. West Ham have a bit of a tradition of enjoying the last game of the season at others' expense. One year we were already relegated when we denied Manchester United a league title, just for a laugh.

On this last day, Spurs arrived looking a bit peaky. They'd had a dodgy lasagne at their hotel at Canary Wharf the night before. Why they were staying at a hotel, I have no idea. Tottenham is in London isn't it? Anyway they had some lasagne that was 'pasta' its best and they turned up at our place with jippy tummies.

I was told that the kick-off might be delayed. This happens occasionally and it's my job to relay the news to the crowd, which is never a popular announcement. Fortunately I wouldn't have to make it this time. There was a stream of Spurs officials going in and out of the referee's room, while simultaneously in the dressing room a stream of Spurs players went in and out of the toilets.

With the thought of the Champions League slipping away, Spurs tried everything to have the kick-off delayed, but to no avail. Any other weekend they probably would have had some joy, but the ref was having none of it. All matches had to start at the same time on the last day as Arsenal were also gunning for the fourth place in the table that led to Champions League football. It wouldn't be fair to them if Spurs kicked off knowing exactly what they needed to do.

Six players in total were affected by the food poisoning, including former Hammer Michael Carrick and goalkeeper Paul Robinson. They all had to play in the match. Carrick looked as white as his shirt.

Lasagne-gate was the talk of the day. The radio bulletins were full of false rumours about the game being postponed. When the teams ran out exactly on time, the Spurs squad were greeted with rolls of toilet paper stacked up on the back of their dugout, put there by some joker.

West Ham won the game 2–1. With the FA Cup Final against Liverpool just six days away, we'd been expected by everyone to lie down and not risk injury. But that's not the West Ham way. We never want to lose and especially not to Spurs. We finished ninth, they finished fifth. We'd both be in the UEFA Cup next season.

At Arsenal, the news was greeted with wild celebrations. It was the last ever league game at Highbury and for the

first and only time the Arsenal fans broke out a chorus of
'I'm Forever Blowing Bubbles'. It was all a bit confusing as
their players wore claret that season as well.

I left the stadium after the last game, having warmed
to Alan Pardew. He seemed to delight in making me look
a prat but he'd instilled a fighting spirit in my team that
I liked. If he could win the cup the following weekend, I
would love him forever.

Sadly the game wasn't at Wembley as they still hadn't
finished building it. We played in the first Wembley final,
but we weren't going to be in the first at the new Wembley.
Instead it was a third trip to Cardiff.

The 2006 cup final was one of the best in years, some
say one of the greatest ever. We dominated Liverpool for
much of the game. When Dean Ashton made it 2–0, I really
thought it was our day. Even when Steven Gerrard pulled
it back to two-all, I still thought we'd win it. West Ham fan
Paul Konchesky put us back in the lead and all we had to
do was hang on. The announcer was just announcing the
four minutes of added time, when Stevie G scored again,
from way outside the box.

I was still optimistic in extra time when a chance fell to
the badly limping Marlon Harewood. Poor old Marlene had
given his all that day, but his injury meant he couldn't find
the touch needed for victory. It would have been perfect if
he had scored, because Harewood was a real trier, with
genuine skill, who just needed to find the back of the net
more often to grow in confidence.

As it was, the game went to penalties. It was inevitable
that we would lose now, it was like England facing Germany
– you just knew it was all over. In our four penalties only
40-year-old Teddy Sheringham scored. The match became
known as the Steven Gerrard Final and rightly so; what a
player that man is, he never gives up. But we played our
part and had a good laugh with the scousers in the bars

afterwards. There was no trouble and lots of good-natured banter.

To be honest, I felt a lot less disappointed that day than I did two years before when we'd lost to Palace in the play-off final. We'd had a good season back in the Premier League and we'd shown that on our day we could be the equal of a club like Liverpool. Even better, with Liverpool having qualified for the Champions League, the UEFA Cup place went to the FA Cup runners-up. We were back in Europe. As long as Alan Pardew didn't lose the plot and nothing happened to Dean Ashton, we were going to be all right.

Season in a Nutshell 2005/06

We finished ninth in the table, qualified for Europe and nearly won our first silverware in years.

Highlight – Nearly beating Liverpool to win the FA Cup Final.

Lowlight – Not beating Liverpool to win the FA Cup Final.

Worst moment – We lost our two greatest managers, Ron Greenwood and John Lyall, within a few weeks of each other.

Hero – The person who first shouted out 'Johnny Lyall's claret and blue army' during the minute's silence for John. That sums up the West Ham way.

Villains – The press for vilifying us for breaking the silence. How we respect our heroes is our business and nobody else's.

Team news – We signed Dean Ashton, a promising striker from Norwich. Teddy Sheringham celebrated his fortieth birthday and carried on playing despite the 'extra yard in his head' shortening all the time.

It shouldn't happen to an announcer – I greeted Jeremie Aliadere's arrival as a substitute by saying, 'He's here, he's there, he's Ally-Addy-Air'. It was greeted with a huge cheer. This was surely going to be a catchphrase that would run for years! He played just seven games for us and left.

New this season – Toilet rolls in the away dugout on the last game of the season.

Missed games – None.

Did we win at Anfield? – We lost 2–0, but it was good to play at Anfield again. Liverpool also beat us at home and in the cup final. Thanks for that.

My bald patch – Still the size of a Snow Patrol CD. I didn't seem to lose any more hair once we established ourselves back in the Premier League. However, I started having it cut very short, because I caught a shot of myself on television where it looked like a flan case just waiting for the fruit filling to be tipped in.

Three-Legged Stool Review

Job leg – I started co-presenting *The World Today* on the BBC World Service. It dovetailed nicely with my TV reporting work.

Relationship leg – Jeanette and I tried to get married but fell foul of tighter laws on marrying aliens. I thought Sigourney Weaver had sorted all that out. We settled for living together until the Home Office granted her indefinite leave to remain.

West Ham leg – We finished in the top ten and reached the FA Cup Final.

THE CRAFT OF AN ANNOUNCER

Attendance

One of the jobs of the announcer is to read out the attendance. It's important to get this right. It will be five numbers and it's important to read them in the right order. Nowadays the Boleyn Ground will hold just over thirty-five thousand when full. At the start of my time as announcer, before the new West Stand was built, the capacity was twenty-six thousand.

In the early days, I was given two attendances to read out. These would be verified by the ticket office. The first figure was the total attendance, with the second figure being the number of away supporters included in that total.

I would say something like, 'Today's attendance 25,308. Away supporters 1,875.'

If we were playing a small team or a team from far, far away then the figure would be small. Sometimes when we played Wimbledon the home crowd would jeer the very low number. I always felt sorry for Wimbledon, they were shockingly treated by their own borough of Merton and had to go and play at Crystal Palace. No one deserves that. Then they were sold down the river by the football authorities in an American-style franchise deal that saw them become MK Dons.

Milton Keynes is a long way from South London especially if you go the roundabout route. There's no other way really, MK has an awful lot of roundabouts. It's right up there with Swindon in terms of orbital traffic systems. I've nothing against Milton Keynes, well, not since Paul Ince was sacked, but you shouldn't be able to just buy a football team. Poor old Wimbledon in their last years in London had pitiful crowds at their away games, and in a sense all their games were away.

It's common in the announcer's world to give travel information that will help fans on their journey home. One heartless stadium announcer once put out the following towards the end of the game, 'A message for the visiting Wimbledon supporters, your taxi has arrived!'

Half-Time Scores

In the old days at football you'd see the letters ABCDEFG etc. painted onto boards alongside the advertising. At half-time scores were placed alongside the letters.

So it might read A 1–0, B 2–0, C 0–0, D 4–1. Each letter corresponded with a fixture being played at the same time as your match. To find out which game went with which score, you had to buy a programme. It was a brilliant marketing device. The home team in the D fixture had obviously had a great first half, but that's all you knew about it. You didn't know who'd scored the goals or if anyone had been sent off. In fact you didn't know anything more until the end of the game when you looked across and saw A 1–1, B 3–1, C 1–0, D 4–4. What happened in the second half at the D game? The only way to find out was to pick up an evening football paper. For some reason these were usually pink or green.

Gradually the papers lost out to the radio after the game. In the stadium itself, the A–Z system was replaced by the announcer reading out the scores. This had the added fun of being able to boo and cheer the results according to local rivalry or league position. The biggest cheer is reserved for defeats for Millwall or Tottenham, closely followed by Chelsea and Arsenal. Any big team losing to a small team would also be cheered. Dagenham and Redbridge results are usually cheered by a few fans from out that way, but not as loudly since they became a league club. Leyton Orient have always been friendly rivals as rivals go, so a lot of people also look for their results.

Now that I sit in the dugout, I'm fed the latest scores over my ear-piece from Russell in the announcer's box. I usually start getting the scores with about forty minutes on the clock. Despite this, there's one footballer who always used to ask me if they were half-time scores. He spent a long period out of action and I won't name him, because I wouldn't want to embarrass him, even though he's now left the club. He was convinced that East London was in a different time zone to other parts of the country. Despite there still being five minutes at least to play, he was convinced that all the scores I'd just written down were half-time scores. How was that possible? I'd always politely say they were the latest scores.

Humorous Announcements

My tip on funny announcements is 'if in doubt, leave it out'. However, if it's funny and it's not going to upset anyone, I think a good humorous line over the PA system can lift the crowd. Where most announcers go wrong, is doing more than one a game. Less is always more in my book.

I once announced the substitution of the ball during a snowy game. 'Leaving the field the white ball, please welcome the yellow ball!' There were huge cheers, and although it was a one-off comment people were mentioning it to me for weeks afterwards. Even my old mate Helen Chamberlain mentioned it on *Soccer AM* on Sky.

But you have to be careful with funny announcements. One Christmas Alfie Moon was married on *EastEnders* on TV. He wore a West Ham shirt in the episode, so the following day I congratulated him over the PA at the Boleyn Ground. There were laughs in the crowd, but because we were on a bad run and lost the match, that comment came back to bite me in the bum. The *Daily Telegraph* reporter wrote that 'West Ham have lost so much touch with reality that the Tannoy announcer congratulates fictional characters on their weddings'.

In reply I'd query the order of the words in 'lost so much touch with reality', mention that I've only ever announced a fictional wedding once and point out that our sound system is not in fact made by Tannoy.

I try not to say anything that will cause problems, especially not in a big game where it might incite the opposition. But I don't always have control over my half-time guests. One match, after London had just won the 2012 Olympics at the expense of Paris, my guest was Sir Robin Wales, the Mayor of Newham. The visitors were Arsenal, our London rivals, who featured a large number of French players as well as manager Arsene Wenger. Sir Robin is always good value and was in fine form about the Olympic win, rounding off the interview with the line, 'We beat the French and we'll beat them again today!' It went down well with the West Ham crowd, while I stood open-mouthed.

I thought I might be in trouble, but I wasn't. Apparently it's OK to say that sort of thing, but only if you're the mayor.

Keeping Everyone Informed

When you are the person on the microphone at an event, your main job is to keep people informed. If you're entertaining as well, that's a bonus, but the main job is to provide information. This was illustrated on a mid-season trip to Denmark. Our friends Lars and Maiken were getting married. Most of the guests were Danish, apart from our table which was international. As the speeches were all in Danish, which is a mixture of Swedish and Klingon, we were given little bursts of translation by the Danish Starfleet officer on our table. It was lovely but it meant our table was a bit noisy and we started to receive funny looks from some of the guests around us.

If there's a problem, I'm a great believer in explaining the situation to crowds. It has served me well over the years. I took matters in hand and passed a note to Lars the groom. At the earliest moment he grabbed the microphone from the best man and explained to the other guests that one table spoke no Danish and were having a simultaneous translation. After that we received nothing but smiles from the guests around us, as we laughed at each joke approximately fifteen seconds after they had. Each speech was greeted at the end with everyone shouting 'wah, wah, wah'. It's like three cheers, except they are pronounced 'wah'. I added a fourth 'wah' when a text arrived with news of David Beckham's second goal for England against Wales. The Danes looked at me strangely; it was a 'wah' too far. I'd broken protocol, but when I explained they smiled. Everyone loves Becks I thought, although I'm not sure they fully understood. A short time later a chilled bottle of Becks beer arrived at my table.

Playing Music After Goals

During the days when Joe Cole was entertaining us with his skills, the crowd would sing Spandau Ballet's 'Gold' substituting the word 'Cole'. 'You've got the power to know, you're indestructible, always believe in Joey Cole.' When the young alchemist scored against Bradford I decided to do something I've never done before, and have never done since.

When Joe scored, I played 'Gold' over the PA system. The fans all joined in and it did sound brilliant. Afterwards I was told by the club not to do it again. So I didn't. On reflection I don't know what I was playing at. I think I was just excited about Joey Cole. I love academy players who've made good, and he was such a brilliant player for us. However, I hate music after goals. It's something small clubs do to generate atmosphere. We don't need to do that, we are always loud. It's not always cheering. It's often shouting or booing, but it's never quiet.

Each season there are requests for us to start playing music after goals at West Ham, but I'm totally against it and I know from correspondence that 90 per cent of fans are with me on this one. I think it's artificial and I hate to hear it when I travel to away games. I go to Twickenham a lot to watch rugby and I can't believe that they've stooped so low as using music after tries there. It's not big, it's not clever and it's not the West Ham way. I did once say to Scott Duxbury that we would play music after goals 'over my dead body'. The mention of my death made him smile, but I got my way.

Congratulating Opponents

I usually wish good luck in the next round to teams that beat us in cup competitions. I am the voice of West Ham and we have a reputation for sportsmanship and doing things right. Officials at the club have always applauded me for the tone of my announcements, but one time I badly misjudged the mood of the crowd.

We'd had a good FA cup run with wins at Walsall, Manchester United and Sunderland, but it all went wrong in our first home game in the tournament. We lost 3–2 against Tottenham. I made the biggest mistake of my announcing career. As the players were walking off, I wished Spurs good luck in the next round. Many supporters have never forgiven me for that.

At the time it seemed like the right thing to do, but I had my fair-minded, sporting announcers head on, not my West Ham head. When you've just lost 3–2 in the cup to your biggest rivals, you don't want them to have any luck in the next round. You want them to be soundly thrashed. So I hold my hands up to that one. I got it wrong.

I still congratulate lower league teams who've played well against us, but now if we lose to rivals from the same division, I just keep quiet.

SILENCING THE CROWD

One of the trickiest things for an announcer to get right is the minute's silence. Keeping quiet is not something football fans are good at. They've looked forward to a game for a couple of weeks, arrived at the ground excited ready to cheer on their heroes. After all the talk with colleagues at work, all the banter with neighbours, the time has come to worship at their footballing cathedral. The excitement builds as soon as the turnstiles open. An hour and a half later, just before kick-off, it's the job of the announcer to try and persuade them to keep quiet for one minute. It's a tall order.

Usually the silence will be in memory of an old player from one of the teams. You know that one set of supporters are going to keep perfectly silent. The problem is the other set.

If you get it wrong, the silence is broken and it creates a dreadful atmosphere. It's the sort of outrage that sparks a war in the real world. It's tribal. One tribe has committed an atrocity. The other tribe wants revenge. An eye for an eye. Not an ideal start to a game of football.

So how do you do the perfect minute's silence?

I always start by trailing ahead to it from an hour before kick-off. That way it gives people a chance to have a think about it. Maybe they didn't like the player in question, so it gives that knee-jerk reaction a chance to surface, before hopefully being replaced by more rational thoughts about the player's family and friends.

Then I write out a tribute to the player. A lot of announcements I will do off the top of my head, but with something like this it's best to have it written down. There's nothing worse than getting someone's name wrong in a eulogy. 'He was a marvellous servant of the club and ... I've got his name here somewhere.'

The biggest thing is to make sure the crowd know when the minute's silence is happening. The players need to be told, but that is really down to the referee to sort out. I usually pop into the ref's room just to make sure we're all singing from the same hymn sheet.

Most refs like the players to come out, line up, shake hands and then break for a kick-about. After the coin toss and the photo with the mascots and captains, the ref will then call the players back to line the centre circle for the silence.

The players will have their minds on the game, so they'll sometimes need herding around like sheep to get them into position. The ref is the shepherd. If necessary I'll join in as his sheepdog, nudging them towards the centre circle with a few well-chosen words. 'Come-bye, come-bye, back, walk on, back, lie down, stand, stop.'

Once everyone is in position, I will read the eulogy and then say, 'The minute's silence will start and finish on the referee's whistle.'

If the silence is not as quiet as it should be the ref will usually blow a little early. A few refs have asked me to say 'period of silence' rather than 'minute's silence' for that very reason. I've politely reminded them that they are at West Ham, and we do things properly here. I know my crowd and I know they won't disrespect the silence. It's not the West Ham way.

One ref, who shall remain nameless because he's a pompous fool, insisted I said 'period' not minute, so I agreed that I would. When the moment came, I said 'minute'. The silence is not about the ref. When he brought it up later, I said that I'd forgotten in the emotion of the moment. But I hadn't.

I think there are too many minute's silences in football. We were instructed to have one for the two little Soham schoolgirls who were killed. It was a story that I'd followed with great sadness. My Dad went to school in Soham. My Auntie lives opposite the house in Littleport where their killer Ian Huntley was found. The little girls had been pictured in their Manchester United shirts in all the papers, but their story had nothing to do with football.

Tottenham had a silence for Glenn Hoddle's Dad. Hoddle was Spurs manager at the time and it was a personal loss for him, but did it really merit a silence? It's hard to turn down someone when they ask for a silence, but in my view it is the best course of action. Otherwise we'll be having one every week and they will be devalued.

We held a minute's silence for Brian Clough when we played Notts County in the Carling Cup in 2004. It was immaculately observed; everyone respected Old Big 'Ead. The following night I was at Nottingham Forest v. Rotherham, reporting on the tributes for the BBC. There was a signed West Ham shirt in amongst them. It was from Rufus Brevett, saying how he wished he'd played for him. It was a nice comment, but I'm not sure Brian would have picked him.

Cloughie had a huge impact on me as a young reporter and commentator for BBC Radio Nottingham in the 1980s. One season started with him punching me in the face and ended with him giving me an exclusive interview, naked in the dressing room at Wembley saying, 'That's because I took your head off earlier in the season!'

I covered his memorial service at Derby's Pride Park for TV. We all got soaked through. Nigel Clough made one of the most moving speeches I've ever heard. He said his Dad would be looking down saying, 'Look at those daft buggers in the rain.'

Cloughie was a special man, completely impossible at times, but a genius at getting the best out of ordinary players. He was the best manager England never had, playing football on the ground, where it should be. If God had wanted us to play in the air, he'd have put grass up there, he always said. I'd have loved him to have managed West Ham.

West Ham were the visitors at Forest's next home game. When the Forest sang, 'Stand up for Brian Clough', all the West Ham fans stood up. Seems I wasn't the only one who'd have liked to have seen him at the Boleyn.

George Best

One of my most challenging games as the West Ham announcer was our home match with Manchester United on 27 November 2005. It was the first game for Man Utd since the death of George Best, one of their all-time heroes. It was my job to introduce the tribute to him before the kick-off.

George Best is one of the most naturally gifted football-ers I've ever seen and I'd once been lucky enough to share a pitch with him in a charity match. I once interviewed him for radio and we arranged to meet him in a pub where he always drank. It was the only way we could guarantee he'd turn up. He did, but rather later than expected.

When George's second liver finally packed in, after years of abuse, the whole of football mourned his death.

I was worried. West Ham fans have never let me down, but this could easily go horribly wrong. You only need one idiot with a grudge against Manchester United or the Irish to ruin things.

Our match was on the Sunday. This turned out to be an advantage as it gave us a chance to assess what had happened elsewhere on the previous day. The authorities had called for a silence at all games that weekend. Most were impeccably observed on the Saturday, but not all. The Manchester City v. Liverpool game saw the silence cut short as shouts broke out. It was even worse from the Leeds fans at Millwall.

I fully supported George Best having a minute's applause. It would allow the silent majority to triumph, by not being silent. I knew most fans would applaud vigorously for a man who'd given football purists so many moments to savour.

Even if a hundred people booed, or shouted, they would be drowned out. It was a no-brainer. It had to be a minute's applause.

Except that I was told from on-high that it had to be a minute's silence. It was Manchester United's call and they wanted the silence. He was their hero, so even though the game was at West Ham, we would obviously bow to their wishes.

It looked to me like being a disaster. Emails flew back and forth. I was contacted by PR people I didn't even know worked for our club, with advice on what to say and how to say it. No doubt someone was getting a huge consultancy fee for this sage advice, but it was my arse that was on the line if it went wrong, and I had no intention of letting that happen. I lobbied and lobbied for the applause.

The day before the game the word from Manchester United was they still wanted it to be a silence. Protocol demanded that we would do whatever they wanted, while hoping they would change their minds.

When I arrived on the morning of the match it was still going to be a silence. Sir Bobby Charlton was coming down onto the pitch to read the eulogy. Sir Trevor Brooking was there to represent us. Trevor is like a trump card that we play in times of crisis. He's so well liked that everyone behaves when he's around.

The Manchester United delegation arrived and they'd obviously had a chance to think about it on the journey. They'd decided that George would have approved of the applause. We were given the thumbs-up for a minute's applause. I breathed a sigh of relief. It was going to be OK.

In the run-up to the tribute I made a few announcements as food for thought for anyone thinking of spoiling it.

'The eyes of the world are on Upton Park,' I said.

'Let's show them we know how to respect a legend in East London.'

A banner in the crowd read, 'George Best and Bobby Moore. God has one hell of a team.'

We walked out to the centre of the pitch before kick-off, two knights of the realm and me. I introduced Sir Trevor and he spoke wonderfully about George's skills as a footballer. Then I introduced Sir Bobby, who looked very emotional and close to tears. He gave a lovely eulogy about his old friend. Bobby thanked West Ham for the marvellous effort they'd made. Towards the end he was filling up and only just managed to finish. Sir Bobby should then have said the words leading into the referee's whistle, but I could see that he couldn't go on. I took the microphone from him and said, 'The minute's applause will start and finish on the referee's whistle.'

Applause broke out all around the ground. Loud and proud from the Manchester United fans behind the goal. I'd expected respectful applause from our lot too, but no, it was just as loud. When it comes to great players, club allegiance goes out the window. The football world stands together in times like this. Manchester and West Ham, united.

The Manchester United manager, Sir Alex Ferguson, later said, 'We owe a big thanks to the West Ham fans. The one lucky thing we have [is] that we came to a football club that appreciates great football players and the minute's applause epitomises the sporting love between two great football clubs.'

So often that comradeship is marred by a few idiots. The minute's silence plays into their hands. It's sad that we have to abandon this fine old tradition, but I'm glad to see it go.

There'll always be a silence on the game closest to Remembrance Sunday, but that is different because it's nothing to do with club allegiance.

The minute's applause when a player dies gives the power back to the majority of sensible, passionate, football-loving people. Long may it continue.

I suspect that a minute's silence would have been respected impeccably by West Ham fans. But imagine if it hadn't. I didn't want to take the risk.

The following week Manchester United did hold their own silence at Old Trafford. You could hear a pin drop. Well done to the West Brom fans who were the visitors on that occasion.

As a footnote to that emotional day in East London, West Ham took the lead just a minute into the George Best game. With emotions running high, Manchester United were caught on the hop by Marlon Harewood.

We still lost. A performance worthy of George Best from Wayne Rooney inspired a 2–1 win for the visitors.

Ron Greenwood and John Lyall

The hardest tributes for me came in 2006 when we lost two people who'd shaped our reputation in the game. In February 2006 the great Ron Greenwood died. He'd been manager of West Ham from 1961 to 1974, leading us to an FA Cup and a European Cup Winners' Cup. He'd stayed on as general manager when John Lyall took over as team manager. So many good things about West Ham can be traced back to Ron Greenwood. Against Birmingham City in a Monday night Sky game we held a minute's silence for Ron. I couldn't look at his image on the screen while I was reading out the eulogy, in case I wobbled.

In April, just two months after Ron Greenwood's death, we lost John Lyall. He managed West Ham from 1974 to 1989, winning two FA Cups and achieving our highest ever finish, third place in the top flight. To lose our two greatest managers so close together was tough to bear.

The FA Cup semi-final against Middlesbrough was one of the most emotional in years. We won it thanks to a goal from Marlon, but that wasn't the tearjerker. There was a moment before kick-off that summed up why West Ham is so close to my heart. It was a great day out at Villa Park. Jeanette came with me and we discussed our marriage plans in the car on the way. I had a terrific idea for a venue that I hoped she'd agree to. Before kick-off they played 'Bubbles' for us, and that Pigbag song for the Boro. The atmosphere was electric in the ground.

The announcer did a really good job of quietening every-one ready for a minute's silence for the great John Lyall. We settled down to pay tribute to a man who we held so dear to our hearts. The announcer read out a few words about John and how he'd led us to cup wins in 1975 and 1980 and then the ref blew his whistle. The silence lasted no more than a few seconds before someone started a chant. 'Johnny Lyall's Claret and Blue Army.' It hung in the air for a few seconds and then everyone joined in, we all sang it for the whole minute. The Boro fans didn't know what to make of it. The commentators and the reporters in the papers the next day didn't know whether to praise or condemn us, but I think West Ham fans felt it was the right thing to do. It was a huge release of all the pent-up emotion of losing the most successful West Ham manager ever, just a few months after the death of his mentor.

I don't know who the person was who started the chant, but I'd like to thank them. It was probably a group of mates who'd planned it beforehand, but it still took one brave person to have the courage to shout out first. Supposing no one had joined in?

My South African fiancée didn't quite know what to make of it. She knew I'd been upset about John and Ron. She also knew that I had a zero tolerance for yobbish behaviour and always wanted West Ham to take the high ground and do things properly. Yet here I was shouting my head off during a minute's silence, with tears streaming down my cheeks. It didn't make any sense, but as everyone around her was singing she joined in anyway.

I wondered later how John Lyall's family felt about us taking over during the silence. He was a hero to us, but he was a husband and father to them. I hoped they didn't feel we'd spoilt it. I spoke to Murray Lyall, John's son, and asked him if he was OK with it all. He said he thought it had been an incredible moment and his Dad would have appreciated it.

A few days later we gathered at West Ham for our own tribute to John. Sir Trevor came down on the pitch with former players who'd served under John. Fortunately we were playing Liverpool that day and they are a club that respects tradition. The Lyall family had asked for a minute's applause rather than a silence, which was just as well. For the first time ever I would have been worried about our fans keeping quiet, not the visitors. To be on the safe side, I said a few words to the visiting fans about how we'd lost our Shankly and our Paisley in the space of a few weeks. But I needn't have worried, the Mickeys all joined in with our supporters in a vigorous round of applause that lasted beyond the full minute. Some fans still have blisters from that night.

Of course, as we were playing Liverpool, we lost the match.

MR MOON ALL OVER THE WORLD

I've been the stadium announcer at West Ham United since 1998, but I've been an announcer on a global stage since 2006, although you'll never see me. Every year I spend a day in Soho in a sound studio, putting down two thousand new messages in my role as the voice of the stadium announcer on the EA Sports FIFA video games.

If you play any of the games, alongside the commentators you'll hear me in the background announcing the team line-ups, the substitutions, the scorers and the added minutes. In fact, everything I announce in real life at West Ham. There is the facility to turn up the announcer if you want to have a really good listen. I sometimes wish that was possible at the Boleyn Ground.

Each time I also record ten 'hidden' messages, which are played at random points. For example on FIFA 08 I congratulated Jeanette on finishing the London Marathon. My good friends Dave Cheeseman and Nicola Underdown were delighted to find their marriage being announced on FIFA 09.

I like to give my nieces and nephews a mention. Christopher, Julian, Kate and Joe have all had birthdays or been lost children who should contact the nearest steward. My youngest niece was also welcomed to her first ever game, before she was even born. At the time of the recording she was just a bump, going under the working title of Lulu Lemon. By the time she was born, my sister had decided to drop the Lemon bit, quite wisely in my view.

But in the game she will always be Lulu Lemon. Once a recording is done, it's done. When you are doing two thousand messages in a day, there's little time to go back and change it.

Every car I have ever owned is given a mention over the stadium PA in the games. Listen out for my first car from my student days, a blue Mini 1000. I seem to remember the announcement is about its lights being left on. Then there's my old white Ford Cortina which is illegally parked. There's a yellow Opel Kadett, a claret Ford Sierra, a blue BMW and a blue Ford Focus, all committing various offences outside stadiums across the world. They're cars I've driven over the years. I should think they're mostly in the big scrap yard in the sky now, but I like to think they live on through the medium of video gaming.

I read out all the number plates as well. I haven't put my current car on, in case some deranged gamer comes round my house. Maybe my announcement put them off during a vital moment when they were about to score against Barcelona. That's the thing with the random messages; they can play at any point in the game. It all adds to the authenticity.

There are a few announcements especially for West Ham fans. I don't mention the club by name, because these messages play out in virtual stadiums across the world. However there's no reason, I thought, why our safety announcement shouldn't receive a wider airing. Gamers have the option to play matches with any teams in any ground, but it's always my voice on the PA. So Mr Moon has been arriving and leaving stadiums across the globe since FIFA 10. There's also a welcome for 'everyone at Knees up Mother Brown' on the last two games, a thank you for the support on the forums I received during the difficult days of the first half of the 2008/09 season.

If you listen carefully there are lots of Canadian youngsters who also get a mention. Electronic Arts is based in Vancouver and the team on the FIFA games get a kick out of hearing their offspring announced.

So how did I get this dream job? Well, like most of the good things in my life, there's a West Ham connection. After the success of FIFA 06 the EA guys decided to bring out a special edition, called *FIFA 06 – The Road to the World Cup*. They were facing increasing competition from rivals like *Pro-Evolution Soccer*, so to keep ahead of the game they added some extras.

Video game consoles were getting more sophisticated. The newly launched Xbox 360 had increased capacity that would allow more layers of audio. As well as the commentators, EA decided to add a stadium announcer and enhanced crowd sounds. I was lucky. The commentators were Andy Gray and Martin Tyler, represented by an agent called Matthew Fisher, who just happened to be a West Ham season ticket holder. When the guys in Vancouver asked him to find an announcer for the new game, he gave me a call. I've been the voice of the games ever since.

I do a lot of corporate event hosting, particularly in the summer months, when there's no football. Once I was speaking at a three-day football event at the NEC in Birmingham. After facilitating at a few sessions with big-name speakers like Graham Taylor, Peter Taylor, Ian Holloway and one of the Alan Smiths, I found I was signing just as many autographs as they were. They couldn't all be West Ham fans and most of the kids were far too young to remember me presenting football on Channel Five.

They were gamers. I realised this on day one when two boys asked me what Mr Moon means on FIFA 10. I said it was a safety message at West Ham and if I told them exactly what it meant, I would have to kill them. At which point they ran off crying.

For the rest of the three days I happily posed for photos and signed autographs for football fans, who'd only ever heard me in the confines of a video game. It was all a bit strange and reminded me of a time a few years back when I'd left West Ham after a match via the players' entrance. A small boy who'd been patiently waiting held up his autograph book and said, "Scuse me mate, are you anyone?' I replied that sadly I wasn't anyone, but he might have heard my voice on the PA and I'd happily sign for him. 'No, you're all right,' he said, and put his book away.

It took a few years to crack the child market. Now that kid must wish he had my autograph. He could have been the envy of his friends. Being the stadium announcer on a video game, it seems, is far more prestigious than doing it in real life! It took a while, but I eventually became a star in stadiums across the world. Well... virtually!

THE SEA WORLD INCIDENT

The trouble with Alan Pardew was that he interfered in everything. He was the manager of the football club, but he wanted to poke his nose into everything else, all the non-football bits. He wanted input into the look of the programme, the merchandise and from my point of view he wanted to pick the music we'd play in the ground.

Once before a game, the manager said he needed a few words about an important matter. He took Sue the marketing manager and me into a small room just off the tunnel. It's the room the broadcasters use for their TV interviews. To a backdrop of sponsors' logos, he outlined his latest idea to raise the atmosphere at the ground.

Pards had been to Sea World in Florida with his family. He'd seen the announcer at the dolphin pool conduct an interactive crowd-pleaser of a quiz. Everyone got involved and it was brilliant, he told me. The TV camera at the pool homes in on someone in the crowd and they are asked some trivia questions to try and win prizes. If it's an adult the questions are hard, if it's a kid, the questions are easy.

To keep it simple, they don't bother with microphones going into the crowd. Instead the answers are all multiple choice, with three possible answers. You held up one, two or three fingers to indicate your answer. Alan loved this simple digital technology and gave the whole idea a big thumbs-up. The look of excitement on his face suggested he was reliving the excitement as he held up his fingers, in case I hadn't grasped the complexity of the format.

I agreed it sounded great, but our game was kicking off in fifteen minutes' time. I was wondering if I wouldn't be better occupied building up the atmosphere in our own ground, rather than reminiscing about Alan's holiday. Especially as the interview room is a very small room, with bright lights and no windows, and I was wearing a thick fleece and coat. I was dressed for sitting outdoors for a few hours, not standing in a windowless bunker discussing Sea World. I believe Pards is a big fan of *Free Willy*, but I am not.

My co-presenter on a late-night phone-in show during the early days of Channel Five was the fabulous Helen Chamberlain. Helen was spotted during her days as a sea lion demonstrator at Chessington World of Adventures. I'm not sure what the sea lions were demonstrating about, but Helen was very funny on the microphone and was spotted by a producer from Nickelodeon, before moving on to the hilarious *Soccer AM* on Sky. Apart from that I didn't think there was much synergy between football and fish-based fun, but it appears I was wrong.

I may have momentarily lost consciousness due to the heat and accompanying dehydration, but when I came to Pards was still banging on about the Florida crowd-pleaser.

'So the kids hold up one, two or three fingers, depending on the correct answer.'

It's brilliant, he said, we should do it here at the next game. It works because the kids always win. Their questions are much easier, Alan explained, just in case I thought Florida children are much brighter than their parents. I've no knowledge of the Miami schools system, but I'd already guessed that, with no need for any fingers.

The more excited Alan became about the brilliant Sea World quiz, the closer he got. He was dribbling with excitement. I hadn't seen dribbling like it since the days of Eyal Berkovic. My face often gives me away and although I was trying my best to look just as excited as he was, my beaming smile may have wilted slightly in the heat.

He was obviously expecting a better reaction to his brilliant idea, because he looked slightly disappointed. Pards is a bit of a spin doctor. In his mind as long as you are enthusiastic about a plan, it will work. It doesn't matter if the plan is flawed and ill thought out, as long as you are positive it will surely work. If it doesn't work, it's because other people weren't enthusiastic about it. They let you down. It wasn't because your plan was a pile of crap in the first place.

By the way, I'm still talking about the Sea World idea, and in no way am I suggesting that Alan Pardew's team tactics were ill thought out. How could I possibly suggest that? He took us to consecutive play-off finals and won us promotion. Without a brilliant plan we never would have finished in the play-off positions. Critics will say that he led the best squad in the division to fourth place and then sixth place in the table. Maybe we should have finished higher, but that was nothing to do with Pards' tactics, that was because some critics didn't believe in the plan.

His game plans were spot on. The players gave their all. It was just that sometimes the supporters who should have been cheering their hearts out decided not to. For some reason fans thought that having paid for their tickets they were entitled to a view, and chose not to behave like lemmings. This saddened Alan.

Anyway, back to that night against QPR in the cup. I tried not to sound too discouraging about the brilliant Sea World idea, but pointed out that our cousins from across the pond are very different to us. While Americans love to be onscreen, the British have a very different reaction to cameras. I know from my TV work interviewing Brits in the street about the hot topics of the day that they often act oddly as soon as you point a camera at them. Some people hate being filmed and walk off, while others clam up. One very typical British reaction is to make mischief. Motorists who drive past a camera crew always honk their horn. I think it's actually in the Highway Code. Question – What should you do if you see a TV crew by the side of the road? Answer – Blow your horn and drive off grinning.

For pedestrians passing a camera there's an over-whelming urge to say hello to Mum. Even completely feral children, with no structured upbringing of any kind, can't resist greeting their long-lost mother enthusiastically via the camera. You can be in the quietest part of the United Kingdom, but set up a camera and it's suddenly noisy. Perfectly normal people are suddenly swearing like dock-ers. One day I'd like to set up a camera in a Trappist monastery, just to see what happens. I bet there'll be lots of noisy swearing.

The shyer types keep quiet but resort to rude hand gestures, reminiscent of the days of Shaker Maker or Gareth Hunt with his coffee bean shaking gesture. Sorry, have I lost some of you? Let me be clearer; they make wanker signs, despite no referee being present. Small children can be obscene but not heard.

My worry with the Sea World quiz would be to do with hand gestures, or to be more specific, fingers. If the answer is one, an American child would hold up one finger. A London child is more likely to hold up the middle finger and a cheeky grin. If the answer is two you can pretty much rely on the Little Hammer to hold up the same two fingers that his Dad might use to wave goodbye to the fore-man at work. We can only pray the answer is three. Even then, there's no telling what the surrounding fans will be doing in the background.

I pointed out the differences in behaviour on the other side of the pond to Alan, but he said it wouldn't be a problem. People are the same the world over, he claimed.

I hadn't realised he'd studied human behaviour to that extent. It almost sounded as if he didn't want his word to be questioned.

I badly needed to take onboard some liquid and besides there was a match about to start, so I made my excuses about going out to talk to the crowd and left. Alan shouted after me that he wanted to try the Sea World quiz at the next home game. It was good to see he hadn't let the small matter of a last-minute team talk get in the way of his mission to bring entertainment to the Boleyn. I would have preferred entertaining football and decided this dolphin-inspired quiz could not happen. Fortunately after consulting with the camera operators at the ground, it emerged that we don't have the ability to zoom in tighter than a section of the crowd four seats wide by three seats high. So twelve people in shot, it just wouldn't work.

I broke the news to Alan, who looked crestfallen. What about the Sky cameras which zoom right in on the players, he asked, with his bottom lip rolling out to full Thunderbird villain mode. Sadly we don't have control of them, I replied. We have our own cameras high in the gantry, but they are no use for a fish quiz.

We never did have any Alan-inspired pre-match entertainment but he did finally get the team playing some entertaining football. I'll always be grateful to him for three consecutive trips to Cardiff. To be fair, he won us promotion and was so close to beating Liverpool in one of the best ever FA Cup Finals, but what happened next was to prove his downfall.

ARGY BARGY

On the day the transfer window slammed shut in August 2006, West Ham signed two players. It was strange because the manager had nothing to do with the signing and they were top Argentine World Cup stars. Javier Mascherano and Carlos Tevez were both twenty-two. We'd had big-name foreign stars at West Ham before, but usually they were old and knackered before we could afford them. It didn't make sense. How on earth had we afforded them?

I still don't fully understand the deal, but there was clearly a problem. A third party owned the players' rights and that's not allowed. It was a guy called Kia Joorabchian, who was actually trying to buy West Ham at the time.

So this should have been brilliant news. I introduced the two Argentinians to the crowd and they waved and received huge cheers from the West Ham fans who couldn't quite believe their luck.

Then we waited for them to play for the team, and we waited and waited, and still Alan Pardew didn't pick them. For some reason Pards couldn't find places in his struggling side for two World Cup stars. Nigel Reo-Coker and Hayden Mullins were preferred in midfield to Mascherano. Whenever I've watched Mascherano starring on the European stage since, I've wondered how on earth he couldn't get in the team. Maybe he wasn't match-fit at first, but even on crutches he should have still earned a place in the starting line-up. Carlos Tevez was kept out of the attack by Marlene, Teddy and Bobby. How was that possible? Looking back at it now, it's laughable that Pards couldn't find a way to integrate them into his side.

The problem of course, was that Alan hadn't sanctioned their signings. He'd built a side around pace and stamina and now these foreigners had turned up with their clever skills and he didn't quite know how to fit them into his team without upsetting his players.

Nigel Reo-Coker had the hump because there'd been talk of him leaving to join a bigger club in the transfer window. The move hadn't come off, and now he was expected to slum it with us, and what's worse he had to fight for his place against Pards' all-time favourite player, Hayden Mullins and some fancy Dan from Argentina. Nigel Reo-Coker sulked for the rest of the season and the fans started calling him Nigel Mediocre. I think he should have been stripped of the captaincy – not only because of all the sulking which affected his performance but because he disrespected my future wife. Jeanette was telling him all about our wedding plans one day, and he just looked at her as if she was mad and walked off. When you are the captain of West Ham there are certain things expected of you like giving 100 per cent, inspiring your team-mates and not disrespecting the announcer's partner.

So we struggled down at the bottom of the table again, the fans started getting restless, the players underper-formed, the atmosphere in the stadium was poor and Pards told me I wasn't doing my job properly. It never occurred to him that no matter what I said or what music I played, if the team played consistently badly, the atmosphere was going to drop. West Ham fans are passionate and vocal, but they're also lovers of good football and watching this rubbish week in, week out was enough to silence anyone.

By Christmas we would have a new manager and new owners, but first I was getting married.

THE OTHER BOLEYN GIRL

I persuaded Jeanette that we should seriously consider getting married at the Boleyn Ground. To my amazement she agreed. As a venue it was ideal, especially since the West Stand had seventy-two hotel bedrooms built in. On a match day they're corporate boxes, but on non-match days the tables and chairs are packed away and beds are put in. It's a neat way to extend the use of the stadium. All our guests could stay at the ground. It was a perfect venue for the wedding service, the reception and there was no taxi needed to reach the hotel afterwards. And the club agreed to give me 10 per cent off, as I was virtually family.

There is one disadvantage to getting married at a football ground: it's often busy on a Saturday. To make sure we could guarantee the ground would be empty we needed to pick a weekend when West Ham were playing away. Club Secretary Peter Barnes rang me the moment he had the fixtures, and I beat the queue booking for a day when West Ham were away at Middlesbrough.

I was married at West Ham on 11 November 2006. It's an easy date to remember, it's Remembrance Day. The Armistice was signed on the eleventh hour of the eleventh day of the eleventh month to signal the end of the First World War.

It was meant to be the war to end all wars. The fact that they called it World War One should have suggested there was always going to be a sequel. Of course in those days it was just called the Great War, but there was nothing great about it. Like all wars it was stupid, bloody and unnecessary. Millions of innocents suffered because the royal families of Europe couldn't settle their sibling rivalries without a few working-class chaps losing their lives. Top author and long-suffering West Ham fan Sebastian Faulks wrote the splendid *Birdsong* about it.

These days we wear poppies to honour and remember the dead. For me the poppy has another meaning. It reminds me my anniversary is approaching and I need to book a table for the evening. My wife does like a game of snooker.

We were married in the Carlsberg Suite, probably the best wedding suite in the world. The photographs were in the changing room and pitchside. We led our guests on a celebratory clockwise lap of the pitch to the reception in the Bobby Moore Suite.

The names have changed since then, but the Carlsberg was in the West Stand and the Bobby Moore Suite is what is now the Greenwood and Lyall Suite, the long thin one at the back of the Bobby Moore Stand. I was warned that a square-shaped room would be much more suitable for a wedding reception, but I wanted a view of the pitch. It was a good choice. At night, with the yellow glow of the growing lamps on the hallowed turf, it was a beautiful sight. It was the happiest day of my life, better than winning the cup in 1975 or 1980, better than promotion, better than anything to do with football. I married my princess.

Before the service we walked down to the World Cup Heroes statue on the corner of Barking Road and Green Street. My bride was in her wedding dress and I was wearing the first made to measure suit I'd ever owned. A red double-decker bus stopped for us to cross at the zebra crossing. The driver gave us the thumbs-up. The Asian shopkeeper smiled at us, his children hiding behind him, waving out the side. A black cab pulled up and the driver parped his horn. It was like a scene from a Richard Curtis film. I was just waiting for a chirpy cockney chimney sweep to emerge from behind the statue to complete the picture. We posed for pictures alongside Bobby Moore, Geoff Hurst and Martin Peters, the three West Ham players who won the World Cup for England almost single-handedly. Ray Wilson of Everton kept trying to get into the shot. He was holding up Bobby, so it would have been churlish not to include him. We could always Photoshop him out later.

On the way back across the zebra an old lady called out to us. 'You look lovely,' she said. I thanked her, but on reflection she may have been talking to my bride.

The registrar from Newham Council had been very firm on the matter of timekeeping in our pre-wedding interview. We were not to be late, as he had other weddings to attend to. We weren't late. He was, arriving very flustered, muttering that he'd got the time wrong in his head. Maybe writing it down would have been a better option. The ceremony started late but it didn't matter.

The registrar was a bit out of sorts all the way through. He called me Jeremany instead of Jeremy. The first time I let it go, but when he did it a second time I corrected him. Jeremany isn't even a name. Besides I didn't want to take the risk of not being legally married, by my name being wrong. I'd seen the problem the wrong name had caused for John Paintsil/Pantsil.

All of my family were there and the bulk of Jeanette's family had flown in from South Africa. One of her sisters had to miss the day because she'd burst an eardrum diving and wasn't allowed on a plane.

My little sister Julie burst into tears during the service. It wouldn't have mattered, except it happened while she was doing the first reading. Fortunately I have plenty of sisters. My big sister Kathryn was out of her seat like a shot and held her hand. Together they finished the reading.

I loved my sisters so much in that moment, Julie for crying and Kathryn for saving the day.

Nothing else could go wrong. The only other reading was by my friend Ella. She's a professional actress, so we knew she wouldn't fill up. We'd worked together on radio at GLR and Mean Country. She'd also played the part of Angst, a Swedish game show hostess in my quiz show on TalkSport. People still ask me about Angst, who had an incredibly sexy voice. Angst was Ella, who went on to star in *Green, Green Grass* on BBC One. It's the spin-off from *Only Fools and Horses* and Ella played Mrs Cakeworthy, who's Boycey and Marlene's lazy housekeeper.

Incredibly a few words into her reading Ella was in floods of tears too. Everyone was laughing. There was a lot of laughter and crying that day. Ella composed herself and continued. Her training at the Royal Shakespeare Company pulled her through.

Once Jeanette and I were legally wed, I held the certificate aloft like a football scarf and we headed off for pictures. We'd already had photos taken in the home changing room. There was a shot of me pointing at the tactics board and Jeanette putting on a puzzled face. We went into the TV interview room for more pictures. We'd made up our own advertising rectangles which we stuck over some of the club sponsors on the board you see behind the managers in the post-match interviews. Our signs said 'Jem and Netta 11 November 2006'. We hoped nobody would notice and they would be left up there. Maybe our wedding signs would appear on Sky TV. They didn't. Somebody noticed and they were taken down on the day of the next game.

After more photographs in the dugout, we sat in the Bobby Moore Stand surrounded by our guests. The official photographer took a lovely shot where everyone was smiling, but it was ruined by my old GLR boss, Trevor Dann, holding up a Notts County scarf. No one likes to see that sort of thing at a wedding, a thieving magpie nicking all the glory.

Then came my favourite moment of the day, we did a lap of the hallowed turf. We paraded around the touchline with all our guests behind us, clockwise for luck, before processing into the Bobby Moore Suite for drinks.

The food was brilliant. If you ever have a chance to have a wedding at West Ham I can highly recommend it. I'm planning to have all my weddings there. My wife and I sat on the top table. My Dad proposed a toast in English and Jeanette's Pa did one in Afrikaans. We had loads of speeches. My best man was my middle sister Mel, she is not a man, but she was definitely the best. Mel, short for Melanie not Melvin, made a brilliant speech. She had blown up lots of pictures of me as a child. When she held up the one of me in my first ever West Ham kit, my big sister Kathryn burst into tears. She says it was the mud on my skinny little knees that pushed her over the edge. Lots more tears followed, during speeches by Jeanette's best man Harish, her cousin Gert and then Jeanette herself. My wife spoke so well, I was so proud of her. I told her she was my rock, my angel and my princess; and she still is.

There was no sound system in the Bobby Moore Suite, another reason why they'd suggested we use a suite in the West Stand. However, I'd controversially sneaked up to the announcer's room and plugged up the public address system for the whole stadium. All of the speeches were on the same radio microphone that I use on a match day. You can select which speakers you want to be live, so I opted for just the Bobby Moore Stand, all apart from the stadium seating area. It meant that our speeches were also going out in the concourses and the toilets. That proved quite useful as the speeches in total went on for an hour. I must take most of the blame. I was the last speaker to take the mike. Well, if you can't headline at your own wedding, when can you? I did twenty-seven minutes. Table seven had a sweepstake on how long the speeches would be, so there was an accurate time-keeping record. Video evidence confirms the timings.

Most members of the family had cried by now. There was just me holding out. I knew I had a tricky bit coming up in my speech. My Nanna had nearly died earlier in the year. She'd pulled through and had made it to my wedding. I was so happy she'd made it and I knew that when I mentioned her in my speech, I would fill up. My Nanna had been one of the most important figures in my life. My Grandad had been knocked off his bike and killed when I was just one year old. She'd held on to me as a baby for hours at a time as she grieved his loss. It meant we always had a special bond.

I could hardly look at Nanna as I came to the bit about her in my speech. But I did look at her and she nodded and I got through it. I relaxed, nothing could go wrong now. On the roller coaster journey I was past the high point, it was all downhill freewheeling now. As a public speaker I should know you can never stop concentrating. A minute later I was filling up and could hardly talk, with tears in my eyes. I'd been so worried about crying about Nan, that my whole body had relaxed, including the muscles that were holding the floodgates back.

At that moment I was talking about how special it was for me to get married at West Ham United, the team I'd supported all my life. People must have thought I loved West Ham more than Nanna. I didn't and I don't. I love West Ham, more than any club in the world, but they are not more important than my family. Anyone who says they put their football team first is either lying or they don't have a very strong family. My family is more important to me than anything. Yet when we watch the wedding video back, it's West Ham that sets me off every time.

We lost Nanna soon afterwards. She'd arranged for a taxi to take her home and left without saying goodbye to me. It was typical of her. She didn't want to drag me away from the guests. I rang her at home from my room late in the night and we had a lovely chat.

Nan's dead now, but she'll always be with me. I always think of her when I have doubts about my ability, because she thought I could do anything. I can always watch her on my wedding DVD. My friend Lisa from the BBC interviewed guests in the Bobby Moore Suite, asking them for advice for the happy couple. Nan said we must never go to bed on an argument, and I don't think we ever have.

My assistant announcer Russell, the man who plays the music on a match day, did the disco for us on our wedding night. Our first song was 'Wonderful Tonight' by Eric Clapton and after much dancing we retired to hotel room 270. I spent my honeymoon at West Ham United. In fact I was the only Hammer to score at Upton Park for a while. While I was getting married, the players were losing 1–0 away at Middlesbrough. I didn't care. For the only time in my life, West Ham lost and I didn't care.

There was no time for a honeymoon as we had a relegation battle to win first. We booked to go to South Africa as soon as the season was over.

EGGY EGGY EGGY

Eggert Magnusson became the new chairman of West Ham, following a takeover by an Icelandic consortium. Eggy seemed like a smashing bloke, enthusiastic about football and a member of UEFA's executive committee. His face looked like one of those trick pictures that are the same upside down. We all thought it was a great move, not suspecting for one minute that he had no idea about money and would spend it like water.

My dad had been saying for years that he wanted a rich benefactor to come in and invest some money into the club. He'd always hoped David Sullivan and David Gold would make a bid for the club they both supported, but they were showing no signs of leaving Birmingham City. The other bidder was Kia Joorabchian, the man behind the Tevez and Mascherano transfer detail. Most people felt the Icelandic bid was the better option, especially with Eggy's clear love for the game, it didn't feel like we were just going to be an investment.

Pards was still calling for Upton Park to become a fortress, but on the pitch his players were showing no signs of battling like soldiers. The new owners decided it was time for a change. Alan Pardew wasn't bringing home the bacon and Eggy decided he'd had his chips. Out went Pards and in came Curbs.

I was delighted, having admired the work that Alan Curbishley and Mervyn Day had done across the river at Charlton for many years. They'd both played for West Ham and knew the traditions and heritage of the club. They knew what the fans wanted and everything was going to be all right. I was genuinely delighted to introduce Curbs and Merv to the crowd before the Manchester United home game. The Sky cameras were there and the new era got off to a flying start with a 1–0 win.

It didn't last. We drew at Fulham and then lost Christmas home games to Portsmouth and Manchester City. We hit rock bottom on New Year's Day, getting spanked 6–0 at Reading. Carlos Tevez kept the bench warm the whole game. Nobody could understand it. We knew Pards didn't want to play the little fellow, but why wasn't Curbs picking him?

Curbs started to get a lot of stick in the press. After one game he stormed out of a press conference, having told the journalists he didn't think much of what they'd been writing about his team. I often pop into the press lounge after the game, to hear the manager's thoughts. I was sat just behind veteran journalist Brian Glanville, who said in a loud voice 'pathetic' as Curbs left the room. It's unusual for journalists to voice their opinions to managers like that. I'd grown up reading Brian Glanville's football reports but I didn't like the way he was sledging our gaffer. The outburst from Curbs was unwise, as you can't win an argument with the press. I've coached many sports people over the years on how to come across well in the media. Give them some good quotes and they'll leave you alone, take them on and you'll never hear the last of it.

Having said that I admired the fighting spirit of our new boss. I had a chat with him about how we could get the crowd behind his team. He mentioned that I'd stopped playing 'Bubbles' as the team came out of the tunnel for the start of the second half. It was something that Alan Pardew had wanted and I'd agreed to, without ever really liking the idea. I think 'Bubbles' can be overplayed. It gets the crowd going, no doubt about it, but how many times do you want to hear the same song? If we play it again at the end, for a win, then it can be overkill in my view. However, Curbs said he thought it would lift us, so I brought it back.

It did noticeably lift the mood at the start of the second half, and we've kept the half-time 'Bubbles' ever since. However, I do personally prefer atmosphere to build naturally. I think if you continually throw paraffin onto a fire, the fire will burn out quickly. It's far better to let the flames take hold naturally, but what do I know?

Dean Ashton was crocked and showing no signs of coming back, and Nigel Reo-Coker was still sulking. Curbs made two great signings: Matthew Upson who instantly settled the central defence and Lucas Neill at full back. Neill's charging runs from defence seemed to inspire the team. He was loud on the pitch, and as Nigel Reo-Coker went further into his shell, Neill effectively became the captain on the pitch, in all but name.

Curbishley built his team from the back. We started to look more solid defensively, it wasn't pretty, but it was necessary. I was disappointed that he still didn't pick the Argentine players. Javier Mascherano was offloaded to Liverpool and Carlos Tevez finally did start getting picked.

It was then that we realised there was a big problem. Liverpool took one look at the details of the Mascherano deal and blew the whistle on us. We were fined five and a half million pounds by the Premier League but were allowed to carry on playing Carlos Tevez. It was a massive fine; in fact it was a world record. But at least that was the end of the sorry business; we'd been given permission to carry on playing Carlos. We'd been naughty, we took our medicine and that should have been the end of it.

Wigan, Sheffield United and, disappointingly, our London neighbours Charlton and Fulham, called for a points deduction, but the authorities said no. We'd paid up the world record fine and that was an end to the matter.

So it looked like that was that. The protests looked to have gone away, especially as everyone thought we'd be relegated anyway, deduction or not.

Our lowest point came at the Valley, where we lost 4–0 to Charlton. It was a funny old game, because the two clubs had swapped managers with Curbs now in charge at West Ham and Pards at Charlton. As we slumped to defeat, the travelling West Ham fans started singing Alan Pardew's name, which I found a little disrespectful to Alan Curbishley. Anyone watching would have been in no doubt as to which Alan was going to be relegated, but they would be proved wrong.

As often happens at West Ham, an amazing story began to unfold. Carlos Tevez started scoring goals and we started winning games. The little Argentine with his scarred neck became a folk hero in the East End. When he was a kid he'd pulled a kettle of boiling water onto himself. He'd been offered plastic surgery when he became a footballer, but refused, saying the scars were part of him. Now the man nicknamed 'Apache' was playing out of his skin. A miracle was on the cards.

A crucial game came straight after the Charlton defeat, a seven-goal thriller against Spurs at home. We lost 4–3, but we played so well, it was a sign of the belief coming back. Six months after joining West Ham, Carlos Tevez finally scored his first goal.

Personally I love a backs-to-the-wall scrap. There's nothing better than fighting your way back, when no one believes you can do it. I grew up reading *Scorcher and Score* comic where heroes like Hotshot Hamish and Nipper Lawrence would overcome the odds to win. My favourite strip was *Billy's Boots* where young Billy Dane became a top player, whenever he wore an old pair of boots that belonged to an old footballer called Dead Shot Keen.

I don't know whose boots Carlos Tevez was wearing, but he suddenly found his scoring touch. He scored seven times in our last ten games. After the Spurs defeat, we won seven of the last nine games and amazingly avoided relegation. Against all the odds plucky West Ham United stayed up. We'd been pronounced dead a few times, but Curbs kept pummelling away on our chest, willing us back to life and, on the last day of the season, the heart monitor flickered back to life. (I've been watching a lot of *Grey's Anatomy* box sets since I grew out of comics.)

Going into the last game, we only had a slim chance of survival, as we were still reliant on results elsewhere. Worryingly for us, two of our rivals, Wigan and Sheffield United, were playing each other. Of course, football is an honest sport and there was never any hint that they might agree to draw, to help each other out and both stay up. Our last match was at Manchester United, who definitely wouldn't roll over and let us win, We'd messed things up for them on the last day of the season too often for that.

The smart money was on a Manchester United win, which meant a draw at Bramall Lane would suit both Sheffield United and Wigan. But then Carlos Tevez scored the goal that according to all the papers kept West Ham up. It didn't keep us up, a draw would have been enough, because Wigan beat Sheffield United 2–1. The Blades were down, but not quite out.

Sheffield United chairman Kevin McCabe was understandably not happy. I could well understand why, but there was a lot of nonsense spoken about West Ham being allowed to stay up because of our standing in the game. McCabe had a very big northern chip on his shoulder. As if we'd been allowed to stay up because we were from London.

However, he did mount a vigorous campaign to have his team reinstated. Blades fan Sean Bean led a delegation to Parliament, which had all the effect of a *Sharpe* style cavalry charge against tanks.

The crucial thing was we'd been told we could carry on playing Carlos by the Premier League, so we did. End of story. One appeal by the Blades cut no ice with the Premier League. It went to the High Court and we won again. There was talk of it being taken to the European Court of Arbitration for Sport, but instead both sides settled for one last Football Association arbitration, with both sides agreeing there was no further appeal allowed.

Having won three times, I think we assumed we'd win again. We didn't, there was no points deduction, but we had to pay Sheffield United twenty million pounds. Remember we'd already been fined five and a half million. In my view the verdict by Lord Griffiths was ridiculous, but I would say that, wouldn't I? His conclusion was that Carlos Tevez was worth at least three points to West Ham that season, and West Ham finished three points above Sheffield United.

He's a clever man that Lord Griffiths, being able to work out how many points a single player is worth. Perhaps he neglected to take into account that Carlos didn't score for months, his arrival unbalanced the team and ultimately led to the sacking of the manager. I would say if you could calculate the effect of his time in a West Ham shirt, it would represent a negative number of points. Yes, he was a hero in the last ten matches, and I'll love the little guy forever, but Carlos did not keep us up that season. To quantify his worth as a points total is nonsense and Lord Griffiths should hang his head in shame.

When Tevez and Mascherano arrived at West Ham, they were reckoned to be worth thirty million pounds. It was a bit like Buy One, Get One Free, except they were both free.

We only had third-party ownership; not even fire and theft. They ended up costing us twenty-five and a half million pounds.

We didn't emerge with any credit at all from the whole sorry business. I believe in truth and fair play and we'd clearly done something wrong, even if it's not 100 per cent clear what that was.

The one thing I've always loved about being a West Ham fan is people, in general, like us. Obviously Spurs and Millwall fans aren't keen, but on the whole the football world has a soft spot for West Ham. I don't know if there is a league table of second-favourite teams, but I reckon we'd be fairly near the top. Or we were until this point. After the Tevez affair we became public enemy number one for a while.

I got fed up with people saying we should have been relegated for fielding an ineligible player. Neither player was ever ineligible. The rules we broke were B13 and E10, which sound like vitamins but are about acting in good faith and third-party ownership. Instead of being known as the club of Bobby Moore and Trevor Brooking, the club who won the World Cup for England, we became branded as cheats.

A Sheffield United fan produced a button badge that he sold on eBay that read West Ham United – Cheating Cockney C***s. I'm not big on swearing, but I admired him for that. If my team had been relegated I would have been furious too. However, the response was typical of the East End banter I love. A West Ham fan posted the eBay shop details on a web forum with an invitation for all Hammers to buy one and then post negative feedback. I'm led to believe the badges sold like hotcakes and the poor old Blades fan's eBay rating plummeted.

I've been saddened to see Sheffield United slip further down the league since. I hope one day they'll be back in the top flight and I don't blame them at all for holding a grudge against us.

Carlos Tevez, having won the Hammer of the Year trophy, left in the summer to join Manchester United and we all wished him well. Javier Mascherano, no longer having to compete with midfield giants like Nigel Quashie, Lee Bowyer and Nigel Reo-Coker, managed to win a place in the Liverpool side. Our benchwarmer ended the season playing in the Champions League final and has never looked back.

West Ham, having survived, now surely looked forward to a great future under Alan Curbishley. He'd sorted out the defence, and we'd played with real spirit. The good times were just around the corner, now where have I heard that before?

Season in a Nutshell 2006/07

Argentinians Carlos Tevez and Javier Mascherano arrived in a 'too good to be true' deal. It turned out to be a disaster. Alan Pardew had no idea how to integrate the World Cup stars into his team which was based on pace and determination not flair and skill. The club were taken over by an Icelandic consortium.

There was discontent off the pitch and Alan Pardew was sacked after losing the dressing room. I don't know what he did, but it was felt it was best that he left. Alan Curbishley took over and stabilised the club. We were fined a record five and a half million pounds after Mascherano left for Liverpool and it emerged that the deal with the Argentinians contravened some rules. We beat Manchester United at Old Trafford to avoid the drop.

Team news – Carlton Cole, Tyrone Mears and the much misspelled John Paintsil joined and that nice Lee Bowyer came back. Carlton proved to be the pick of the bunch.

Highlight – A storming end to the season, winning seven of our last nine games.

Lowlight – What were we doing at that end of the table in the first place?

International highlight – Signing two big-name foreign stars.

Awful moment – Realising our manager had no idea how to utilise players of that quality.

Nightmare moment – Dean Ashton was called up for England and was crocked in training by tiny winger Shaun Wright-Phillips. He was out for the season and though he did play again he was never the same.

Hero – Carlos Tevez, who took forever to find the net, but then couldn't stop scoring.

Villain – Nigel Reo-Coker, who sulked his way through the season after being denied a move to a bigger club. He was a disgrace and should have been stripped of the captain's armband. In the end Lucas Neill became the skipper in all but name and took over officially the following season.

It shouldn't happen to an announcer – At the end of the season I traditionally ask the captain for a few words on the microphone to thank the crowd. Nigel Reo-Coker refused to say anything.

New this season – The matchday programme grew a bit, became square and went up to £3.50. It was a good read but it didn't fit in your pocket very easily. Jimmy Walker's column 'Walker's World' was hilarious. Despite playing just thirteen times in goal in five years at West Ham, he was worth his wages for that column alone.

Missed games – None, we saved the honeymoon until the end of the season.

Did we win at Anfield? – No the Mickeys beat us 2–1.

My bald patch – The size of a Keane CD, possibly *Hopes and Fears*. In other words it was still the same size as before, although there were signs of erosion into the hair either side of the front bit.

THREE-LEGGED STOOL REVIEW

Job leg – The World Service radio work dried up due to cutbacks in budget, but the TV work held firm. I was compère for a big corporate event at the Guinness head-quarters in Dublin, proving it is possible to organise a piss-up in a brewery.

Relationship leg – Jeanette and I were married, so I think it's fair to say it was a good year for the relationship leg of the stool.

West Ham leg – We survived in the Premier League on the last day of the season.

STOCKINGS AND PANTS

I t's the responsibility of the two captains to hand the team sheets to the referee an hour before a game. The West Ham skipper and his counterpart walk down the tunnel from the changing rooms and go into the ref's room, which is on the left, just before you emerge from the tunnel to the pitch. The sheets are handwritten. All the players' names and numbers have to be correct.

The team sheets are then read out in the tunnel by one of the media team, for the benefit of the TV and radio commentators, producers and floor managers. There's always a hush as everyone notes down the numbers. The team sheet is a very formal document and a little dated in style. The kit colours are always referred to as shirts, shorts and stockings. It always makes me laugh when they say 'stockings', especially if the team is wearing black. It's all those years of watching Benny Hill. I imagine the team running onto the pitch in black stockings, to the Benny Hill theme tune, being chased round and round the corner flags at double speed by the referee.

The thought of footballers wearing stockings is not something anyone would enjoy. Not even Sepp Blatter, a fan of both football and classic hosiery. As well as messing up football, the FIFA boss also served for a time as the President of the World Society of Friends of Suspenders. They had one aim: to fight the wearing of pantyhose. Sepp usually wins his battles by whatever means, but tights versus stockings was not a close contest. Even with his support for stockings, after a good run, tights won comfortably in the second leg. Despite that, every match day with just under an hour to go before kick-off the mention of stockings still makes me laugh. Even Sepp can't stop that, well not yet anyway.

After the team sheets have been read out in the tunnel, the TV and radio people head off to tell the world the news. I move on to the photocopier room, where the sheets are typed into the computer by the media team, and then checked, once, twice, three times, to make sure there are no spelling mistakes.

Occasionally the handwriting on the original sheet is hard to read, so that makes it difficult. One time Paul Scharner was wrongly typed up as Paul Schamer. He was a new player at the time for Wigan, so I read it out. I was ridiculed by someone on a message board for getting his name wrong. He might be a household name now, but I hadn't heard of him at the time. I hadn't followed his career in Austria or Norway. Neither of those countries were big on my football radar. He might have been voted footballer of the year by the supporters of Brann, but I thought he was called Schamer, because that's what was written on the sheet. On subsequent visits with Wigan and West Brom I've referred to him as Scharner, but the shame of the Schamer incident continues. Especially in the eyes of the Norwegian and Austrian-based Hammers.

It helps if the writing on the team sheets is neat and easily legible. Former goalkeeper and then goalkeeping coach Ludek Miklosko was always a man for neat hand-writing. Especially if he took his gloves off. Ludo would invariably fill in the details of substitutions.

It's also common for players' names to be misspelt on the sheets. It's up to us to spot them. I don't think I've ever got a West Ham player's name wrong. Sometimes there's a bit of controversy over the exact pronunciation. For a while Julien Faubert was 'Faw Bear' before settling on

'Fo Bear'. Frank Nouble was first suggested as 'Noo Blay' before being anglicised to 'Noo Bull'.

You'd think it would be easy enough to just ask the player himself, but that doesn't always work. Frank, for example, was born in London, but his parents are from the Ivory Coast. So the Ivorian pronunciation has been adapted for the London market. I imagine growing up in Lewisham Frank found it much easier to fit in as a 'Noo Bull' than 'Noo Blay'.

This brings us to John Pantsil, the lively Ghanaian defender who became a cult hero at West Ham. I call him Pantsil, because that's how I announced him in all his time at West Ham. But that is not his name and never has been. He should have been 'paints' as in Van Gogh, not 'pants' as in Calvin Klein.

He was born John Paintsil in Ghana, but there was a cock-up about his birth registration. The letter 'I' was missed out, and he was registered as John Pantsil. That was fine, everyone still called him Paintsil. It didn't make any difference to him. Except young John grew up to be an exceptional footballer. Foreign shores beckoned and so he needed a passport, which was made out in the name on his birth certificate. After a spell in Israel he arrived at West Ham.

We all knew he was called Paintsil, but because his registration documents had to be the same as his passport, we were duty bound to call him Pantsil. There was a lot of fuss about his name being misspelt on his shirt, but if we'd put that extra 'I' in his name we'd have been fielding an ineligible player.

I had to laugh when I saw him play for Ghana at the World Cup in South Africa against Serbia. They'd spelt his name 'Panstil'. Not only had they taken a letter out, they'd swapped two of the others around. His shirt had become an episode of *Countdown*.

However his name was spelt, John Pantsil was one of the most enthusiastic footballers I've ever seen in the claret and blue shirt. He particularly loves a celebration. Whenever I've seen him play for West Ham, Fulham or Ghana, he's always the first person on hand to congratulate the goalscorer. He loves leaping all over them. John does a lap of honour at the drop of a hat.

West Ham players always do a lap of the pitch at the end of the last home game of the season. It's not a lap of honour; it's a way of saluting the crowd, to show how much their support has meant over the previous nine months. Over the years this has become a tradition at West Ham but it has evolved. The coaching staff like the players to return to the dressing room for a debrief, and more importantly to have a drink. Once they're hydrated and wrapped up warmly they emerge for the lap.

One season, while the players were disappearing down the tunnel to down their drinks and pick up their kids, there was one notable absentee. Celebrations specialist John Pantsil had set off for a lap on his own. Clearly worried that a few fans might start to leave, John was flying round the pitch waving his arms in all directions. He was like a whirling dervish and was getting a great reception from the Hammers faithful. However, the coaches were shaking their heads in disbelief. They wanted him off. So it was down to me to be the party pooper.

'Could Mr John Pantsil please return to the tunnel. Mr John Pantsil to the tunnel, thank you,' I said over the PA.

Johnny Pants was by now more than halfway round. He cut the last two corners and ran for the tunnel, still waving wildly and grinning from ear to ear. He received a standing ovation. West Ham fans love a bit of passion and spontaneity. Best of all we love a nutter and whatever he's called, JP is certainly that. He's not a bad player either and he's always warmly applauded when he returns.

'He comes from Africa, He's better than Kaka, John Pantsil, whoooooa, John Pantsil, whoooooa.'

CELEBRITIES

West Ham can rightly claim to be top of the Celebrity League, surely no other club has so many famous fans? They're real fans too; we don't attract many glory hunters as we haven't won anything since 1980. Not unless you count the Intertoto Cup and I don't.

Inside the West Ham family are global leaders, Hollywood legends, rock stars, TV actors and authors. There are also lots of comedians, because having a sense of humour is common amongst our followers, as a kind of safety valve.

Let's begin at the top with two of the most famous people in the world, the Queen and Barack Obama. Both are believed to be West Ham fans, but how serious are those claims?

Let's start with the leader of the free world, the Queen. Her Majesty has certainly been to West Ham, indeed she opened the new West Stand. There wasn't a match on that day, because it was during the week, so I can't claim she's ever sung 'I'm Forever Blowing Bubbles'. However, the *Mirror* newspaper revealed in 2009 that she supported West Ham. When a member of her staff revealed an allegiance to Millwall, the Queen allegedly let slip that she's a Hammer. It's claimed she fell in love with the claret and blue, because of an admiration for legendary West Ham and England boss Ron Greenwood.

The Palace doesn't comment on this sort of speculation, so I can't confirm that she is an Iron maiden, but I like to think she is. I know she greatly respects the spirit of the East End. She's often spoken about her admiration for the 'backs to the wall' attitude during the blitz. I've never seen her at a match, but she would probably come incognito. I imagine she'd sit in the East Stand wearing one of William's Aston Villa scarves so she doesn't get spotted. Of course, she can't let the rest of the country know her true allegiance. She has to remain neutral and I respect that. But I saw that smile when she handed Bobby Moore the World Cup and she was smiling again when she made Ron Greenwood a CBE. Not conclusive proof, but I love the Queen and I like to think she loves my team, so I'm putting Her Majesty top of my list of famous Hammers. After all, she's never denied it!

Next most famous Hammer would have to be the President of the United States of America. Some may say he should be top, but I say come back when he's been in charge of his country for sixty years and we'll have a recount.

Barack Obama has certainly been to a match at West Ham.

In 2008 he was quoted at odds of ten thousand to one by William Hill to replace Alan Curbishley as West Ham manager. In the end he opted for the *West Wing* job instead.

If you're still not convinced that we have the best celebrity fans in the world, check out this little lot. If you're talking Hollywood, we have Ray Winstone, Richard E. Grant, the late, great Alfred Hitchcock and Keira Knightley. Check out Keira's film *Pure* to see the Boleyn Ground in all its glory.

On the musical front there's David Essex, Chesney Hawkes, Billy Bragg, Keith Flint, Louise Wener, Steve Harris from Iron Maiden, Phil Collen from Def Leppard, Roger O'Donnell from The Cure and Dave Grohl from the Foo Fighters.

If we're talking funny guys there's John Cleese, James Corden, Phill Jupitus, Nick Frost, Lee Hurst, Simon Day,

Russell Brand, Richard Digance, Reg Varney and the much missed Linda Smith. On the soap opera front, Nick Berry, Todd Carty, Ross Kemp, Perry Fenwick and Leslie Grantham are all East Enders in real life.

Boxers Lennox Lewis, Frank Bruno, Terry Spinks, Steve Roberts, Colin McMillan, Kevin Lear, Kevin Mitchell, Mark Kaylor and Nicky Cook all follow West Ham. And if you're wondering why we're always in the papers, it could be because journalists Martin Samuel, Rob Shepherd, Denis Campbell, John Cole, Jim Munro, Lee Clayton, Nigel Morris, Simon Walters, Tony Gallagher, David Croft, Bob Ballard, Mark Webster, Martin Kelner and Matt Lorenzo all swear allegiance to the claret and blue.

And that's without mentioning: Graham Gooch, Glen Murphy, Billy Murray, Kenny Lynch, Billie Whitelaw, Dame Anna Neagle, Martin Brundle, Johnny Herbert, Kriss Akabusi, Sean Day-Lewis, Frank Dobson, Noel Edmonds, Martin Hancock, James Gaddas, Simon Geoghegan, Paul Ross, Tommy Walsh, Len Goodman, Ben Shephard, Bryan Forbes, Nanette Newman, Paul McGinley, Danny Dyer, Donald Sumpter, Adrian Mills, Scott Maslen, Jo O'Meara, Sally Gunnell, Ade Adepitan, Steve Jones, Terence Stamp, Katy Perry, Sebastian Faulks, Max Lewis and Martin Hancock.

Plus there's loads more that I've probably forgotten and others which I can't say for sure, like Morrissey, Paul Gascoigne, Dizzee Rascal, Kyle McLachlan, Nicolas Cage, Matt Damon and Macaulay Culkin.

Brand Recognition

It's surprising who you meet at West Ham; there's so many celebrities knocking about. I met comedian Russell Brand for the first time in the toilets. At the time he was quite famous, but not ridiculously famous. It was before

Hollywood, before he'd met Katy Perry and before all the malarkey with Manuel from *Fawlty Towers*. I think it was round about the time he was presenting the *Big Brother* spin-off on Channel Four.

I nodded to him as we both pointed Percy at the porcelain. I wondered what he was doing in the club toilets, which are not for general use. These toilets were fancy ones, where the big nobs hang out. I'd always assumed Russell would be a nob in real life. He certainly looked like one, with his ridiculously tight black jeans and his massive hair. He was like an oversized Ramone who'd been in cold storage since the 1970s and had now been released onto an unsuspecting public.

I ended up really liking Russell, but I never liked the Ramones. Two sixth-formers would play them loudly in the Common Room at lunchtime and I couldn't really see the attraction. I liked Blondie, the Stranglers, Roxy Music and more tuneful stuff. I didn't mind a bit of punky music, like the Clash and the Undertones, but there had to be a tune, not just a racket. I never saw the attraction of the Sex Pistols, but I loved the Buzzcocks. The Ramones passed me by. The only Ramones song I liked was 'Baby I Love You'. The two sixth-formers, I wish I could remember their names, let's call them nob one and nob two, said that wasn't proper Ramones because it was too commercial. I was delighted to hear that Sheena was a punk rocker, but I needed a few more insightful lyrics about the rest of her personality, rather than just that statement repeating over and over again. Music alone does not define us. I only knew two Ramones fans and they were both nobs, but that does not mean all Ramones fans are nobs.

So anyway I'm in this toilet with Russell and we've both got our hands full and we've nodded.

'You're the announcer,' he said. I admitted that I was and realised that despite him being on the telly he was a little bit in awe of me because of my association with West Ham United. It turns out Russell was allowed to use the club toilets as he was mobbed when using the regular loos. By the time he'd finished signing autographs he'd missed half the match. Time was short as this was in the half-time interval and I had to get back out ready for the start of the second half. Russell said he had an idea he wanted to discuss with me and would I like to come on his Radio 2 show to talk about it.

So it was that the following Saturday evening a car arrived and drove me to Radio 2's studios at Great Western House in the West End. Russell had this mad idea that he'd like to sing Billy Joel's 'Uptown Girl' on the pitch at West Ham. Except he wanted to change the lyrics to 'Upton Park, We're the Hammers, we're from Upton Park, whoooooo, oooo, ooo, Upton Park etc.' You get the idea. It was a pretty weak idea to be honest. The sort of thing that fans scribble in their rough books at school and when they try and get it started at the ground, everyone just looks at them with disdain. A good terrace chant has to be simple, so people can remember it. It also helps if it's spontaneous, or at least not too contrived. The more it looks like you've spent ages writing the words, the less chance there is of others joining in.

However, with his charismatic personality, Russell would be just the person that could pull it off. I told him he would be welcomed onto the pitch at the next game to sing the song. He was very excited. This was to be the fulfilment of a dream. As a boy he'd always wanted to start a chant at the ground. The thought of having the power to start a song that thousands would sing was intoxicating to the young boy from Grays. My Dad nearly became manager of Boots the Chemists at Grays, but after a family visit to the town on one bleak weekend, he decided to stay at the Barkingside High Street shop. Russell is the best thing to have come out of Grays in years, apart from the A13 and Joe Pasquale. Mind you, a lot of people speak highly of Joe, including himself.

I'm sure Grays has its attractions, but for the young Russell the glitz and glamour of the big city was too much. He dreamt of playing the West End and hearing the audience applaud him. And he fantasised about the crowd at the Boleyn Ground singing a song that he'd started. Now his moment had come. He had an invitation to join me pitchside to kick off the Billy Joel song with his amended lyrics.

It never happened. He bottled it. The man who would later host the MTV music video awards and call George Dubya Bush a 'retarded cowboy', was too scared to sing his song at West Ham. He was worried that nobody would join in. With good reason, I suspect. West Ham fans don't like a smart arse. While many would admire him for coming down and having a go, there would be just as many who would enjoy sitting back and watching him fail on his arse.

So he never did it. I told him I fully understood and I do, but I watch him now, as a Hollywood movie star, wowing audiences wherever he goes, and I wonder why he couldn't overcome that fear at West Ham. This is a man who turned up for work at MTV on 12 September 2001 dressed as Osama Bin Laden. OK, he was sacked as a presenter, but he had the nerve to do it, however ill advised. When he hosted another MTV awards show he caught the eye of a beautiful American singer, the daughter of a preacher. The next time we see Katy Perry she's hosting an awards show of her own wearing a claret designer basque, lovingly crafted out of West Ham shirts with Russell's nickname, Rusty, embroidered on the back of her pants.

So Russell can catch a pop princess, fight off the demon drugs and insult the American President but he can't stand up at West Ham and start a song, in case no one joins in. How amazing is that? I think it shows the power of our childhood dreams and memories. The first time I had to interview someone famous from my childhood I was tongue-tied. Fortunately it was Bobby Charlton and he was very understanding. We sat on two footballs on a training pitch and just chatted into a microphone. Anything to do with our childhood instantly makes us become children in our minds. I've spoken at many events across the world over the years, but if I was asked to speak to my old school assembly I would find it very daunting.

The Mummy's Henchman

It's one thing to talk to celebrities on the pitch at half-time, it's quite another to go with one to a game. I don't travel to many away games; I spend enough of my week on the road as it is. I'd never see my wife. But I like to go to the London games. I once went to Chelsea with Omid Djalili, the actor and comedian. He played a slave trader in the film *Gladiator* and was in *The Mummy* too. He specialises in large, scary Middle Eastern henchman types.

Omid is a big Chelsea fan, really big. He was great company, but the trouble is he has a very loud voice. He'd forgotten that I was a West Ham fan and we were surrounded by Chelsea fans.

'Who's that little number thirty-two playing for you, he's a bit tasty?' he boomed.

I replied that it was Carlos Tevez and he was indeed a bit tasty. He gave Chelsea a lot of problems that day and caused us even more problems down the line. Omid made a few other enquiries, about our tactics and our bench. There were two people in between us, a comedy promoter and one half of the Raymond and Mr Timpkins revue. Omid has two voices, the cheeky Iranian voice that he uses at the start of his performance, and the cultured Home Counties voice that he uses after a few minutes of his show. Both are incredibly deep, and every time he asked me a question Chelsea fans would turn around to identify the West Ham fan in their midst.

No matter how many times my companions tried to shush him up, he still kept talking very loudly, asking me questions about 'your team'. I only got away with it because I was with the Mummy's henchman and because we lost, so there was no chance of me standing up and cheering. Even Omid might have had trouble protecting me then. I've always found the best way to cope if you ever find yourself in the wrong end and your team score is to bend forwards, put your head in your hands, smile and silently cheer. Everyone around you will assume you are crying. It works every time.

HEROES AND VILLAINS

Paolo Di Canio

The best goal I've seen in my time as the man on the microphone was scored by Paolo Di Canio. Nine minutes into a game against Wimbledon Paolo scored a fantastic volley with an acrobatic kick in mid-air. It was the most incredible piece of timing you are ever likely to see and rightly won the BBC's Goal of the Season. My way of announcing Paolo's goals became a bit of a trademark, with so many syllables to get my tongue around, I elongated even further to POW LOWWWWW DEE CAN YOWWWWWW.

Paolo Di Canio played Champagne football, or at least Frascati football. The fans would sing his name to the song 'La Donna è Mobile', from Verdi's opera *Rigoletto*. I started playing the song as a tribute to our Italian superstar before games.

He was a flawed genius, as he often seemed to be injured in the days before a difficult trip to the north. There was speculation that he suffered from northern flu. He also had a habit of returning to Italy for treatment, as if nobody in London had the ability to treat him. Once he missed the last game of the season because he'd gone back to his homeland, and then moaned when I didn't mention him over the microphone as I commentated on the lap of honour. I think if you want to receive your applause you have to turn up to collect it.

Paolo was responsible for my first run-in with Scott Duxbury, who at the time was the club lawyer. We all knew Paolo was leaving for Manchester United as the Champions League transfer deadline approached. As he left the field for the 'last time' he kissed his badge, waved to all four stands and did a beating-heart gesture. I urged the fans 'Let's hear it for Paolo, we might never see him again.' Everyone sang his song, and he left the field in tears. I later received a letter from Scott Duxbury reminding me that it was not my job to comment on transfer speculation. It was addressed to 'Jeremy Nicholls', which is nearly my name, but not quite. But it's easy not to spot mistakes in documents, isn't it?

Julian Dicks

I was very honoured to be the announcer at Julian Dicks' benefit match against Athletic Bilbao as he'd always been a favourite of mine. That might surprise a few people, as I'm not known as a fan of the crunching tackle, but Julian was so much more than that. Outside of Upton Park, I don't think he ever received enough credit for his skill. There was so much nonsense spoken about the rough stuff, with speculation that he'd have played for England if only he'd ditched the skinhead look.

In my days as a season ticket holder I'd watched some pretty grim games. To be frank, junior or senior, we were often rubbish. But week in week out, one man was head and shoulders above the rest. That man was Julian Dicks, a real gem, not only as hard as a diamond but also as cultured as a pearl. He was Hammer of the Year in 1990 and 1992, before heading north to join Liverpool. A stream of red cards meant he made the headlines for the wrong reasons. Many scousers, who of course invented comedy, claim he saw a red shirt hanging in the dressing room on his arrival, and he thought it was his because it had 'Fowler' on the back. Despite hilarious gags like this,

Julian never fitted in at Anfield, so we welcomed him home with open arms. He wasn't as good as before and he kept getting into trouble. He had bust-ups with Ian Wright and Steve Lomas, which isn't as bad as it sounds, as they were playing for Arsenal and Manchester City at the time. But he knuckled down and if you want to see him in vintage action take a look at the second half of the 1995/96 end of season video. He received no cards from late December onwards. He won Hammer of the Year again in 1996 and 1997.

His career was cut short by injury after having eight knee operations. He'd had so much keyhole surgery, I was expecting Loyd Grossman to turn up at his testimonial. What made the day even more special for me was getting a phone call of thanks from Julian the following day. He left us to try his hand as a professional golfer. He was always good at whacking balls as hard as he could. Sadly the knees put an end to the golf career as well, but he's moved into football coaching and I'm sure we've not heard the last of Dicksy at West Ham.

Rio Ferdinand

I used to have regular arguments with Tommy Docherty about Rio during our double-handed Sunday after- noon show on TalkSport. Tommy insisted Wes Brown of Manchester United was a better defender. I championed Rio's case and I like to think time has proved me right.

I was sorry to see Rio go, having watched him move up from the youth team to establish a regular first-team place. Like all West Ham fans I love to see the academy players come through. It's the West Ham way. We don't buy big- name players, we prefer to grow our own. Rio departed for Leeds United for eighteen million pounds. It's hard to turn down that kind of money. Leeds later sold him on for thirty million to Manchester United. Fans criticised the board for not having built in a sell-on clause, so we would have got some of the money from the second transfer. But at the time we received a British record fee for Rio, a world record for a defender. I think Leeds would have laughed if we'd then asked for a sell-on fee as well.

Dean Ashton

We signed Dean Ashton from Norwich for a club record fee of just over seven million pounds. He was terrific with a deadly eye for goal we'd not seen for years at West Ham, but he had dodgy hamstrings and struggled with his weight. When I introduced him to the crowd he was one of the calmest people I've ever met. When I was explaining to him in the tunnel the order of events, I honestly wondered if he could speak English. He didn't react to anything I said, and just nodded his head very slightly. I've never met a professional assassin, well not to my knowledge, but if I did, I reckon they'd be like Dean Ashton. Maybe they wouldn't have dyed blond hair, because that would make them easier to spot on the top of buildings. Dean was an awesome player who showed all the signs of being a West Ham legend in the making. He was clever, skilful and clinical, but sadly his career was to be cut short by injury. There had been talk of signing Benni McCarthy, the South African striker, but it was felt that we'd be better waiting until he was older, slower and fatter.

Dean Ashton made the England squad, which turned out not to be such good news for him or us. He was crocked by tiny little winger Shaun Wright-Phillips during training. He didn't even get to play for England against Greece, how unlucky is that? When you look at the size of Dean Ashton compared to SWP it doesn't seem right. Deano was never the same again, one of our best prospects in years was ruled out before the season had even started. It wasn't fair. When you lend something to a friend, you don't expect it to come back damaged.

Deano spent hours working on his own in the gym to regain his fitness. His injury meant he'd spent longer doing weights than he had doing cardio, so he came back looking like a boxer. That aside, Deano was everything we needed in a player. He was a great target man, who was strong enough to hold the ball up, but he was also deadly with his finishing. It's rare to get both in a striker. Having found ourselves a real gem of a player, we'd lent him to England and they'd broken him. Now he'd come back and although he scored some cracking goals that season, including a lovely overhead kick against Manchester United, he was never going to recover fully from that injury. He later had to retire from football tragically early at the age of just twenty-six.

SHAUN NEWTON

A regular in the cheap seats in the dugout with the doctors and me for most of that season was Shaun Newton. He'd tested positive for cocaine after the Middlesbrough FA Cup semi-final. It had only come to light in July and he was banned for seven months. Personally I would have sacked him, but the club chose not to. To be fair to him he came to a lot of games, some players would have been tempted to stay away on a match day. He'd have seen a lot more of the action if he didn't spend all his time texting, but at least he'd made the effort.

During a match I have two flasks of tea, one for each half. In those days I had a claret one for the first half and a blue one for the second half. They were very battered steel travel flasks. One day Shaun asked me what was in them; when I told him it was tea he looked disappointed. What could I say? I have a caffeine habit! He said he thought the club would have given me some smarter flasks as they looked a bit bashed up. I smiled to myself. Footballers are so mollycoddled, they have no idea how the real world works. Everything is given to them, so the idea that I might have been to a shop and bought the flasks just didn't occur to him. How many jobs can you think of, where you break the law, are banned from doing your job and instead of getting the sack, you spend the next seven months watching others do your job, while you still get paid?

FRIENDLY FIRE

In August 2008 West Ham United made a fantastic gesture in tribute to our greatest ever player. We retired the number six shirt worn with distinction by Bobby Moore over so many years.

It happened at the start of the second half in our pre-season friendly against Villareal, designated the Bobby Moore Cup. The teams came back onto the pitch and I welcomed Bobby's widow Stephanie Moore, who does brilliant work for the Bobby Moore Fund, the cancer charity she set up after his death. This is the announcement I made:

'When I was a kid the first West Ham shirt I ever had was a number six. In those days we didn't have names on the back, but everyone knew what the number six meant ... it was Bobby Moore. From today, West Ham will never again play with a number six shirt.'

(Applause as Matthew Upson handed over the number six shirt he'd worn in the first half to Stephanie.)

'In the second half, Matthew Upson will wear the number fifteen shirt. Let's hear it for the fantastic gesture that he's made.'

(More applause).

Matthew Upson wore the number fifteen for the rest of his career at West Ham. No West Ham player has worn a number six since, but every new West Ham shirt I buy still has a six on the back.

In the game itself, Carlton Cole's early goal was

cancelled out and the game ended one-all. A highlight was young Freddie Sears coming on as a substitute and looking like another academy player who would step up to the first team.

The pre-season friendly often throws up a few teething problems for the announcing team. The stadium is used a lot during the summer months, for all sorts of events. The microphones and sound equipment have been used by lots of different people, so the faders and settings on the mixing desk are often all over the place. Of course we'd do a sound check in the morning, but some tests can only be carried out in a full stadium, so I'm used to sounding a bit odd in the first game, until they've had a chance to tweak the controls.

Video Killed the Radio Star

The independent team operating the big screens had a few ideas for the new season, which included team sheets that looked like sticker books and zooming in on each player's picture as I read their name out. It was talked up to such an extent that I was expecting something really fancy, but it was pretty basic to be honest. On the day, the video team up in the box played the sticker book graphics far too early and it was hard for me to synchronise my words with the visuals. Instead of enhancing the matchday experience, it dragged it down in my view. No matter, we could tweak that and make it better for next week's season opener, or so I thought.

It may have looked bad to me at pitch level, but to West Ham's chief executive Scott Duxbury, watching in the stands, it looked downright terrible. He left his seat during the first half, stormed into the box and sacked every member of the video team, the lot of them. After the game I commiserated with the video guys, who were understandably upset. I told them it would blow over, and I was sure they'd be back the following weekend.

They were, but I wasn't. Without me knowing, a meeting was convened at the ground on Monday where they begged for their lives. Scott granted their request for one last chance against Wigan on the opening Saturday. The video team facing the firing squad had one last request; they wanted to bring in their own announcer and have him sit in the box with them, to make absolutely sure nothing could go wrong. In fact that was a complete smokescreen as the problem was little to do with contact with me, as I have a walkie-talkie and a mobile phone with me at all times. I suspect I was the fall guy.

However, I'd had a few conversations with Scott Duxbury the previous season about a few aspects of the match day. There were questions asked about whether 'I'm Forever Blowing Bubbles' was a bit dated and also defeatist. The possibility was mentioned of music being played after goals were scored. I'd dug my heels in on both of these suggestions. While they were only discussions it appeared that I hadn't won any friends with my intransigence.

PLAYING OUT OF POSITION

Oblivious to the fact I was being carved up, I went about my business reporting on sports features and funny stories to cheer up the end of regional news magazine show BBC *East Midlands Today*. Living in London it wasn't ideal freelance work, as I was in the car in Nottinghamshire, Leicestershire and Derbyshire a lot, but I really enjoyed the work and met lots of interesting people. On the Friday there was a shortage of heavyweight reporters on the rota and so a lightweight like me was despatched to cover a story about the British National Party. I was a bit out of my comfort zone as I have little knowledge of politics, but it was nothing compared to what followed.

My story wasn't about politics as such, but rather the inconvenience caused to the villagers by a BNP rally. As often happens in regional television, my mission was to ignore the big picture and find the local angle. I was under instructions to interview locals about being trapped in their homes. Under no circumstances was I to interview Nick Griffin, the leader of the BNP. That was stressed very strongly as it required editorial clearance from London. I think the producer was worried about sending the And Finally Guy to a serious story.

I sat in my car in a lay-by, waiting for my cameraman to arrive. A lady in the house opposite told me I couldn't park there. When I showed her my BBC pass, she relented, happy that I was there to report on the problem, not cause further problems. Then came the phone call from West

Ham which spoilt my day. After ten years I was on the way out. I couldn't believe it, I felt physically sick. How could this be happening? This was not the West Ham way to do things, or at least it didn't use to be. The club had changed a lot since the Icelandic consortium came in. Scott Duxbury, the lawyer who'd failed to spot the problems with the Tevez and Mascherano contracts, had somehow avoided the sack. Incredibly he'd instead been promoted and was now the chief executive. Scott had a manic smile like the Joker from *Batman*, but this was no joke. He was a northerner with no sense of the traditions of West Ham United and he was not well liked at the club. Anybody who stood up to him was soon out of the door. I'd held my ground a few times, about the idea of playing music after goals and doing away with 'I'm Forever Blowing Bubbles'. Now it seemed that my time had come.

I felt empty inside and just sat in my car for ages and ages. Gradually that void was filled with anger and righteous indignation. I'd been brought up to believe that if you did your best you would succeed in life. I'd given everything to the role of announcer over the previous ten years. Sometimes I'd been ridiculed for doing things in what I perceived to be the 'West Ham way', but largely I like to think I was acknowledged as one of the better announcers in the game. Now I'd been discarded without a second thought by a man who'd proved himself inept. I was confident that I was better at my job than he was at his, but on a whim I was out, a lifelong fan of the club sacked with as little thought as any other employee that stood in his way.

As I ended the call, there was a tap on the window. It was a policeman telling me I couldn't park there. In a leafy green country lane, with no yellow lines, I was moved on from a lay-by, having just been given the push by my beloved West Ham. At times like this you can either crumple or you can get on with your life. I chose life, found my cameraman, interviewed some locals about the disruption and then headed off to the field where the rally was being held. It wasn't billed as a rally, but rather as the Red, White and Blue Festival, at Denby, near where they make the pottery.

We filmed the flags flying at the gateway, but couldn't really see into the site, which was a couple of fields back. I was full of adrenaline. West Ham were playing Wigan tomorrow and I'd been looking forward to the start of the season all summer. Now I'd been told I could go and watch, but they wouldn't let me talk on the microphone.

Some burly guys with big arms, lots of tattoos and very little hair walked towards us. They were clearly the security wing of the event. We stopped filming and I strode towards them to say hello. I always think you should treat people as you find them. I didn't really want to be there but I had a job to do, even if I was feeling gutted about West Ham.

We chatted for a bit and they seemed friendly enough. Perhaps they bonded with me over our short hair. They had shaved heads while I had a balding head.

They asked if I would like to interview BNP leader Nick Griffin. I found myself saying yes. Well, what was the worst that could happen? I'd just lost my dream job, how much worse could it get? My cameraman nearly fell over his tripod in amazement. A few minutes later we were marched into the site. My cameraman looked very worried as he had longer hair than me.

Nick Griffin asked us to record the interview favouring one side of his face, as he has a glass eye. When I claimed not to know this, he looked at me with suspicion. What kind of reporter wouldn't know that? It was the sort of thing that would be uncovered with the most basic research. I explained that I usually cover sports and funny stories. I must have looked helpless, because he smiled and we filmed the interview. I'd sort it out with editorial policy later, I thought. I stuck to questions about the disruption to locals and pointed out that we might not be able to use the interview at all, if it wasn't cleared by the bigwigs in London. He was aware of this restriction, so all seemed well.

Still angry and hurt about losing the West Ham job, I decided to go a bit further. I looked him straight in the eye and asked to film the camp. He agreed, which gave us lots of colourful footage of flags to use in the story. In TV news you always need pictures to show when you are telling a story. The only tricky bit now was explaining to the producer of the day why I'd gone against instructions.

I drove back to the studios to edit my feature for that evening's news. It was a long drive and gave me plenty of time to think. I realised that being the announcer at West Ham had been such a huge part of my identity. I'd been a journeyman in the world of broadcasting. Yes, I'd presented shows on Channel Five and BBC Radio 5Live and GLR. I'd won a few awards, but I'd never been as successful as my peers. GLR was a hothouse of fresh broadcasting talent. I'd worked alongside Chris Evans, Chris Morris, Danny Baker and Fi Glover who'd all become stars in the broadcast world. I'd also co-presented with Garth Crooks.

The one thing that defined me was being the voice of West Ham. Whenever my career took a dip, I still had my beloved West Ham to keep me going. Now that love had turned against me.

I didn't get too much of a ticking-off at work. The Editorial Policy team listened to the interview and gave it the thumbs-up. My feature on the traffic disruption caused by the rally/festival ran high in the bulletin and the next day my interview with Nick Griffin featured in the Saturday programme. I wasn't around to see it as I'd long since left for London. I was on my way to West Ham, even if it was just to sit in the stands.

GRANDSTAND VIEW

Gutted as I was to lose my dream job, I looked forward to being a fan again and watching the games without having to worry about what I was saying. To be fair, the club gave my wife and I decent seats. Singer David Essex, ten years on from that 'pick and mix' day at Sheffield Wednesday, was sitting in front of us, with comedian Phill Jupitus just behind. West Ham star of the 1960s Brian Dear was in the seat next to me. These were comfy seats, ever so slightly padded, but not where I wanted to be. I wanted to be out there in the middle announcing the arrival of the teams. Ten years before in August 1998 I'd made my debut on that pitch and I'd been scared stiff. Now I'd have given my right arm to be back out there.

The teams ran out. I didn't stand up. I didn't feel like cheering, I was hurting too much. I sang the West Ham anthem 'I'm Forever Blowing Bubbles' from a seated position for the first time ever. I recognised the voice of the new announcer as Martin Godleman, a friend of mine. He was a good choice, I thought. But it should be me. He did a decent job of reading the teams out, giving slightly too much emphasis to Dean Ashton. Much as I liked Deano, I didn't think it was right to favour one player more than another.

Dean Ashton scored twice in the first ten minutes to set up a 2–1 win. I should have been delighted, but all I could think was that I wasn't announcing those goals.

Over the next months Jeanette and I watched West Ham from the stands. The club were true to their promise of giving us free tickets, but each game our seats were a little further back from the pitch. The days of the padded seats were a distant memory as we moved to regular plastic seats and then the upper tier, gradually creeping higher and higher. Week by week the players got smaller and smaller and I felt less and less part of the club.

Things were bad for manager Alan Curbishley too. As Eggy's overexuberance on the wages front began to hit the coffers, Curbs was forced to sell Anton Ferdinand to Sunderland against his wishes. He'd thought he had final say on player sales, but it appeared he was wrong. When George McCartney followed Anton out of the door and also joined Sunderland a few days later, it was too much for him to bear and Curbs resigned. In my view he was very harshly treated, he'd stabilised the club, saving us from relegation and then taking us to a top ten finish. OK, the football hadn't been as pretty as we'd have liked, but he had a lot of injuries to deal with. Curbs later won a constructive dismissal claim against the club and although it was money we could ill afford to pay, I don't begrudge him a penny of it. He was a good man, a West Ham fan, who played for his club and then managed them. I'd have him back like a shot.

Gianfranco Zola became the twelfth West Ham manager in history. He was the first manager to be younger than me, and he looked tiny in the dugout, but that might have been because we were now so high in the West Stand that we had oxygen at half-time instead of a cuppa. I was disappointed Gianfranco wasn't introduced to the crowd over the PA. This was not the West Ham way. The story goes that Franco felt he might not get a good reception, because of his links with our rivals Chelsea. What nonsense! Any manager of West Ham will be applauded warmly, maybe not forever, but at least at their first game. For heaven's sake, even Lou Macari and Glenn Roeder were applauded at their first games! If I'd have been the announcer, I'd have thanked Gianfranco for his fears, and made the decision for him. I believe everyone is an expert in their own field; I don't tell the manager how his team should play and I don't expect him to tell me how to do my job. I think I know the West Ham crowd well enough to anticipate how they'll react. There are worse crimes than playing for Chelsea and without fail everyone in football admired Zola during his time there.

By now I was given seats behind the goal in the noisy corner next to the away fans. Usually I love this part of the ground, as it's the most passionate, but it wasn't ideal for me and the wife. In one game Jeanette was pulled backwards over her chair by joyful supporters celebrating a goal. It was a far cry from the padded seats behind David Essex.

On the pitch West Ham were having a mixed season with some good wins and some disappointing defeats. The new announcing team, though, were consistently having a nightmare. Martin Godleman lasted just eight games before he was given his marching orders too. He'd been good but suffered from us not being able to hear him that well. Martin's a good mate of mine and he said he'd found it tough going in the announcer's box. Of course he did, what a nightmare situation, behind double glazing trying to project his voice above crowd noise he couldn't hear. Plus there were six to ten other people in the box, from the various other media like the video screen, the digi-boards and the plasma screens in the concourse, all run by different firms, all chatting and rarely about the game.

After that West Ham tried out another announcer who I didn't know. I was trying not to be bitter about it but it was hard not to be, it was awful. It might seem a bit odd but I carry a notebook around with me all the time and I scribbled down all the mistakes they made. I usually like to make notes of things that I can use in my after-dinner speaking, but this was more a form of therapy. Here's a few extracts:

> An England international was mispronounced. A West Ham player was announced with the wrong number. James Collins and Jack Collison were twice muddled up, so it appeared we had a player called Jack Collins.
>
> 'I'm Forever Blowing Bubbles' was not played as the team ran out. Then Bubbles started being played at strange times in the build-up, but not at the end to celebrate a win. On one occasion Bubbles was far too quiet to hear and then faded down mid-flow for no apparent reason. There appeared to be a random rock version of Bubbles that can only have been done by someone's garage band, it was that bad.
>
> An attendance was announced that is more than twice the ground capacity. I suspect the digits were transposed. Worst of all a Spurs defeat was announced, with no pause for the crowd to cheer. What's the point of that? It's the first thing you learn at West Ham announcer school.

I then heard from sources within the club that a third new announcer was being given a go. It was like the *X Factor*. You don't audition people during live games – it was a disaster. The new guy sounded scared stiff, with a high-pitched voice, and he was prone to errors. He sounded so nervous against Spurs that he seemed to develop a stammer. Against Fulham Dickson Etuhu was given an extra couple of syllables in his surname – Etu-hu-hu-hu.

Aston Villa's Gabriel Agbonlahor might look scary when written down, but there's no excuse for getting it wrong, he's not exactly an unknown. Gabby was 'ban' all afternoon instead of 'bon'. I was furious when Villa's Marlon Harewood's name was read out and there was no welcome back for him. He had his ups and downs at West Ham, but he sweated blood for us in that FA Cup Final and deserved a cheer from our fans. Instead of pausing, announcer number three ploughed straight on with the rest of the line-up. Amazingly, when Nigel Reo-Coker's name was read out, he did pause. You didn't need to have that much knowledge of West Ham to know which of the two former West Ham players was likely to get the better reception.

I began to doubt if the announcer was a West Ham fan. I later discovered that he actually supported Liverpool. Imagine how hard it was for me to hear all these mistakes. I pride myself on my meticulous research and after ten seasons of establishing a reputation for West Ham doing things right, our reputation was being dragged through the gutter. It was embarrassing and heartbreaking.

One thing that struck a chord was 'Please welcome your team, West Ham United.' When I'd started at West Ham in 1998, I'd said exactly the same thing at my first two games. One day an envelope dropped on the doormat with a House of Commons logo on it. The MP for Poplar and Canning Town, Jim Fitzpatrick, was writing to ask me to say 'our team' instead of 'your team'. Jim's a lovely bloke, a great MP and a proper West Ham fan despite the disadvantage of being born Scottish. He was spot on of course, why was I being so formal? Now, though, the new announcer was perfectly entitled to say 'your team' as he was just doing his job, not announcing his own team.

Craig Bellamy was once announced as wearing the number eleven shirt, which was a surprise as it said ten on his shirt, in the programme and on the big screen. In fact he'd been number ten all season. Hybrid player Jack Collins was no longer getting a mention, but then it went horribly wrong during a substitution, when the player leaving the field was announced as 'John' Collison. That was followed by an announcement of 'fort added minutes', which is presumably a military version of 'four added minutes'.

From my seat high in the stand it appeared that there were two announcers being used, one in the box and one that came on the pitch pre-match and at half-time. The pitchside announcer wore a Dennis the Menace type jumper with red and black hoops, not exactly the dress code for a West Ham announcer. 'Dennis' conducted an interview with Olympic rower Mark Hunter that sounded like two blokes in a pub having a chat.

We lost the Villa game but it was our best home performance in ages, yet the team were allowed to leave the pitch without any acknowledgement of their efforts. There was no mention at all from the announcer, instead there was loud music and then a recording of fans singing 'Come on you Irons'. How two-bob did we look to the Villa fans? We'd lost, let our team shuffle off the pitch and were now playing a tape of our fans singing from a previous game. It was just rubbish!

The West Ham fan sites picked up on all the mistakes and a campaign began to grow for me to return. I watched with interest, having previously kept off the message boards, because I was usually being criticised for playing the wrong music or generally 'ginksing' things.

The problems with the club's finances increased as our shirt sponsors ran into trouble. Icelandic airline XL went bust, and their logo was instantly covered up on our shirt. The kitman cut out square claret patches from other shirts to put over them. It meant the team ran out for their next game looking like Teletubbies, with those little TV screens on front. Sadly they played like Teletubbies too. Rumours that the club shop did a roaring trade in replica shirts with the names Dipsy, Laa-Laa and Po on the back were greatly exaggerated.

It wasn't a good look, so a marginally more stylish solution emerged. White squares were placed over the XL logo and the player's number was put on the front as well as the back of the shirt. It still looked rubbish but it made it easier for the ref to book them.

The team were winning a few games at home and Zola had them playing some lovely passing football, but the atmosphere in the stadium was terrible. I won't say it was all to do with the announcing, but it certainly didn't help. The message boards stepped up their calls for my return. The same forums where I'd been slaughtered for the past ten years for all manner of things were now backing me as the devil they knew, over this array of hopefuls.

Things came to a head against Fulham, which was live on Sky. We won 3–1 with goals from David Di Michele, Carlton Cole and Mark Noble, yet the atmosphere in the stadium was very low-key. The Sky commentators picked up on it, saying it had been like that all season and wondered why. At this point the club decided enough was enough. The live *X Factor* announcer auditions had to stop; they needed a voice of experience.

HULL AND BACK

One day, completely out of the blue, I received a call from West Ham, asking me to return as the announcer. It felt like a cloud had lifted. The gloom that had been over my head for the last five months was suddenly gone.

It's being a bit overdramatic, but it was like losing a loved one, grieving for five months and then finding out that they weren't really dead after all. I don't know if you watched the BBC drama series *Mistresses*, where one of the characters loses her husband in the 9/11 attack on the World Trade Center? When he turns up alive and well a few years later, she's still in love with him, but she's just the tiniest bit annoyed that he deceived her. And that he'd had a child with another woman.

My love affair with West Ham was complicated. I loved them because they were my team. I hated them because they sacked me. Hell hath no fury like a woman scorned, but that's nothing to the fury felt by a supporter who loves their team.

I've lost jobs before. I don't think I've ever been sacked, because it doesn't really work like that in the media. I lost my show on TalkSport because I was 'too BBC' and kept giving 'both sides of the argument'. I lost my late-night show on Channel Five because my co-presenter Helen Chamberlain wasn't released by Sky. I lost a show once because I looked too much like my co-presenter, James Richardson, the chap who presented *Football Italia* on Channel 4. I look nothing like him, he's far better-looking!

I was replaced by my mate Phill Jupitus, who still feels guilty about it.

The man who rang me from West Ham was Ian Tompkins, who'd taken up his position as head of corporate affairs after I'd been kicked into touch. He hadn't been part of that decision, which made it much easier for him to pick up the phone. We could both shake our heads in amazement at the decision earlier in the season and then get on with making it better.

I told Ian I was delighted to be asked back and I was sure it wouldn't be a problem, but I just needed to talk it over with my wife. I also needed to see how it would affect other jobs that I had in my speaking diary.

A few days later I was sat in Ian's office at West Ham with a list of demands. I always knew I was going to go back, but I wanted to go back on my terms. No matter how many speaking engagements were in that diary, I'd always bump them out for a West Ham game.

I made a list of requests that I would like agreed before taking on the job again. Only a few of them were deal breakers, most were just to get a bit of pride back.

Condition number one was a seat in the dugout as in the most recent seasons. The three announcers in my absence had all worked from the confines of the double-glazed box on the third floor. This caused problems, as it's hard to lift your voice above the crowd if you can't hear them. Ian wasn't keen to start with, but when I explained my reasons he agreed that it made sense.

I asked for two season tickets, so my wife could go to games with a friend. That would not be a problem I was told. True to his word, Jeanette watched the rest of the season from the West Stand Upper.

I wanted assurance that we would always play 'Bubbles' before the kick-off. And that we would never play music after goals. A lifelong West Ham fan, Ian not only agreed with these, he heartily endorsed them. I liked this man.

My final demand was for a West Ham coat, like the subs wear, with my initials on the chest. This was a demand too far. I didn't really care, because we were both smiling by now. In the end I was allowed the coat, but not the initials, as that's just for players and coaches.

My first game back was on 28 January 2009, a midweek game against Hull City. It was a magical night, my favourite West Ham game ever. A floodlit game at Upton Park is always a bit special, but for me this was more special than usual. As I walked into the ground it seemed everyone stopped and welcomed me back. 'It hasn't been the same without you.' 'Thank goodness you're back, we couldn't understand the other guy.' 'Sort out the atmosphere, Jeremy, can't you?' 'Are you going to play "Bubbles" again, the other guy didn't play it.'

In fact there had been three announcers since I last spoke on the microphone, but nobody seemed to realise that. 'Bubbles' had been played, but not always at the right time or at sufficient volume.

Before kick-off I walked round the pitch, clockwise for luck. It is the slowest pre-match lap I've ever made. So many people came to the front and shook my hand. I even went into the Hull supporters for a chat with my mate Dave who follows the Tigers. On reflection it perhaps wasn't the wisest thing to go into the away supporters as I was wearing a claret and blue tie and holding a microphone, but on a special night like this I felt nothing bad could happen.

The stewards were very kind, especially Mark and Michael, the two brothers who've run the tunnel and dugout area throughout my time at the club. It was just so lovely to see everyone again. I felt quite emotional as I took my seat in the dugout. I shook hands with Gianfranco Zola, the manager who'd joined in my absence. What a charming man he was, not as small as he'd looked from high up in the stand, but still shorter than me.

By the time I'd shaken hands with the doctors and the rest of the back-room staff, the game was under way. Zola had the team playing some lovely passing football and we scored after half an hour.

'Goal for West Ham scored by David Di Micheleeeeee.'

On that wonderful night under a moonlit sky we beat Hull by two goals to nil, Carlton Cole adding the second. Mr Moon was back in the stadium.

END OF SEASON GALA

That season the club introduced the first end of season gala dinner. I went along with my wife. My job was to interview people for WHUTV, the club's web-based pay channel. I interviewed old players and famous fans, particularly about the Zola factor. The answers would be edited together to make an interesting feature on the future going forward with the little Italian.

I spotted Hollywood tough guy Ray Winstone walking by and asked him if he had a quick word for West Ham TV. He actually had two words and they were very quick. He grinned and disappeared around the corner sharpish. I've always been a bit scared of Ray since watching the film *Scum* when I was a boy. I had nightmares about the scene where he whacked a kid over the head with a sock containing snooker balls. Since then he's gone on to great success in films like *Sexy Beast* and he's a regular at West Ham.

After a few seconds he came back round the corner. 'Did you say West Ham TV? Of course I shall be delighted,' he said, putting on a mock posh voice. I asked him to put his cigarette out first. He refused.

'I am having a fag,' he said, this time in a 'Kathy Burke as Waynetta Slob' voice. The smoking ban had been in force for a few years, but it didn't seem to apply to movie stars. He'd clearly partaken of a few jars of falling-down water, so I decided to let it lie.

We started the interview. Ray used my microphone as an ashtray. Each time I asked a question he would tap his cigarette butt against it. A crowd had gathered to see the famous man in action, especially as I was interviewing Ray Winstone.

I asked him what he thought of the Zola effect. 'Well between you and me, Jel,' he said, 'when he first joined, I thought he's f***ing Chelsea. But to be fair to the fella, he's got us playing all right.'

With lots of laughter from around us and more ash on my microphone, I was mentally editing which bits I could and couldn't use. There wasn't much left, so I tried to cut the interview short, but Ray was having none of it. Worried about socks and balls, I persevered. I knew we couldn't use any of it, but it was fun. Ray is a natural wit and raconteur, with a way of telling a story that makes you listen. Sadly the interview never made it to WHUTV because of all the smoke and swearing, which is a bit of a fag, but let me tell you it was hugely entertaining. I was especially good in the supporting role as the fall guy.

It was a great night with Phill Jupitus an excellent host on the stage. I've known him for years and I've never known him so keyed up for an event. That's the thing about being called up by your club, it turns even the most seasoned professionals to jelly. Phill didn't wobble though, even if he did admit to being completely in awe of Zola. I think we all were; he'd been the best overseas player ever to play in the Premier League. For West Ham fans to admire a Chelsea player you know he must have been a bit special.

The evening was rounded off by Scott Duxbury cornering me. He'd had a few drinks but there was no doubt in the sincerity of his apology. He said getting rid of me was the worst thing he'd ever done at West Ham. It was kind of him to say that, although I think his role in the Carlos Tevez affair would have won the vote in most people's Scott's Worst Mistakes Ever Top Ten Countdown.

That had led to us paying out millions in fines and blood

money. My sacking as announcer had probably cost us a few dropped points at home due to the reduced atmosphere, but it's hard to gauge how many. Maybe we missed out on a European place because I wasn't there, possibly even a Champions League spot, but it's not for me to say.

Scott told me that I was back for good now; I had a job for life. I was delighted. I went and found my wife to tell her the good news, and then Scott spent ages apologising to her as well.

My three-legged stool had finally stopped wobbling on all fronts: relationship, career and West Ham. My wife and I had moved to leafy Twickenham to be closer to her job and were enjoying the walks along the river into Richmond. We'd bought a lovely home under the Heathrow flight path, next to the sewage works. It was a real bargain, we couldn't believe no one had snapped it up. My career was evenly split between 'And Finally' news reports for BBC TV, after-dinner speaking and event hosting. And the third leg, West Ham, had wobbled, fallen off and was now firmly stuck back on with super glue.

Things were looking up. I was back at the club I loved, and I had a job for life. Scott had said so and surely he wasn't about to leave the club any time soon. He was the darling of the owners. We were bankrolled by one of the richest men in Iceland. Players had been signed on huge wages. Everything must be fine.

As always I was optimistic about the future. So long as nothing happened to Scott or the Icelandic economy, what could possibly go wrong?